Does she know she's there?

For Catherine,

who made this necessary, and

for Ted and Dominic and Benjy,

who made it possible.

ACKNOWLEDGEMENTS

While I have been writing this chronicle over the years, many kind people have given me helpful suggestions and much-needed encouragement. I am grateful to each one of them and hope they won't be offended by a general, but deeply felt THANK YOU! Particular gratitude, however, is due to Andrew Allentuck, Ramsay Derry, John Snidal and Heidi Harms.

In looking over this book as it was first published in 1978, I cringe at some of the terminology I used, e.g., "the retarded," "the multiply handicapped." Tempted though I am to sneak in a few changes, I've not done so. I would not want to diminish or dishonour the profound influence my daughter has had on me as I've grown up with her.

Nicola Schaefer
July 1999

PART ONE

1961–82

1

My seven-month-old daughter Catherine lay droopily in my arms. She was dozing peacefully for once, as I sat waiting on a yellow plastic chair outside the office of a child-development specialist in the Children's Hospital. I had arrived for my appointment half an hour earlier but his door remained shut.

I seemed to be in the physiotherapy department because I could see into one of the rooms leading off the corridor; within it were parallel bars and huge floor-length mirrors on the walls with rubber gym mats beside them. A small boy was on a slanted bed, head down, feet up, being thumped on the back by a determined girl in a split skirt.

"What's wrong with that little boy?" I asked the receptionist, not really feeling conversational, but needing distraction from my thoughts about the forthcoming interview.

She looked up briefly from behind her desk.

"Cystic fibrosis," she said disinterestedly. "They have to get the mucus up out of his chest."

"Every day?"

"Every six hours."

"Good God! Will he get better?"

"There's no cure for it." Her face vanished. The child was now being told to cough and spit. I didn't pursue the subject but continued to observe the activity in the corridor. Every now and again a child wearing leg braces or walking with crutches would be led clanking or stumbling past me into another room. Behind yet another door I could hear a girl called Lisa being exhorted to stand up.

"Now push up, there's a good girl. Push, Lisa, no *push*. We want to get your legs strong, don't we? No, no, not all floppy like that. *Push up*. No, you can't go back to the ward yet. We want to get you up onto those legs first, don't we?"

"No." The answer was faint but rebellious and was followed by tired crying.

I was getting hot. Having lived in Canada for only eighteen months, I was still not used to the high temperatures at which Canadians kept their houses. Public buildings seemed even hotter. I tried to shift myself into a more comfortable position on my plastic chair but gave up when I found myself stuck to it. I didn't want to jerk Catherine awake into one of her terrifying and inexplicable screaming fits. I eased my wrist round to look at my watch. God! We'd been there an hour. A doleful-looking boy with an enormous head wobbled past, holding the hand of another split-skirted girl with a sign on her bosom, "Physiotherapy-Miss Phipps." My supposition had been correct. The two disappeared into a room at the far end of the corridor from which emanated more noise and activity than from the other rooms.

"What's down there?" I asked the receptionist.

"The CP class."

"CP?"

"Cerebral palsy."

"Oh." I had heard the term, of course, and knew vaguely that it meant brain damage and caused spasticity. Right now I didn't want to know any more. I was here merely to establish that my daughter was a slow developer; that there was nothing basically wrong with her. Nevertheless it was uncomfortable being in the midst of obviously handicapped children when I had been expecting nothing more than a reassuring chat with the doctor in his office.

Would his door never open? We'd been waiting nearly an hour and a half now, and Catherine was bound to wake up soon. My left arm was aching from supporting her, I was hot and, horror of horrors, would soon have to find the Ladies. I wiped off a moustache of sweat. Catherine began twitching. I peered down into her basket on the floor beside me to make sure I had her soother and Billie Bee honey, which sometimes quelled her screaming. They were there, of course; this was the fifth time I had checked since our arrival. Ignoring the teenage girl shuffling jerkily past me down the corridor, I stared at the door ahead and continued the confidence trick I was playing on myself. Why on earth was I getting into such a state when all I was going to be told was that my baby was a slow developer; that there was nothing fundamentally wrong . . . ?

The door opened and a boy of about five with crossed eyes emerged accompanied by a placid-looking woman.

"Thank you, Dr. Hall. We'll try what you suggest," she said. She didn't look particularly enthusiastic about whatever it was he had spent the last hour and a half suggesting.

"Mrs. Schaefer? Come in please." I stood up with a squelching sound and looked back at the plastic chair with distaste. Dr. Hall struck me as impersonal and imposing, though I was totally unable to conjure up a picture of him when I got home.

"Child's name?" There was no welcoming smile, no expression at all. His face was, in fact, totally blank.

I remember only isolated incidents of that interview. My main ambition was to get out as quickly as possible. I needed to find a Ladies and wanted to phone my husband to tell him all was well. I do know I answered the case history questions as precisely as possible, trying to read the doctor's reactions on his face. Just how odd did he find it that Cath still couldn't hold her head up, for instance? He remained impassive.

"I believe I was a very slow baby," I said, attempting a casual air, "and a friend of mine says her first baby didn't sit up till she was over a year."

He ignored me. After his questions, he shook a tinny-toned bell in Catherine's face. The handle was red and the paint was chipped. I felt a wave of alarm. I suspected that this inscrutable man's opinion of my daughter's abilities depended upon her reaction to the bell.

I hugged her closer to me and hissed in her ear, "Grab it, silly." I knew she wouldn't. Turning to the doctor, I said as calmly as I could, "Give her a chance, she's only just woken up. She often doesn't seem to notice things, you know." He jangled the bell repeatedly, insistently, but Catherine stared past it, one eye wandering slightly. "She's very selective," I said. "A sign of intelligence, I would have thought." Tring tring. Tring. Tring tring tring. "She doesn't like your beastly bell," I finally exploded. "OK?"

The doctor pressed his lips together and put down the bell. He wrote something on his sheet of paper. Suddenly Catherine stiffened in my arms. Oh hell, I thought, here goes. The screaming. She arched her back as I reached down and tried to fish for her soother but the doctor interrupted me. He held up a flashlight and pointed to a closet, apparently indicating that we were all going in there. He could barely make himself heard above the baby's yelling.

This just isn't possible, I thought as I moved like an automaton towards the closet. This felt as if I was in one of my more surrealistic dreams. We crammed in. The door shut and we were in total darkness. Catherine stopped crying abruptly. Clutching her to me, I could feel Dr. Hall's breath on my face. I was speechless. There was a blaze of light as he turned on the flashlight. Cath's piercing screams filled the closet as the doctor put the beam close to her head, shining it over her entire skull.

When we emerged I was beyond asking questions and, as far as I remember, Dr. Hall offered no explanations. Much later I found out that this procedure is called transillumination of the skull and is commonly used as a rough guide to determine the size and shape of the brain, and also to see if the baby's head contains anything superfluous, such as blood or cerebrospinal fluid.

Then there was a physical examination of Catherine, during which she continued to scream frantically. When I had dressed her, she quietened down and we sat and awaited judgement.

I was superficially calm while Dr. Hall spoke. I thought I was listening intelligently but only certain words and phrases really penetrated my consciousness. Grossly abnormal . . . cerebral palsy . . . neuro-muscular disorder . . . extensive brain damage . . . never walk or talk . . . will become an increasing burden to you . . . no hope . . . no hope . . . no hope . . . institution. . . . "I suggest you go home, put this baby in an institution and then have another," the doctor concluded.

I think I smiled. I didn't let myself react emotionally yet. The things this madman in a white coat had said to me were so ludicrous that they didn't deserve a serious response.

"I don't really fancy having another, actually," I finally got out. "Oh, a normal one, you mean. Sorry, my mistake. What are my chances of having another dud?"

Dr. Hall seemed relieved that I was taking it so well.

"Judging from everything you've told me, this baby is about one in a million," he said quite cheerfully. "Your chances of having normal, healthy children hereafter are excellent, I'd say."

"I see," I said. "Thank you very much. Now could you tell me where the toilet is, please?"

I stared at myself in the mirror over the basin in the Ladies. I still looked the same. Continuing to keep my emotions at bay, I picked up Catherine in her basket and went to phone my husband.

"What did he say?"

"I'll tell you when I get home."

Still dry-eyed when I reached our apartment, I gave Ted a synopsis of the last few hours. He looked down at Catherine, sleeping in her basket.

"But she looks so . . . normal," he said with the mild puzzlement born of total disbelief. Then he turned to me. "Oh, my God," he said, "what are we going to do?"

We clung to each other. "Don't," I said. And we howled.

That was, I think, the moment at which I accepted the truth. I cried nearly all night, but as I did so a curious relief edged its way into my chaotic thoughts. No pretending any more, I said to myself. No more comparing Cath to other babies. Now there is something definite to face, not just vague fears.

And I went back in my mind to Catherine's birth and the subsequent events, and non-events, that had led up to my making an appointment with Dr. Hall.

2

On July 26th, 1961, I waddled out of our local supermarket and realized I was leaving a trail behind me. Aha, I thought, this must be the famous waters. I glanced backwards and then glared at my shopping bag, hoping to indicate to onlookers that I had a leaky package. Hastening home to our pleasant basement apartment overlooking the river, I made supper and decided to pack my bag, knowing this was the first step one took towards going into hospital to have a baby. The trouble was, I didn't know what, exactly, one was supposed to pack. I ended up with my toothbrush, a hairbrush, two nighties, six books and as many packets of cigarettes as I could ram into the corners of my case.

To my everlasting regret my own doctor was on holiday. All his replacement said when I gave him my dramatic news was, "This your first? Well, get down to the hospital when the pains are coming regularly."

Ted came home and we had supper. I was ravenously hungry but he ate very little. He was nervous, he said. Well I wasn't, I said; excited yes, but not in the least nervous. I was supremely confident that I would have a lovely little baby in a few hours.

After supper I began to get bored. When were labour pains going to start? Nothing had happened by nine o'clock that evening so we went over to see Wilf and Ann, Ted's brother and his wife, and played cards until everyone except me was exhausted.

I had just started to fall asleep at about two o'clock when the first contraction started. Good, I thought, it'll be soon now. Little did I know that it would be thirty increasingly miserable hours before Catherine was born. The pains were short-spaced and fierce right from the start, so there was little chance of sleeping. My excitement waned as the hours passed and by lunch time the next day I was tired and fed up. Ted stayed at home and I lay in bed eating cherries and trying to read. The poor man was fidgety and anxious and didn't know what to do to help. Eventually he pushed aside the paper he was working on.

"Do you think you'll have it if I go out for a minute?"

I said it was doubtful, so he took off and returned quite soon with a fan—our apartment was fiendishly hot, up in the nineties—some flowers and more fruit, all of which cheered me up.

By supper time I'd had enough of lying in bed convulsed with pain as Ted scribbled equations at his desk. It was time to go to the hospital. While I was "being prepared," as the revolting ritual of shaving and enemas was euphemistically known, Ted left for a while. I clambered with difficulty onto the high hospital bed in the labour ward and felt desolate and sorry for myself. What on earth was I doing here in a strange country, surrounded by strangers, at what should have been one of the most thrilling moments of my life?

Ted and I met while he was finishing his D. Phil. at Oxford, which was my home town. He was nearly a foot taller than I, wore corduroys and penny loafers, was shy and studious, had the softest variety of Canadian accent, and was absolutely intriguing. When he returned to Winnipeg to be an assistant professor at the University of Manitoba we corresponded for a couple of years until he came to England again to spend the summer working at the National Physical Laboratory in Teddington, London. I was working in London at this time, and living close by in Hammersmith. That fall he sent me a one-way air ticket to Winnipeg. Happily bidding my tearful family farewell, I flew off to start a new life. It was lovely being married and in a new country. Everyone, including Ted's family, was as welcoming and friendly as could be, but I did inevitably miss my family and friends in England. I was delighted upon discovering myself to be pregnant; a baby would help me to transfer my roots.

Right now, though, I felt alienated and intensely lonely. I rang the bell for a nurse.

"You're not nearly ready yet," she said and, when I started to cry helplessly, "What's the matter? You're only having a baby, you know." Curious words of comfort!

The next few hours seemed endless but finally I was carted off to the delivery room. I was so dopey by this time that I barely remember the baby being born, but I did ask the conventional questions.

"Did it go all right? Is she normal?"

"Absolutely. A normal delivery, even if it did take you a while, and a nice baby girl." The doctor was kind but distant. I don't remember seeing him again.

Up in the ward I fell asleep instantly and dreamed I was just going into labour. It was a considerable relief when I opened my eyes to see a huge bunch of chrysanthemums looming towards me with a grinning Ted behind.

"Have you been to see her?" I mumbled.

He nodded. "Briefly. She looks just like a mouse."

I was enchanted with my funny little mousy-haired daughter. When friends came to visit, I told them I loved her dearly but knew she looked like a caricature of Ted without his glasses. They were shocked. Why she was sweet, they said, just adorable.

Catherine was very sweet but with the arrogance of ignorance I had always been determined that having a baby would not affect my life style. The baby would accommodate itself to us, not vice versa. Not that I planned to be one of those mothers who keep their babies on a four-hour feeding schedule come what may, or refuse to pick them up when they are crying for fear of spoiling them. She would be fed when she was hungry and cuddled when she was unhappy (and when she wasn't) but having her would not stop us from going out and leading our own lives. She would simply go everywhere with us in her basket. I hadn't bought any baby books, either. Instinct and good sense were to be my guides.

Thus, when Catherine was three weeks old, the three of us set off on a two-week holiday in the Rockies we had been planning for months. Our friends were unanimous in their disapproval. Good grief, they said, it's madness to take a three-week-old baby on a trip like that. Babies don't like being shifted around just after they're born; they need stability. What if one of us got sick? Or the car broke down? And what about feeding her? I waved aside all their objections. The motion of the car would relax her and since I was feeding her myself there would be no problem about heating bottles. And there was no reason to suppose that any accident or illness would occur. The only thing that was worrying me, privately, was the baby's crying. Ted thought Cath cried a great deal when he was at home, but what he didn't know was that she rarely stopped crying. I, being an optimist, assumed she would settle down tomorrow or the next day.

Now, nearly fifteen years later, I can finally admit that ours was, by any standards, a truly terrible holiday. Driving from Winnipeg to Calgary on the Trans-Canada highway in heat 90 degrees or more was not, I decided, the best initiation into the wide open spaces of the Canadian prairie provinces. Having only ever known the pleasant countryside of England, I found this heat unbelievable. On the first day out I got sunburnt and sunstroke. We had an umbrella arranged over the baby in the back seat and I continuously sponged her down with wet face cloths. Nevertheless, she yelled almost unabatedly all day.

After several hours of driving through flat, sunbaked land with no sign of life anywhere, I noted in some surprise, "Wow, this is a desert, isn't it?" After that the conversational efforts were as sparse as the scenery. Every hundred miles or so I'd venture an offering: as we shot past a grey, collapsing frame house all by itself in the middle of nowhere, "Golly, is that what one could call a grim reminder of pioneer days?" Or, miles later, "I wonder what those bones are?" And finally, "Is there really eight hundred miles of this?" I blew down the front of my shirt. "Haven't seen anything green or moving for hours. Too hot for birds, I suppose."

"Want to turn back?" asked Ted over the baby's crying. Despite his clenched jaws I felt that he wanted to go on.

"No, no, no, only let's stop if we happen to see a tree and I'll try feeding the baby again." I was feeding Cath more often than I had been at home but it made no difference to her crying. She did seem thirsty, however, and drank a lot of water from a bottle. This blew her stomach up, which at least provided a reason for her screaming and in a daft way made us feel better.

When we staggered into a motel late that night I bathed Cath and fed and cuddled her but nothing seemed to calm her down. As I paced the room with the howling baby on my shoulder, I felt terribly sorry for the poor scrap. I blamed the heat and, reluctantly, myself for having embarked on this crazy trip. And I was concerned about Ted, who had looked forward to this holiday and was now lying on the bed after a hard day's driving, his face screwed up in a concentrated effort to ignore Catherine and sleep. Eventually he went and slept cramped up in the car while I snatched what sleep I could when the baby dozed off periodically.

The next day, I swallowed my snobbish pride and bought a soother before we left Medicine Hat. It worked for a while, too. Driving towards Calgary with Schumann's Fourth Symphony in the background instead of Catherine's screaming, we were able to enjoy the long-awaited pleasure of watching the foothills of the Rockies gradually taking shape in the distance.

We spent that night in Calgary. Ted slept in the car again, however, because Catherine was awake most of the night after a relatively peaceful day. The following morning, when it became obvious that I was getting very little sleep, Ted felt guilty and said he would carry Cath around that night and let me sleep. This in turn made me feel guilty; I didn't have to drive, and felt a mother should instinctively know what was wrong with her baby and how to stop her crying. I capitulated around midnight. When I suddenly awoke later in the night, Ted was in an armchair with his feet up on the bed. Cath was asleep along the length of his thighs.

"Tie my ankles together," he whispered. "Carefully. I've been jiggling her for hours and she's just quietened down, but if I move at all she jumps. I daren't fall asleep because my legs might shift." He was talking as if our baby was a bomb ready to go off at the slightest movement, but in a sense that was how we felt about her. Ted was pleased to have discovered this unorthodox method of placating Catherine. For the rest of the holiday, he spent as many hours with his feet tied together in motel rooms as I did pacing.

During the next few days we explored the area around Banff and I did manage, though light-headed with weariness, to marvel at the Rockies. Once, Ted and I risked leaving Catherine sleeping in the car and took a ride up a mountain on a chairlift. Twin pictures taken at the top show Ted with a tight smile and me looking stunned. We had a number of picnics at roadside scenic view sites, but if we wanted a proper meal we had to take turns. We didn't dare take the baby into restaurants.

We left Banff and headed for Glacier National Park for a few days, returning through Iowa and Montana, where we got lost in the wilds. Catherine's noise frazzled us so much that neither of us could read the map properly.

The odd memorable or funny incident still stands out from the worry and exhaustion we suffered during the trip. Most of our energy, though, was directed towards either praying that Catherine's shrieking would stop or waiting on tenterhooks for it to start again. This was the beginning of a pattern that was to last until she was about eight months old. Eventually we learned to block out the thought of the next shrieking jag and relax while we could.

The relief of being back home was enormous. We no longer had to enjoy ourselves, for one thing. Ted was able to escape to his lab whenever he could no longer stand being at home. Come to think of it, I saw very little of him at that time.

Ted's work has always been a mystery to me. To the question, "What does your husband do?" I answer that he is a physical chemist who teaches and does research in the field of nuclear magnetic resonance. To the persistent, I add that he is a spectroscopist who measures and analyzes spectra. But that is as far as I can go, because my knowledge of chemistry stops at the fact that if you let too much gas out of a Bunsen burner before you light it the result is an explosion. The only thing about Ted's work I really understand is that it is highly cerebral and that, even when he's not actually in his lab or scribbling equations at home, his mind is almost constantly preoccupied with chemistry.

While it has always pleased me to know that Ted is internationally respected by others in his field, sometimes I have found it hard to accept his frequent physical and mental absences. During the first few months of Catherine's life, however, I was grateful for his absorption in his work. I don't think I was mature enough to understand fully how difficult he found it suddenly having to be the loving father of a baby who spent most of her time screaming. All I knew was that when Ted was around I bore his anguish and frustration as well as my own.

He did try. "My turn now," he would say as soon as the screaming started, even if he'd only just come home. "You've had her all day." He spent hours carrying Catherine around the apartment and would suffer any discomfort to maintain her peace and ours. I remember one evening just before supper she fell asleep face down on his stomach when he was lying on the floor. He remained motionless for two hours, until his stomach rumbling finally awoke her.

When I took Catherine to the pediatrician for her six-week checkup I asked him about the screaming. He checked her over and seemed satisfied that nothing was amiss.

"But there must be," I said. "As I've told you before, the noise she makes is almost inhuman sometimes and she keeps it up for hours on end." He smiled and nodded.

"Wind," he said comfortably. He had obviously played this scene a thousand times.

"Well, look at her eyes," I said. "They keep crossing and she doesn't seem to register anything."

He nodded again. "Quite normal at this age," he said. "Now go home and stop worrying."

I took him at his word and didn't seriously think there was anything wrong. I decided I was simply ignorant about babies at that stage.

The question I am most often asked about Catherine is when did I first suspect that there was something wrong with her. I used to say it was when she still couldn't hold her head up when she was six weeks old, or when she failed to show any interest in toys held out for her. I realize now it was the amount and the quality of the crying she did in the initial months of her life that first aroused my suspicions. I have since encountered women who claim that their normal babies cried as frequently and for as long as Catherine did, but never, before or since, have I heard a baby cry in the *way* she did. It was a high-pitched, agonized scream. She would do it for hours on end. Her record, I masochistically recall, was twenty-one hours non-stop. My pediatrician, though I phoned him repeatedly, was sympathetic but not disturbed. We did everything we could think of to keep the baby comfortable and contented, but her screaming fits really seemed to bear no relation to anything. I did notice, however, that they were often immediately preceded by a twitch or jerk in her body, almost as if she had been given an electric shock. In retrospect I realize that some horrible form of convulsant activity was going on in her brain and that when Catherine screamed she was, just as she sounded, in agony.

During the next couple of months or so, I remained generally optimistic that Cath's screaming would diminish. She would soon turn into a proper baby who smiled at us and played with toys and only cried for identifiable reasons. I tried to infect Ted with this optimism, and he tried hard to catch it.

But the screaming continued. It dominated our lives and ruled our actions. Still clinging to the by now forlorn idea of taking Catherine everywhere with us, we would sometimes visit friends on autumn evenings. However, it seemed the screaming would start as soon as we got happily settled with drinks. Initially, we tried passing the baby around because people were eager to help and to show their expertise but that soon proved embarrassing. "I don't understand it," one grandmother said rather crossly, "I'm famous for comforting babies." Eventually we decided it was best to leave as soon as she started. She never cried for just a few minutes, it was always for hours.

How desperately I wanted to comfort her! But there were moments when I felt I hated that poor baby—hated her because she made me feel so utterly useless. Then, of course, I would be overcome with guilt and think what an unnatural mother I was.

One day during this period I read a newspaper story about a young couple who had accidentally suffocated their baby when they put tape over its mouth to stop it crying. A horrifying story, but I understood what had led them to take such a measure and had often felt like that myself. I would now classify continuous, high-pitched noise, particularly in a confined space, as physical torture, and a person can act very oddly under such stress. I vividly recall getting so frantic with the noise drilling through my head that I used to bite my arm. And I literally tore my hair out by the handful more than once. Ted now says he had a permanent headache in those days. I think Catherine must have addled his brain slightly, too, because one day when I had given up on her and left her crying in the bedroom he came charging in saying, "Look what I found stuck behind her ear—a ball of fluff off her nightie! I'll bet that's why she's been screaming!"

I looked at him incredulously. "Well then, why," I said, "is she still crying?"

"Well, it'll take her a while to calm down, won't it? That's obvious, isn't it? It must have been driving her berserk."

"Oh, bugger off," I said.

Our relationship was taking quite a battering.

Kind friends, particularly my sister-in-law Ann, offered to look after Catherine for a few hours at a time but I rarely took them up on it because I felt it unfair to subject them to her. For that same reason I didn't like to get babysitters. Catherine was on tranquillizers for a few weeks, but soon became immune to them. Anyway, it disturbed me to treat her symtomatically.

Even apart from the screaming, Catherine was behaving oddly. She always seemed to lie with her head turned to the left; in fact the back of her head on the left side was getting quite flat. This puzzled me but I figured it was just a habit she had formed. She was putting on weight satisfactorily but feeding her was difficult because she never seemed to be really hungry. She often cried so much after eating that she sicked up most of the meal. She shattered my belief that all babies naturally like to be breast fed by showing a marked preference for the bottle. It seemed ridiculous to force her to breast feed so, rather than frustrate both of us, I gave up the struggle when she was three months old. Besides, with a bottle I could see the nourishment going into her. Maybe she had been starving all this time, I thought. I tried her on tinned baby foods but I enjoyed them more than she did. She wouldn't touch the meats and vegetables but she did go for some of the fruits. It was fortunate she liked prunes, because she was always constipated. Needless to say, she still had her soother and, when its effectiveness wore off after a few weeks, Ann suggested dipping it in honey. Catherine loved it, of course, but it became an addiction. As it was cumbersome and sticky to carry a jar of honey wherever we went, I was delighted to find a squeezy jar in the shape of a bear at the local store. Billie Bee Honey, it was called, and we bought so much we probably kept the makers in business.

Another thing that helped to pacify her was a shawl my mother had sent when Catherine was born. Now that there was an autumnal chill in the air, I used it to wrap around her and I felt she missed it when it wasn't nearby. At night I tucked it around her in her crib and she looked lovely and cozy and just how a baby should look.

When I took her for her three-month checkup the doctor said she was a little slow, perhaps, but just fine. Ted and I told each other that she'd had no time to develop so far because all her efforts had gone into screaming.

When she was calm Catherine looked adorable, particularly when she smiled. I don't remember exactly when she first started to smile and laugh, probably because it was a more protracted affair than usual, but I do recall feeling slightly uneasy because her smiles seemed rather uncommunicative. She would quite often, it's true, smile at us when we played with her but it was difficult to catch and hold her eye. We would frequently see her smiling vacantly and gurgling with pleasure at nothing at all. The same applied to her laughter, which was often completely irrelevant. We would hear her chortling away in the darkness at three in the morning, but she showed absolutely no sign of amusement at rattles or squeaky toys. She appeared to enjoy only private jokes. I was also upset by how crossed her eyes were. It wasn't as if one was turned in; that I would have understood. But her eyes appeared to work independently of each other, sometimes one turning in and sometimes the other, and only rarely did I get the feeling she was looking at me directly with both of them together. I mentioned these concerns rather too casually to Ted one day and he rather too casually said he hoped she hadn't inherited his awful eyesight and warped sense of humour.

We were beginning to whistle in the dark.

Catherine was still as floppy as a rag doll by the age of five months, unless, of course, she was having a screaming session, in which case she would be bent stiffly backwards into a bow shape. She hardly ever attempted to hold her head up and only moved her limbs feebly. Yet the funny thing was, her arms and legs were sometimes difficult to move, as if she were resisting some unseen pressure. She seemed fascinated with her left hand and would wave it gently in front of her eyes, staring at it with a preoccupied expression. We were greatly encouraged when she started holding onto an object with the hand for a few seconds at a time. Nevertheless, she was still not exactly progressing by leaps and bounds.

Wilf and Ann's daughter, Loni, was eighteen months older than Catherine. I plagued Ann with questions about Loni's activities from birth to five months. She found it hard to remember but, sensing my worry, said the only thing she could say. "Look, Nix, all babies are different and I guess Cath is just a little slow, that's all." I knew nobody at that time with a small baby so I couldn't compare Catherine to anyone. Besides, my feelings were ambivalent; I wanted to reassure myself by checking with other babies but I was also scared to.

We spent Christmas day with Ted's father and stepmother in Gretna, a small prairie town eighty miles south of Winnipeg where Ted had done much of his growing up. Wilf and his family were there for the day, too, and Ted's older sister Lily and her large family. It should have been a happy occasion, but for Ted and myself, at least, it was more of an ordeal. Catherine screamed nearly all day, and when she wasn't screaming she was floppy and unresponsive. Ted's father adored his grandchildren and Cath, being the newest, received a lot of attention. I was mortified that she didn't respond to his eager overtures.

"She's a bit sleepy today," I noted more than once. "The crying tires her."

"The doctor says it's just wind." Ted tried to put conviction into his voice. "She seems shy of everyone except Nix and myself," he added as

Cath turned away from his father's puzzled gaze. I liked Mr. Schaefer very much, and as he answered the call of another grandchild I thought back to the first time I had met him.

It had been shortly after I had arrived in Canada and I was nervous. Ted was clearly very fond of his father and admired him, and I wanted to make a good impression. "Just be yourself," he had advised, adding in contradiction, "and don't smoke or swear." In fact he had already told me enough about his father's life to make the latter piece of advice unnecessary.

In 1925, Mr. Schaefer, who was a Mennonite of German origin, had emigrated to Canada from Russia with his wife and baby daughter. Life as an immigrant on the bald, bleak prairies was tough but, despite the Depression and three more children, Ted's father had managed not only to support his family but to learn English and get a BA, whereupon teaching became his career. Mennonite schools in Canada have an enviable reputation for high academic achievement and the Mennonite high school in Gretna, of which he became the principal in the late forties, was no exception. He loved his job and was more than just good at it. Mr. Schaefer inspired several generations of students to go out into the world and do well, including his own four children. He had also been a Mennonite minister for many years and was now a prominent church leader, known and immensely respected throughout the Mennonite community of Manitoba, and further afield in Canada and the States.

Ted's father was probably as nervous about the forthcoming encounter as I was. Here, I imagined him thinking, was his beloved but deviant oldest son introducing him not to a nice Mennonite girl whose family tree could be traced but to an unknown quantity whom Ted had picked up in England.

If he was indeed filled with such trepidation he hid it most effectively and there wasn't a trace of the polite reserve I'd half expected. His welcome, as Ted nudged me over the threshold, was a combination of enveloping warmth and lively curiosity. We got on well and when a few months later he performed the wedding ceremony for Ted and myself, I felt that he and Ted's stepmother had decided I might make an adequate wife for their son after all.

I wondered what he thought now. Did he, like me, feel I had produced an enigmatic granddaughter who was causing him and his family suddenly to feel uneasy with each other? Mr. Schaefer returned his attention to Catherine and held out his arms in a smiling invitation. As

I handed her over she miraculously attempted to hold her head up and then smiled. It wasn't a direct smile at her grandfather but it was a smile.

"Look! She's getting stronger and she's smiling!" he said. "What a fine girl! Ted, come and see!" I refused to allow myself to think of his delight as inordinate.

Ted seemed to feel the same. "So?" he said. "There's no reason why she shouldn't."

A few weeks later I was invited for coffee to the house of an acquaintance. We had met briefly in the faculty wives' club at the university when I first arrived in Winnipeg. Cath was nearly six months old, and it transpired that this woman had a six-month-old daughter.

"Where's your little one, Germaine?" I asked my hostess. Catherine was lying quietly on the sofa beside me. She was studying her left hand, the fingers of which were hooked through her shawl. I felt myself tensing all over as I asked the question.

"I'll go and get her. She should be awake now." Germaine returned with Juliette perched on her hip in a way that I could never have held Catherine; she would have slumped over. When Germaine put her on the sofa, there was no doubt that Juliette looked very much more wide awake than Cath. She sat gazing around at everything with interest and chomped at a rusk Germaine gave her.

"Would Catherine like a rusk?" Germaine asked.

"I don't think so, thanks," I said. "She's a bit lazy about feeding herself. And she's rather sleepy at the moment."

Later, Juliette was placed on the floor, where she did a few preliminary pushups and then rolled onto her back.

"Goodness, she's very advanced, isn't she? Cath hasn't started rolling over yet." I laughed uneasily. "She seems to find her head as heavy as a cannonball."

"Oh, I guess she's just a bit slow," said Germaine pushing Juliette over again with her foot.

"How's your thesis coming along?" I said, changing the subject.

The next day Cath was due to have her six-month checkup. I tried to look forward to it, telling myself and Ted that the doctor would consider her progress satisfactory.

It seemed wise to give the doctor a chance to reassure me right away.

"I'm really sort of wondering about Catherine," I said cautiously. He didn't say anything but examined her with care while I tried not to bite my nails too obviously. "She seems a bit odd to me," I added. It was the first time I had voiced my fears so specifically and it terrified me.

"I must admit," said the doctor finally, "she does seem to be developing very slowly." He paused and my ears started to hum in the most peculiar way. "Look," he went on, "I'll phone you in a couple of days when I have the result of the urine test."

I shook my head and banged each ear with the palm of my hand. "What is the urine test?" I asked.

"It's one we do at birth to catch and check a certain form of retardation—"

He'd said it. Retardation. God almighty. Sweat spurted from all my pores. I had to blink to bring his face back into focus.

At his next words I recovered, however. "I'm pretty sure it will be negative. Her original one was. This is just to make sure."

Phew. A reprieve. I was cold all over.

He phoned with the news that the test had been normal again.

"Thanks," I said. I cleared my throat ready to say goodbye when I suddenly found myself asking a question. "Do you think there's anything wrong with her?" My voice was a monotone.

There was the slightest pause. My ears were humming again and sweat trickled down my sides. It was hard to concentrate on his answer—something about being a slow developer. "We do see them sometimes," the doctor finished.

"I see." My whole body was shaking. Of course, Catherine was just a slow developer. What on earth had made me ask such a stupid question? I hadn't planned to; the words had just popped out. The doctor must think me a dreadfully neurotic mother. I almost stopped worrying. By the time Ted came home that evening I was able to report both the visit and the phone call with equanimity.

"I suppose I was a bit worried about her too," said Ted. "But look at her now. She's been holding that rattle for a good five seconds. She's smiling at it, too. Great going, Cath!"

"When she's grown up we'll tell her how we used to worry," I said cheerfully.

Our whistling was getting louder.

We started to formulate plans for the summer. Ted suggested that while he was working at the National Research Council in Ottawa I should go to England to see my family. It was extraordinarily generous of him and I demurred at first.

"You need it," he said firmly. "You've had a pretty rotten time of it here so far and I know how homesick you get."

"I've not had a rotten time. What nonsense—"

"Besides," Ted continued, "it'll stop me feeling so bloody guilty about dragging you out here to the wilds. I'm sure Cordelia will never forgive me."

"What's Mum got to do with it? I wanted to come and she was very happy for me. You'll have to produce a better argument than that."

"OK, I'll get more work done if you're not around."

We laughed, and a few days later it was all arranged. I was able to end my letters to England with "See you soon."

Apart from the odd stab of acute anxiety my worrying thoughts about Catherine were almost buried. Any time now, I told myself, she'll surprise us and get going.

We coasted along uneasily in this way until two weeks after her checkup, when I received a letter from a school friend. Enclosed was a photo of her first baby. I turned it over. "Patrick at seven months," Gillian had written. Good God, he was standing; hanging on to a table with one hand, but standing. In a complete panic I phoned the pediatrician.

"Listen," I blurted, "I'm worried sick, I can't pretend any longer. There's something terribly wrong with Catherine. She should be standing but her legs are all floppy. You saw them the other day when you tried to get her to take her weight on them, didn't you? They're completely floppy except when they go stiff at the wrong times. She never tries to use them for standing. She's floppy all over except when she stiffens up in that purposeless way she has—" I realized I was babbling and repeating myself and stopped abruptly.

There was a long silence at the other end of the phone. Then the doctor's discomfited voice came stuttering over the line.

"I—ah—yes. Look, normally I wouldn't send you to see a specialist until the baby was nine months old because one hates to worry the parents—"

"Worry the parents!" I interjected. Dear God! What was the man talking about? "I couldn't be more worried than I am now! I want to see someone at *once*—"

"Yes. Ah. Yes, I see. Yes, well, in view of that and the fact that you're going to England I'll fix up an appointment for you to see Dr. Hall as soon as possible."

"Dr. Hall?"

"Yes, he's a child-development specialist down at the Children's Hospital."

"Oh."

Later that day Dr. Hall's nurse called me to say that an appointment had been arranged for March 15th.

"But that's a month away!" She must be joking. "I want to see him today, tomorrow at the latest!"

"I'm sorry," said the nurse crisply, "Dr. Hall is a very busy man, you know."

I dreaded telling Ted I was taking Catherine to see a specialist. I had been getting used to the idea all day but he would have to face it all at once. My whistling had temporarily petered out but I suspected Ted would deafen us both with his.

I was right.

"For God's sake what on earth *for?*" he said furiously. "Didn't what's-his-name, the pediatrician, didn't he tell you she's just slow? Try and get that through your head—she's *just slow.*" He stalked off and I went miserably into the bedroom to pick up Catherine. She wasn't crying but I needed something to do. Ted came in later and said he hadn't been cross so much as sick with worry. I said I knew.

I remember nothing more about that waiting period and neither does Ted. We both seem to have erased it entirely from our minds. I do recall, however, phoning the pediatrician the day before seeing Dr. Hall.

"Is it possible," I asked, "just possible, that there's nothing wrong with our daughter? That she's just slow?"

The silence stretched to infinity. "It's just possible," he said.

I put the phone down and sat quite still, staring at a patch on the knee of my jeans. I found that in my mind I could shorten the silence, replace the "just" with "quite" and add a cheerful expression to the doctor's voice.

By the time Ted came home I was able to greet him with, "Hello sweetheart. Supper's nearly ready. Oh, and listen, I'd nearly decided not to bother taking Cath down to see this Dr. Hall but I think I'd better go. You know, just in case. Here's a cup of tea—"

"Thanks, I'm parched. Hey, is that roast pork I smell? Yes, I guess you'd better. Incidentally, I think I've found somewhere to live while I'm in Ottawa."

"Gosh, that's good. Let's have a bottle of wine tomorrow to celebrate. It can be a double one—that and finding there's nothing wrong with Cath."

We were whistling again but it seemed the only way to cope with the thought of the next day. When I set off for the hospital I felt almost jaunty.

3

How does one react to being told that one's baby, one's precious first-born daughter, one's hope and joy, is a useless mistake of nature who should probably be dumped in an institution and forgotten about?

Even after discussing this subject with many other parents of severely handicapped children, my own reaction is still the only one I can speak about in any depth.

There are several stock phrases to describe my initial reaction—"stunned disbelief," "impotent rage"—and I certainly felt these emotions. But my very first reaction was one of overwhelming self-pity. Why us? Then, within a matter of hours, I thought why *not* us? I was on the way to facing the situation, intellectually if not emotionally. There was a strong element of relief present; having a definite situation to face helped enormously. It was the months of suspecting there *was* a situation that had been intolerable.

It still took me a day or so to face people. I didn't mind telling them what was up but I dreaded the sympathy and pity that was bound to come our way. The morning after our appointment with Dr. Hall I called Ann. I broke down and became incoherent, but managed to give her the basic facts, adding, "Please don't tell anyone else yet." Ted phoned a close friend of ours in the chemistry department. "It's not good, Ernie," was all he could say before he hung up. "I sounded like a bad film script," he told me.

Within half an hour Ernie was on our doorstep with a bottle of rye in a paper bag, a gesture for which we will always be grateful. None of us said very much at first because there was extraordinarily little to say. We just sat and demolished the whisky. I drank not because I wanted to, but because I couldn't think of anything else to do. I got very drunk and maudlin but retained enough clarity of mind to know that this wasn't really me. I was acting like this because it was expected. I gave myself a mental shake. All right, I thought, this is a lousy blow we've been dealt but what's the point of moaning and moping? Let's accept and enjoy Catherine for what she is and take things step by step. We'll not worry about the future for the time being. As for people's sympathy—well, that's fine. But let's make it absolutely impossible for anyone, ever, to pity us.

And this, roughly speaking, was the attitude I adopted.

Ted now says he was grateful I took the lead about Catherine, although I didn't consciously do so. He was completely at sea. I have always felt that in many ways Ted had a tougher time of it than I did during that grisly period. For one thing I am quite loquacious and have always been willing to bore my friends with my problems. Ted is much more private and withdrawn, preferring to sort out whatever problems he has by himself. Secondly, I had a much more definite role to play with Catherine and a more immediate responsibility for her. I found that my daily routine with her helped to keep me going.

Telling friends in Winnipeg about Catherine was painful enough but telling Ted's parents was, naturally, far worse. They were horribly upset at the news but admitted they had been concerned about her. They tried hard to adopt our *que sera sera* attitude. Although it was illogical, I felt oddly guilty about having produced such a failure of a grandchild for them. I promised, rather wildly, that we would have lots of other babies, respectable ones, in the future.

As I discovered later, the innate sense of guilt I experienced is almost universal amongst people who have a child born seriously abnormal, particularly if there is no explanation for the abnormality. And it is not a reasonable guilt, so no amount of reasoning can dispel it. Men sometimes have a worse time with this than women. If the abnormal child is their first they often feel humiliated. "I was bursting with pride when my son was born," one friend told me recently. "I strutted around thinking I was Superman. Then we discovered he was severely retarded. Pow! I was impotent for months." Ted didn't react quite so drastically, but he did experience a feeling of guilt at having fathered a useless offspring who would ultimately become a burden to society. The guilt was touched with fear and he thinks both these emotions were primitive ones harking back to the days when weak members of the tribe weren't tolerated.

I still needed to tell my family in England about Catherine, of course. I found that letter to my mother the most difficult I have ever written.

After presenting the doleful facts, I stressed that Ted and I had accepted the circumstances and so should everyone else. I went on to say how adorable Cath was and how much we loved her and how we planned to enlarge our family quickly and that everything would be all right. I awaited my mother's response with trepidation. She sent a loving cable and in the letter that followed she said something that surprised me. Apparently she had been worried about the baby because she could tell from my letters that she wasn't developing normally, even though I had always minimized Cath's screaming and made the most of her merits. She loved the photos I sent her but they worried her as well. This made me remember ruefully the hours we had spent hovering around Catherine with our five-dollar camera waiting for her to smile, or at least have her eyes pointing in the same direction.

I also wrote to my mother's sister, Mary, who is a doctor. She and I have always enjoyed a close relationship and she was one of the mainstays of my childhood. Perhaps she might have some practical suggestions about seeing a neurologist, or whatever sort of doctor was appropriate, when Cath and I got to England. I knew another doctor wouldn't make a different, more cheerful diagnosis but I was accumulating a number of questions that required a doctor's opinion. What exactly was wrong with Catherine's brain? Cerebral palsy and neuromuscular disorder were so unspecific. What had caused her condition? This was the first thing everyone wanted to know but I could only parrot my pediatrician and say, "These things just seem to happen sometimes." I had been perfectly healthy during my pregnancy, as far as I knew. What areas of her development were likely to be affected? What was her prognosis?

Mary responded immediately saying, amongst other things, that she would arrange for Catherine to be seen at the spastic clinic in Edinburgh, where she lived. Apparently there was a bright young doctor there whom she and my uncle, a biochemist, knew.

Once my family had been informed about Catherine, I began to look forward to going to England. We found a lodger for the apartment and Ted wrapped up his year's work at the university. I wrapped up Catherine and myself and off the three of us went to Montreal where Ted was to put us on the boat.

There was, incidentally, some exciting news I had not imparted to my family and kept up my sleeve, as it were, in case people ran out of nice things to say about Catherine when they met her. I was two months preg-

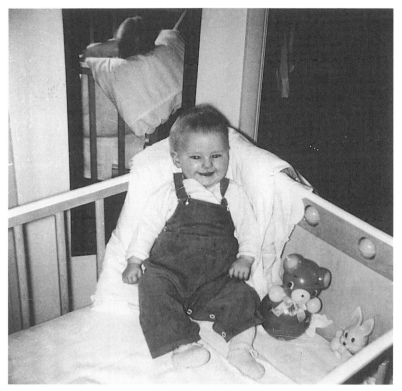

Cath, aged nine months, with her favourite toy, Ding-dong.

nant. One of my reactions to Cath's diagnosis had been an urgent desire to have another baby, and nature had obliged. Our son Dominic was born almost exactly nine months after the momentous visit to Dr. Hall.

By the time we went to England, Cath was nine months old. Her screaming had become more managcable. I could usually pacify her within a few minutes if I caught her in time. If I didn't, she would get herself wound up and hysterical, and the ensuing session could last for over an hour. Whenever I noticed her beginning to twitch and breathe faster, I would pick her up and hold her tightly against my chest with my left arm, while rubbing and thumping her back vigorously with my right. This was an energetic exercise in itself but only worked when I would simultaneously jiggle her up and down like mad while striding around.

It was an exhausting procedure, and I sometimes felt I was in physical battle with whatever devil it was that caused Catherine to scream.

A bottle of phenobarb plus the above strategy saw us across the Atlantic. A gang of relatives met us off the boat train and and we piled into a taxi. We were heading for the house in Hammersmith where my mother and stepfather, an actor, lived with my young brother Edgar and a curious assortment of lodgers and cats.

"Why isn't Mum here?" I asked my older sister, Veronica, through the gabble of conversation.

"She's dealing with the drains," she answered. "It poured last night and the bath won't run out because the outside pipe's choked up with leaves. Mum nearly had a fit. The kitchen sink backed up this morning and she'd just finished dealing with that when she discovered the bath. She's convinced there's a conspiracy to stop her from coming to meet you." Veronica and I giggled.

"Any changes in the house?" I asked.

"Let's see. A new lodger in the ex-convict's room and an enormous hole in the roof at the back. Oh, and a smart hi-fi set. That appeared a month after the hole," she added succinctly. We both giggled again. Neither of us had ever understood Mum and Harry's system of priorities.

"Well, things sound reassuringly chaotic," I said happily. As we chattered and giggled, I peered out at the familiar landmarks gliding by. Ted had been right, although I hated to admit it even privately. I had missed my daft family and my old habitat acutely. And the drawn-out strain of Cath's first few months hadn't exactly helped.

The taxi drew up to the unchanged, crumbling doorstep. My mother appeared at the top in men's gumboots. "Darling!" she shouted and came charging down waving a stick. "All unblocked. Oh, how marvellous to see you!"

Once inside, I changed a soaking Catherine, fed her, then put her down to sleep in Edgar's old cot. I was in my old room that Harry had redecorated in our honour. He came in and hugged me. "Oooooh, it isn't half good to see you, love. And your Cath." He looked down at her. "I don't give a bugger what's wrong with her, she's an absolute little beauty, isn't she?" Dear Harry, he could be wildly irritating at times but he never failed to find exactly the right thing to say.

"You're her favourite step-grandfather," I said gratefully. "Harry, you've done a smashing job on this room. Hey, I really like that sort of splattered effect. How did you manage it?" I nodded to the one wall that was painted instead of papered.

"Yerse. Well." Harry cleared his throat. "I used a spray gun you see, and they're a bit tricky—"

"Ah," I said, light beginning to dawn. He had always loved gadgets but tended to encounter difficulties with them.

"They go off all over the bloody place—" he started to pantomime what had happened—"not just where you aim. I had to go and get my eyes washed out at the hospital at one point. Shocking business, they thought I'd be blind. Gor! And," he concluded, "I've got the only green-spotted evening shoes in the business. Yes, yes, I know, I meant to change them before I sprayed. I changed everything else, mind you. I just got carried away one night after doing a variety show. Oooo! Seen the downstairs lav yet? I've had a go at that too—nice plastic tiles. Your mother says she misses the graffiti but I think she was upset because I accidentally happened to spill a bit of the glue down the lav and she had to unclog it. Now then," he said suddenly serious, "I could easily go over that wall with a brush—"

"Oh Harry, no," I laughed. "I love it. It'll be like sleeping with Seurat."

Downstairs there followed two hours of lovely confusion while six or seven of us crammed around the kitchen table, talking and downing spaghetti and wine.

"That was a delicious meal, Mum," I said later while my mother was helping me with Catherine, "absolutely first-rate. Gosh, I've missed your spag!" My mother finds cooking onerous and requires abundant praise when she makes a meal.

"Thank you, darling," she responded graciously. "Sorry I wasn't up to doing a pudding but there was plenty of fruit, wasn't there? Now, give me all Cath's dirty nappies and I'll wash them. You're not to wash a single one while you're here. No, don't protest, you naughty girl, you know I'll be blissfully happy doing them." She paused. "If you ever felt like cooking a meal—" We struck a happy bargain and I went to bed that night feeling more relaxed than I had for nine bewildering and frightening months.

Those three and a half months in England were highly restorative to my battered psyche. There was a constant stream of people through the house—interesting, funny, sometimes mad—which suited my gregarious nature perfectly. Judging by the number of people who commented on how much less strained I looked as the weeks went by, I must have looked awful when I arrived. I realized I had been subconsciously scared of facing everyone with Catherine. My mother had obviously done an excellent job of sowing in people's minds the idea that Cath should be accepted for what she was. I don't know what, if anything, was said when I wasn't around, but certainly nobody overtly pitied me.

Shortly after I arrived I went to the local ante-natal clinic and was thrilled when the doctor said he could feel the heartbeat of my new baby. My appetite was gargantuan but I indulged myself because Ted, sweet man, had made me promise to do so. My spirit blossomed and my body bulged.

Catherine, meanwhile, was changing slightly too. Her terrible screaming fits began to diminish in number if not in quality and she smiled and laughed more frequently. Her laugh was becoming delightfully infectious. I was pleased to discover that if I caught her in one of her laughing-at-nothing moods, I could increase her laughter by tickling her and flapping her limbs around. This was really the first time I had felt any definite response from her. Until then I had known there was some sort of communication between us but it was intangible. She also began to smile directly in response to a smile from me more frequently. My overall impression at this time was that she lived in her own private world, a world she would only occasionally allow me to penetrate. I was constantly having to dismiss from my mind the idea that she didn't really notice whether or not I was around.

She was also changing physically. She still appeared to derive great pleasure and comfort from holding up her left hand and staring at it whimsically but now she evidently decided it might be put to some practical use; I would sometimes spot her pulling things towards her mouth with it. I had discovered some time before this that she enjoyed having her face covered up. Indeed, one way of encouraging her to sleep was to put her shawl—it was a lacy one—loosely over her face. Now Cath was struggling to do this for herself. Her muscles were becoming a little stronger, I thought, because she was moving her legs more and trying to roll over onto one side. I encouraged this, of course, and I also placed her over cushions on her stomach and then nudged her to see if she could get the idea of rolling over onto her back. She didn't enjoy this, though, so I concentrated on what she herself had initiated. She was putting on weight and eating quite well, but still mostly baby foods because she choked violently on even a minute lump. I had carried her everywhere from the time I had left Winnipeg but as soon as I arrived in England I bought a stroller. If I put the back down I could lie her in a semi-sitting position on a pillow and she was quite secure. In this way we were able to go for long tramps down the Thames Embankment and in the park nearby.

One sunny afternoon when I was sitting under a tree in the park reading and Cath was asleep in her stroller, a woman passing by paused to ask me the time. I told her and as she left she remarked, "Lovely baby you've got there. Cheerio." She didn't notice anything odd about Cath, I thought. She assumed she was a normal baby out for a walk with her mum. And out of the blue I found myself plunged into a state of profound bitterness as I started to think uncontrollably about what might have been. My hard-won philosophical outlook on everything was being shaken out of me by great wracking sobs. I was enveloped in hopelessness.

I was frightened and bewildered. What was happening? And why? It seemed as if an outside force was dragging me down, holding me beneath my normal self. At the time I thought I was having a nervous breakdown but after it was over, I felt calm and refreshed. Since then it has happened quite regularly about every six months: half an hour of tears and despondency usually precipitated by a tiny incident that shouldn't bother me at all—a chance remark like the first time, seeing a normal girl who resembles Catherine, and so on. But I understand it now, and am no longer frightened. I know I'll recover; in fact such bouts are therapeutic and necessary. I'm supremely grateful that I seem to be quite straightforward emotionally. It is, after all, one of the factors that made accepting Catherine, and keeping her, possible.

Due to the dearth of good concerts and concert halls in Winnipeg in the early sixties (the scene has changed dramatically now, I should add), I had had to assuage my concert-going urges by listening to the radio and my records. Now that I was in London there were excellent concerts virtually on my doorstep every night. I tried to put the idea of going to any of them out of my mind, because Cath refused to take food from anyone except me. She was also prone to crying sessions in the evenings. However, my mother was determined that I should manage to go to at least one while I was visiting.

"You're never away from her, darling. She's got to get used to being without you sometimes. It can't be good for you, either."

So one night when I noticed a particularly enticing concert advertised I poured my mother a hefty gin and tonic, and a friend and I took a taxi to the Festival Hall. But I was unable to concentrate and enjoy the evening, because I kept visualizing Catherine screaming as my mother paced up and down, eyeing the gin bottle. When I panted in later on, Catherine was indeed screaming and my mother greeted me with her hair standing on end and a wild look in her eye.

"Oh God am I pleased to see you back!" She tried to modify her words later but I could see that her nerves were jangling. It was a long time before I dared to leave Cath with anyone again.

Catherine and I spent a week with Mary and David in Edinburgh and I was delighted to find that their daughter, Julia, was staying there too. After greeting each other with much hugging, I said proudly, "And this is my daughter Catherine," thus instituting a greeting pattern between us. It would be firmly established over the years as I increased my family and Julia began hers.

My aunt had arranged for Catherine to be seen by Dr. McInnes at Rhuemore Hospital where there was an out-patient clinic for spastics. I was disconcerted as I walked into the room to be faced by several people sitting at attention with pencils and notebooks. I felt as if Catherine and I were on exhibition and for an instant I wanted to turn tail and run. I have taken her to many clinics since then and have learnt to accept the presence of other doctors, therapists and students, but that first time I found it difficult both to ask and answer questions.

I liked Dr. McInnes immediately. He was straightforward without being unpleasantly blunt and he was also sympathetic and intelligent. But possibly the nicest thing about him was that he treated me as though I, too, was intelligent. He was more edifying than the doctors in Winnipeg but none of the things he told me filled me with joy.

First, he said that the cause of Catherine's brain damage would never be ascertained. I have, however, always accepted his explanation that there are many viruses knocking around which, if caught by a woman during the first three months of her pregnancy, may damage the brain of the embryo she is carrying even though the virus may only cause an unremarkable sneeze or a slight sore throat in the mother. It is an incomplete conclusion, but better than "these things just seem to happen."

Second, Catherine's brain was, it seemed, extensively damaged and this would affect every area of her physical development. The damage to the right side of her brain was not so severe as that to the left side, hence the budding use of her left hand while her right one remained curled into a fist. Dr. McInnes pointed out that although Cath's muscles were developing somewhat, they were showing marked signs of spasticity—stiff, uncontrolled, jerky movements. This was particularly true of her legs; the inside thigh muscles were contracting more than the outside ones when she kicked, causing her legs to pull together. This would lead, eventually, to scissoring, dislocated hips and various other complications.

Third, he said she was experiencing epileptic-type seizures in her brain which, when they occurred, interrupted any tiny train of thought she might be having. This made sense to me. I had often noticed that she would embark on a course of action, such as reaching for her shawl, and then her body would twitch several times in close succession. Afterwards, she would look blank and forget about the shawl. They were the same sort of twitches she had had when she was smaller but they no longer seemed to cause her terrible pain. The doctor said he would do an electroencephalogram later in the week to see exactly how much seizure activity was present and whether it could be controlled by drugs.

Fourth, in answer to my urgent enquiry about what I could do to help Catherine, Dr. McInnes said there wasn't much beyond physiotherapy and as much stimulation as possible.

"Get a dog, perhaps," he suggested.

"My husband doesn't like dogs," I replied.

"Oh. But you're having another baby, aren't you? Well, that'll do just as well."

Fifth, she would be more prone to serious chest infections than usual but her prognosis was normal. And finally, her mentality was severely affected. I had left this question to the end because I dreaded the answer. I actually knew perfectly well that she was very dim but had been hanging on to the possibility that Dr. McInnes would say her motor difficulties were preventing her mental powers from showing. He did me a tremendous service when he said, after observing my crestfallen, tearful response to his answer, "She will be happier. Try to think of it that way. She'll never know, you see. It's you who will bear the anguish, I'm afraid."

Why is it less impossible, which is not the same as easier, to accept gross physical impairment in one's child than severe mental retardation? I know I'm not alone in finding this; certainly almost every parent I've talked to on the subject has felt the same. Possibly it's due in part to the enormous emphasis placed on achievement in our society, and this seems to apply more in the intellectual field than in the physical. Consequently, there is still more of a stigma attached to mental retardation than to physical handicaps.

Assimilating the confirmation of Catherine's mental retardation was helped greatly by being with Mary and Julia, although they were both so empathetic that I sometimes felt they were having a worse time than me. Mary took time off from her work to drive me and Catherine around, first to have the EEG, X-rays and other tests done and then to see Mrs. Wallace, the physiotherapist at the clinic. She was a solicitous woman and spent ages talking to me and showing me developmental exercises to do with Catherine. I didn't think there was much in Winnipeg in the way of therapy for children like Catherine, so she wrote everything down and drew diagrams of what I should be doing. We also saw Dr. McInnes again. He gave me a supply of a drug called Ospolot, unavailable in Canada at that time, to help control Cath's epileptic seizures, which he referred to as myoclonic jerks.

All the way down from Edinburgh in the train I thought about the letter on its way to Ted. I had couched the news in the most optimistic terms possible but nothing I said could disguise the salient point.

I accepted Catherine's diagnosis and prognosis but didn't then sit back and expect nothing of her. Neither did I plan to exhaust myself financially and emotionally by chasing around the world forever seeking a different opinion, a cure, a miracle. I tried to view the situation with open-minded realism. I would do everything in my power to help her to progress but not at the expense of my marriage, any normal children we might have and, last but not least, myself. Achieving this balance may not sound difficult but it most assuredly was, and still is.

If I ever had only two days to spend in England, I would spend one of them in Oxford. That city has an attraction for me that never diminishes. It may become more industrial and some of the Victorian mansions may disappear to give way to modern additions to colleges. Oxford may change in many ways but it will always be my favourite city. Not only are parts of it unparalleled in beauty, but it also holds a deep nostalgia for me. I spent a happy childhood and adolescence there and a number of my old friends still live nearby.

When Julia's sister, Chloe, invited me down for a week just after I returned to London I was on the next train. Chloe, a good friend as well as a first cousin, is a domiciliary midwife. Although by that time she had a car to do her rounds in she still had her old bicycle in the cellar. I hauled it out and oiled it and, when I knew Catherine was settled for a while, would take off on bike rides all over the city. What a wonderful sense of freedom that ancient contraption gave me as I pedalled around all my old haunts! I also walked with Catherine for miles along the river, eating blackberries off the bushes as we went. Christ Church College is just down the road from Chloe's house and Cath and I spent hours ambling around the Meadows. It was midsummer and the gardens were at their best. Catherine seemed to catch my happiness. I remember only one occasion when I had to rush home with her because her screaming was attracting more attention from the tourists than the college was.

The last part of our holiday was spent with my mother, my brother Edgar and my sister's two children, Richard and Eleanor, at my mother's cottage in Sussex. About two miles from this cottage, deep in farming country and close to the foot of the South Downs, is what might be described as our family compound, Greatham. My great-grandparents on my mother's side had bought it, a farmhouse set in eighty acres of land, in 1911, as a summer home for their large family. The core of Greatham comprises the original house, with a large library built on, the family having a literary bent, plus three other houses that were added soon after the property was bought. Surrounding the houses is an extensive garden, with a swimming pool and tennis court, and this in turn is surrounded by woods and fields. It is a beautiful place and I spent nearly every summer there as a child. A few members of the family, mostly of my mother's generation, live there permanently but it is mainly used as a holiday place for my great-grandparents' numerous descendants, over a hundred of them. As early as the fifties space was becoming limited, so my mother very cleverly bought a cottage nearby for a few hundred pounds. We can now enjoy the family and the amenities of Greatham but remain independent.

It was several days before we walked over to Greatham. Knowing there would be swarms of relatives, including several cousins who had babies Cath's age, made me a little apprehensive. However, since I badly wanted to see everyone, and Greatham, I put on my casual look and we went. It was fine, of course, though I do recall taking a somewhat defensive attitude and talking about my next baby rather too much at first. I remember at one point Julia and Chloe's sister, Rosalind, coming towards me across the lawn with her year-old son crawling behind her. She said, "I feel almost guilty having such an obviously healthy baby!" I told her not to be ridiculous and not to think that way because I certainly didn't.

I was glad she had said it, though. It made me realize how thoughtlessly selfish I had been since finding out about Catherine's deficiencies. I was constantly worrying about what I would feel when meeting people and not paying enough attention to their feelings. Thenceforth, I tried to put myself in other people's shoes so I could try to dispel their embarrassment and fear of hurting my feelings.

Our weeks at the cottage were lovely. The days idled by, we ate mountains of vegetables from the garden, Cath lay by the hour on the lawn under the apple trees, her diapers lost their grey London look and flapped whitely on the line, friends dropped in and we soaked up the sun of a generous summer. On most days some kind relative with a car would come and take us over to Greatham because it was too hot to walk that far. I took Catherine with me into the swimming pool on one particularly hot day but it terrified her and her feet turned purple.

Enjoyable and rejuvenating though our months in England with my family were, I had missed Ted immensely and began to be restless as the date of our departure drew close. I was, inevitably, sad to leave, but looked forward to being with Ted again and resettling in Winnipeg. And to the birth of our next baby.

4

Soon after we arrived back in Winnipeg I had a nasty thought. What was going to happen to Catherine during the five days I would be in the hospital? The only person with whom I might possibly have left her was Ann, but she was due to have another baby a month before I was and her daughter Loni was now an active three-year-old. Theoretically, Catherine could have gone into one of the hospitals with a special wing for the care of severely handicapped children but leaving her with strangers was unthinkable at that time. I wished I were back in Oxford, where, with Chloe's help as a midwife, I could have had the baby at home. I thought fleetingly of staying in the apartment until it was too late to go to the hospital, but knew the idea would upset my nice obstetrician, Dr. Friesen, who had promised to be around this time.

What was I to do? I hesitated to worry Ted about it because he had worked hard all summer and was now preoccupied with a new year of

Nicola and Cath just before Dominic was born.

teaching and research. It was he, however, who surprisingly came up with the solution. I was bathing Catherine one evening and he appeared at the door and watched me.

"That looks a complicated business," he said.

"It is," I muttered briefly. I was concentrating on not drowning her. One moment she would lie limp and vacant-eyed as I held her head above the water with one hand and washed her with the other. Then, without warning, she would emit an excited shout and simultaneously arch backwards and kick spastically. Then she would return just as unexpectedly to limp inactivity.

"I could do it," said Ted nonchalantly.

"Mm? Cath, if you swallow any more water you're going to choke and bring up your supper. *What* did you say?" I removed the plug and pushed my hair back from my face so that we could see each other.

"Well, I guess she'll need a bath while you're in hospital—"

I stared at him. "Of course, yes, but—good God, you don't seriously mean—"

Ted seemed surprised. "But that's what I've assumed all along. It'll be the Christmas break so there's no reason why not. I'll probably never look after her again but five days won't kill me." He looked thoughtful. "I don't think," he added.

So, as the time drew near I laid in a supply of canned baby and grown-up food, ordered Dial-a-Diaper service and wrote twenty-seven illegible pages of instructions on how to look after Catherine. Ted later told me he couldn't even decipher the pediatrician's phone number.

A short while before I had the baby I took Cath down to see Dr. Hall, wanting to arrange some professional physiotherapy for her at the hospital. I went feeling cheerful and returned home in a fury.

"That bloody man," I said to Ted as I handed Cath over to him and sat myself down, splay-legged and panting, on the sofa. "I cannot seem to convince him that I've accepted what's wrong with Cath and that I know she's never going to amount to much! I suppose because he gets some mothers who kid themselves there's nothing wrong with their wonky children he thinks they're all like that. He just sits there going on and on about what a terrible burden Cath's going to be, then looks at me gloomily, writing in his notes and shaking his head. God!"

Ted then told me, not for the first time, what he thought of the medical profession in general. "Did he at least fix up physiotherapy for Cath?" he asked at the end of his diatribe.

"Yes. Reluctantly, I might add. I'm to take her down periodically so that my methods can be checked up on." I started to get steamed up again. "Hell, it's hard enough getting to the point where you've accepted the situation without people then implying that you haven't! And I will not even entertain the idea of sticking her into an inst—"

Ted held up his hand. "OK, OK," he said. "Let's have a cup of tea."

I removed Dr. Hall from my mind and concentrated on looking forward to having the baby.

When the time came, Ted had to take me to the hospital during a snowstorm in the middle of the night. He went back home muttering rude things to the effect that it had taken me two bloody days last time so why the rush now? This time I knew it was going to be different. The whole thing, from first spasm to first squawk, took three and a half hours and I enjoyed every minute of it.

"Is he all right, Dr. Friesen?" I gasped a split second after the baby was born.

"How do you know it's a boy, Mrs. Schaefer?" I could hear him smiling.

"Of course it's a boy—it has been right from the start. If you see what I mean."

"Yes, it's a boy, and he looks perfect. I don't think you need worry for a minute about this one. He's big, too. Look!"

"Oh, let me hold him. Oh, he's stunning. Look at that great thatch of black hair. Oh, thank you, Dr. Friesen. Good God, look at this, he's holding his head up already, he really is, just look at this. Oh, he's the most beautiful thing—" I was delirious with joy.

"Now calm down, Mrs. Schaefer, for heaven's sake," said Dr. Friesen from between my legs. "You're jumping around and I haven't finished yet."

"I can't calm down! Don't you realize what I've done? I've made a proper baby at last! It's the most wonderful feeling I've ever had. Can I phone Ted? I must tell him right away, he'll be so happy!"

"Yes, you can, Mrs. Schaefer, of course you can." Dr. Friesen came and kissed me on the forehead. "I'm so happy for you," he said smiling at me. "I wouldn't have missed this one for anything."

I was wheeled out on the trolley into the hall and a nurse dialed the number. It was some time before there was an answer. "Yes?" said Ted's sleepy voice.

"Hi," I said slowly, and then, savouring every word, "you have got the most gorgeous son imaginable." I paused. "What do you think of that?" I shut my eyes and smiled expectantly.

"You've got the wrong number," said Ted. And he hung up.

I phoned back indignantly and we got things sorted out. Poor chap, he'd assumed it would be well into the next day before he heard from me and had just got off to sleep when the phone went.

I was very curious to see what, if anything, Catherine would do when she saw me again and prepared myself for the worst—a blank. Ted left her propped up on cushions in the back of the car while he came to help me out of the hospital with the baby. I opened the door and slid in beside her. "Hello sweetheart," I said. "How's my precious girl?"

She turned and looked at me and turned away again. Then, in the slowest double take I've ever witnessed, she turned back and her face gradually lit up with the loveliest smile. Her eyes shone and she produced every excited noise in her repertoire, waving her arms and kicking madly. I picked her up and hugged her.

"You sweet, adorable nitwit," I said. "Chuck the baby in the front with you," I shouted to Ted through the window. "I'm sitting back here.

Apart from having been squashed into a garment she'd outgrown months before, Cath looked fine. Ted had managed very well during my absence, though he confessed that he was relieved to throw the reins back to me. The fridge was full of extraordinary things like shrimps and avocados, none of which I would ever have dreamed of buying. I decided he should do the shopping more often, particularly when I came across pounds of steak in the freezer.

I have never ceased to be grateful to Dominic for being the perfect baby that he was. Not only was he patently strong, healthy and interested in life, he was also exceptionally good-natured and contented. I unashamedly showed him off to anyone who was interested, and probably quite a few who weren't. I was usually too besotted to notice. We wanted to rush out to Gretna and show him off to Ted's parents but they beat us to it. How delighted they were with the baby! How delighted we all were with him, and with each other!

I didn't know what Catherine was going to make of the baby and at first she didn't make anything of him at all. If I held him up in front of her she seemed pointedly to ignore him, her eyes rolling around and refusing to settle on him. When I put them together on the floor or a bed, though, she sometimes took quite an interest in him, turning over onto her side and touching Dominic delicately with her left hand while making cooing noises. Every now and again her interest would be aroused to the point where she would grab at him and try to pull him towards her.

I had to be careful not to let her grab Dominic in the wrong places because I knew how painful it could be. As she grew more excited Catherine's hold became more spastic, until her fingers were so tightly clenched that it was almost impossible to unhook them. One of her favourite games was tangling her left hand up in my hair, and another was getting hold of my nose and slowly but inexorably trying to twist it off. The best part of these games, as far as she was concerned, was my loud protestations. Ted and I endured considerable pain to amuse and gain a sense of communication with her. Her right hand still resisted all my attempts to make it useful and remained curled up like a new-born fern, except when I unrolled and exercised it.

Ever since seeing the physiotherapist in Edinburgh, I had been doing the exercises she had suggested and written down, occasionally checking in with a physiotherapist at the Children's Hospital. The passive ones—massaging and stretching her muscles—were no problem, but the more active ones were tricky. They were designed mainly to help Catherine follow the normal developmental pattern of holding her head up, rolling over, kneeling, rocking, sitting, standing, and so on. The secondary aim was to create in her a sense of balance and self-preservation. There were two main problems. First, she still couldn't manage the all-important first step of holding up her head. True, she was beginning to show signs of wanting to hold it upright but she found it very tiring. Second, her muscular system had only two speeds, totally floppy or seized up in spasticity. I would sit her cross-legged with me supporting her from behind and shove her gently to one side, with the idea that she should stretch out her arm to the floor to save herself. But she would either flop over with a giggle or transform herself into something closely resembling a twisted-up bicycle wheel. However, I persevered, though I felt constantly guilty because I suspected I should really be working on her for much longer each day.

When Dominic was about a month old, Cath did do something that thrilled me. She rolled from her stomach onto her back. I often left her on her stomach, even though she disliked it most of the time. I think it made her feel helpless, like an upturned turtle. However, it did encourage her to lift her head up and to use her arm and trunk muscles to do push-ups. I hoped that pure fury might eventually induce her to roll over, though I had to be careful not to leave her struggling so long that she became hysterical. One day I had left her on the sitting room floor straining her head up to look at herself in her mirror. I suddenly realized that her angry squawks had stopped. Leaving Dominic half changed I dashed in and there she was on her back, beaming and kicking. I hugged and kissed her and told her how incredibly clever she was. Then I put her back onto her stomach and held my breath to see if she would repeat the performance. She did, and I was fascinated to observe her unorthodox method. Instead of starting with her head she evidently found it easier to hitch her shoulders and bottom over first, then her legs and finally her head, which would roll over with the momentum of her body.

I usually tried not to phone Ted at the university but I felt this achievement warranted a call.

"Any message?" asked the student who answered. Ted was grappling with the plumbing of his three-ton magnet and I knew he would find it tricky to disentangle himself.

"Tell him Catherine got from her front to her back," I said. "He'll understand."

"What's all this about Cath being back to front?" asked Ted a few minutes later. "You're kidding!" he said when I'd explained. "I'd resigned myself to her never making it!"

Trying to stimulate Cath mentally was frustrating, largely because there appeared to be so little mentality to stimulate. Someone had given her a bright red plastic teddy bear which rocked and rolled but was weighted so that it wouldn't fall over. As it moved it made a noise, which resulted in it being known as Ding-dong. When I left her alone on the floor or in her crib I would often leave Ding-dong beside her so that she would have something to amuse her. She never played with it in a conventional way, of course, but she enjoyed being close enough to lick it. She would do this for minutes on end, gurgling with pleasure as it ding-donged. I liked to think she was discovering the cause-and-effect principle but in view of her other activities I wasn't so sure.

She took no notice of the ingenious and frequently changed arrangement of toys strung across her crib. True, she sometimes bashed at them spastically but she was almost totally uninterested in the noise and movement unintentionally produced. Because of her budding interest in the baby we fixed up a mirror on one side of her crib. This was more successful and she loved to make funny faces at herself. It was at this time that I realized her crib gave her a sense of security. If she was unhappy and I put her into it, she would quite often spontaneously stop crying.

The physiotherapist had suggested that I give her different textures to feel—silk, sacking, stones, foam rubber and so on—to stimulate her senses of touch and feel. This was fine until the day I decided to try one of her more improbable ideas, which was to lie Cath in a bath full of cooked porridge. At least, I think she meant cooked, but on reflection she might have meant raw oats.

I spent the morning making porridge. It soon dawned on me, though, that even if I used every pot I possessed there would still be barely enough porridge to line the bottom of the bath, and the idea was that

Cath should lie in, rather than on, the porridge. This problem was solved by wedging a piece of wood across one end of the bath, shortening it to Catherine's length. Even so, it would still be difficult to have enough porridge at the right temperature all at once. I tipped the first lot into the biggest roasting pan I could borrow and put it in the oven while I made a second batch. Finally there was enough and I staggered back and forth unloading it into the bath. By stirring it up with a wooden spoon and adding some water from the tap, I soon had a grey glutinous mass at the right temperature. Having lashed myself around with rubber sheets, I undressed Catherine and told her cheerfully what I was going to do.

She was not enthusiastic. She seemed to know this wasn't going to be an ordinary bath, which she loved, and started to cry and cast nervous glances around. Normally I would have picked her up and held her close to reassure her, but being pressed against cold rubber would hardly be comforting. So I picked her up and, holding her at arm's length, rushed into the bathroom and plopped her down in the porridge. Her eyes darting around in terror, she took a deep breath, stiffened up and let out the longest and most blood-curdling shriek she could manage. My vision of her delightedly exploring this new texture vanished abruptly. Now that we had got this far, however, I pushed her further down into the porridge and scooped handfuls of it all over her body. I hoped she might gain something from the experience despite herself. It was a revolting business and Cath didn't help when she rubbed porridge into her eyes and hair. Her screams became even more ferocious. I managed to stretch over to the basin and get a damp cloth to wipe her eyes clean and suddenly wondered how I was going to dispose of all the porridge. I couldn't hope to send it down the drain without blocking it up. Plastic bags? No, they would burst. Into the incinerator? It would bung up the works. Down the lavatory? Ah, that was it. It would have to be done tactfully, a bit at a time, but it should work.

"You're supposed to be enjoying this, for God's sake, Cath," I shouted through her screams, "but you'll be glad to hear I've just given up." I wiped some porridge off my nose with my wrist. My left arm was beginning to shake with fatigue as I was having to hold not only Catherine's head up but her chest too; otherwise the stuff would have sucked her down like quicksand.

I now faced a crisis. With the bath out of commission, how could I clean Catherine off? Damn. I lifted her out, still stiff and shrieking and now festooned with grey slime, and wrapped her in a towel while I had a think. Our basin was tiny but we did have a good-sized sink. Had I washed up that day? I squelched into the kitchen. Damn again. All the breakfast things plus myriad saucepans were still in it. However, I cleared the actual sink and decided the best idea would be to hose Cath off with a hair-washing spray. This should have worked nicely, only I hadn't allowed for the fact that congealed porridge is probably the most efficient glue in the world.

I should imagine that de-scaling a twenty-pound fish alive would be similar to the operation I had to perform. Spraying and picking, I thought of the globs trailed all over the apartment. And of the baby, who was due to wake up any minute. And of having to go out and buy food for supper. In desperation I turned the water on faster but, because I only had one functioning hand, I couldn't hold the hose at the same time. It reared up and water shot across the kitchen and into the hall. My wits had by this time scattered out of reach and instead of shutting off the taps I lunged at the hose, missed it, lunged again and finally trapped it. But of course I had to release it to get at the taps and this time the water hit the ceiling, clattering down all over Cath and myself.

That evening Ted came home and found us all asleep. "Where's supper?" he asked, "and what have you done to Cath's hair? It looks all moth eaten"

"Oh, that," I said, "she somehow managed to get some of her breakfast into it and it was a bit sticky so I had to cut it out."

I t is a lonely feeling having a child who has been classified as a useless nuisance and I was anxious to meet other people who were in the same boat. Maybe they would have some ideas and advice. Perhaps I would find that Catherine wasn't such an oddity and that there were hundreds of others like her around. I found that most of the organizations in Winnipeg catered to specific disabilities. There was one for mental retardation, one for physical handicaps, one for the blind, and so on. I eventually heard about a cerebral palsy parents' group which I thought sounded more suitable. Accordingly, I went to one of their meetings.

I was expecting a roomful of people enthusiastically discussing ways of improving the lot, private and public, of severely handicapped individuals. I was disappointed to find a mere handful of people scattered

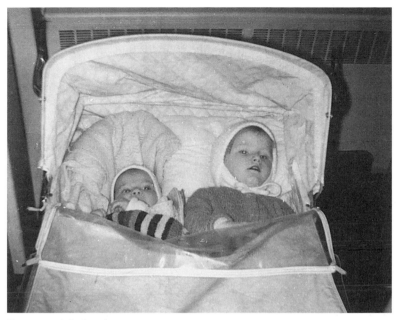

Dominic and Cath in the twin carriage.

around a large school gym. Feeling shy, I sat at the back until a nice woman spotted me and introduced herself. She had a ten-year-old version of Cath. I learned that all the people belonging to the group had children much older than Cath but that newcomers were welcome to join. In the end I never became more than superficially involved. I was very busy with the two babies and, apart from making the odd cake for the odd tea, there was nothing I could contribute. Meeting these parents made me realize several things. First, there were very few kids around as badly handicapped as Cath who were living at home. Second, apart from the meagre physiotherapy service at the Children's Hospital, there was absolutely nothing going on in Winnipeg for such children. There was, of course, custodial care, and a huge waiting list even for that. Nobody in authority thought it worthwhile to do anything at all with our children. My conclusion was that if one was daft enough to keep a child like Catherine one just coped as best one could.

And this was what Ted and I did for the next ten years.

As the lung-shrivelling cold of winter diminished and the snow melted into street wide puddles I put my mind to how I could get Catherine and

Dominic out for walks. At first I balanced Dominic in his basket on the end of Cath's pram. She, with her passion for being covered up, thought this was very amusing, but it was such a precarious arrangement that I soon bought a second-hand twin carriage. Judging from its appearance it had served several sets of twins. Once Ted had fixed up the wheels and I had patched the bodywork together with masking tape and string it was perfectly usable. In fact, I used it for one or more of the children until our youngest could walk, after which Ted used it for collecting firewood.

When Catherine was nearly two I made a third appointment with Dr. Hall because he had said he wanted to see her again. I had never wanted to set eyes on him after my first two experiences, but had tried to rationalize his curious attitude towards me. I now felt better about him. To begin with, I couldn't really count on my original impression. At the time I was under such enormous emotional stress that I could not be objective. I decided that during our second visit he must have misinterpreted me. I thought I'd done a pretty good job of showing that I was being totally realistic about Catherine but was far from being down in the dumps about everything. He evidently thought I was too bright-eyed and bushy-tailed to be genuinely facing up to things. Finally, I decided that dealing with people like Cath and myself must be a difficult and depressing part of a doctor's job and that he was doing the best he could.

When our appointment came up I walked into his office feeling composed and cheerful. Catherine was draped over my shoulder like a scarf.

"Good afternoon," I said and settled Catherine on my knee. Dr. Hall sat quite still behind his desk, his chin propped up with his hands. He looked at me with an expression of gloom.

"Well?" he said at last. "How are things going?"

"Fine thanks," I said. "We've got a super baby boy now and Catherine's doing quite well, all things considered." I smiled.

"Mm. What can she do?" His tone was discouraging.

"Well, it's not exactly a long list to reel off," I answered, "but she's much happier for one thing. She only has a really bad screaming fit every couple of days or so. The Ospolot seems to be helping her other fits, the myoclonic jerks, and her attention span appears to be a tiny bit longer as a result. What else? Oh, she's exploring with her left hand much more, too, and playing with toys a bit. She looks more or less *at* things more often. And I'm certain she recognizes me now, and my voice, and I think she knows my husband, though she doesn't see so much of him, but he spends hours carrying her round and rocking her on his knee while he's reading. And . . . she can hold her bottle for a second or two, especially if I support her arm." I heard myself braying a nervous laugh. I was gabbling, I knew, but this wretched man didn't seem to respond to anything. He just sat and stared at me impassively over his knuckles.

He let ten seconds elapse before speaking. "Mm. Nothing else?"

God almighty, I thought, how bloody negative can you get? "Yes," I answered petulantly, "yes, there is something else. She can roll from front to back." Damn him, this was going to be Catherine's little moment of triumph and he'd forced me to produce it in a defensive whine.

"Really?"

I leaned forward. "Yes. Really," I said. "Only she won't do it now, I'm quite sure, but she absolutely can." I could just imagine him writing "mother claims Catherine can roll over" in his notes. He put down his pen and heaved a great sigh.

"Why don't you," he said in a tired voice, "just give up and accept it?"

I was so shaken that I think my mouth actually fell open.

"Accept what, precisely?" I realized with a sense of fury what he was getting at. For some unknown reason he still couldn't bring himself to believe that I had realistically accepted Catherine's condition. How dare he not grant me a modicum of intelligence! Insensitive bastard! I hung on grimly to my boarding school manners and made a desperate effort not to break down and cry.

"I'm fully aware," I said carefully, "that Catherine is never going to win the Olympic high jump or be an intellectual challenge to Einstein. But she is my child and I love her. She is developing at an extremely slow rate, I know, but even the almost imperceptible progress she has achieved proves to me that she has the potential to continue developing. I shall do everything I can to help her and to give her a happy life. And I shall never, never put her into an institution to rot." Brave words, those last, but it was the idea I was trying to get across.

Judging from the way he looked at me, Dr. Hall obviously decided I was a hopeless case. And I decided he was almost as half-witted as Catherine.

A year later I forced myself to go back once more and see him. I felt that some specialist should take an interest in Catherine and he was the only one I knew at the time. I got no further with him than on the previous occasions. In all likelihood he didn't mean to cast gloom and despondency. Maybe, even, his heart bled for me, but if it did I never got the message. Maybe he had personal problems and was unintentionally taking them out on his patients. I don't know. But I do know he could have caused me considerable psychological damage if I hadn't been so sure of myself. I should have told him just what I thought of him but I didn't have the guts. Instead, stalking out of his office, I vowed never to return and eventually found another doctor in the same field.

I have described in some detail my bitter and negative experiences with Dr. Hall because I know that parents of handicapped children are to this day being treated by some doctors in the same clumsy way that I was. And it's not necessary.

We were loath to leave our apartment. The other occupants of the block had been extraordinarily nice about Catherine's screaming, claiming they never heard her. Also, the view of the river was magnificent and we were unlikely to find a house in similar surroundings. However, the day Dominic learnt to crawl out of his basket we found a two-bedroom bungalow and bought a second crib.

Watching that child develop so naturally, so fast, was a constant joy to Ted and me. We enjoyed him as a first baby, really. Having him also made me realize I would have known something was amiss with Cath almost as soon as she was born had she been my second child.

Catherine, meanwhile, was coming along too, at her own very sedate rate. By the age of two, when we moved, she had acquired one more definite skill: she had learnt to wriggle around on the floor on her back, undulating her whole body sideways and using her heels and the back of her head as pivots. Using this method she could move quite rapidly, particularly if the floor was wood or lino. The only trouble was, she often set off across the room purposefully snorting and grunting with effort, only to stop halfway and look blankly surprised, as if she hadn't the faintest idea why she had started moving.

I tried to dot interesting objects around the room to encourage her to move around but there were very few things she found interesting enough to bother with. One was Ding-dong, the only toy out of dozens that she really liked. Another was a large leather floor cushion, or pouffe, to which she had formed a great attachment. She would often wriggle towards it and lie curled around it, licking or chewing it. The only other things that interested her were the radiators. One day she had wriggled up to one, touched it and was slightly burnt. Ever since then the sight of a radiator had intrigued her. Giggling and gasping she would work her way up to one and then dare herself to touch it, ending up in paroxysms of laughter when she finally did.

This fascination with being scared cropped up constantly. Catherine loved being whizzed around by her feet, and being jumped a little way into the air. Once she fell off our bed and ever since then another favourite game was wriggling to the edge of it, waiting for me to pretend to give her a little shove. She would seize up and hoot with terrified laughter and then cast an eye back at me to see if I was going to do it again. To this day, she has never fallen off anything again. If she figures she's close to the edge of something she turns herself away from it. The only reason I can't believe this shows brilliant intelligence as well as instinct is that she reacts the same way when she's on a two-inch mat on the floor.

Another activity she enjoyed immensely was being held upright with her feet on the floor. This couldn't be called standing because it required enormous manipulation on my part to support her under her arms with my left arm, push her hips forward with my knees and push her knees back with my right hand. Once we were all set she would tense every muscle, which of course increased the bends in her hips and knees, and hoot with excitement. She wasn't supposed to be trying this and Mrs. Wallace in Edinburgh would not have been pleased. But Cath loved it so much I couldn't resist it.

To enjoy any of these activities Catherine had to be in what we came to think of as her "switched on" mood, when she was lively and ready to get what she could out of life. When like this, the slightest thing could cause her enormous amusement, even just a curtain flapping in the breeze. She also greatly enjoyed being handled in any way—tickled, hugged, exercised, shoved or dragged across the floor. The trouble here, of course, was that all these things had to be done by someone else; her active, self-created enjoyments were extremely limited. The thing that made her laugh most of all was any sudden loud noise, the louder and closer the better, the sort that makes me leap into the air with an oath.

However, Cath was only switched on for short periods of the day. A great deal of the time she appeared to be only semi-conscious of the life going on around her. Often she seemed to cut herself off from life entirely, probably a result of convulsant activity in her brain. When she was "switched off" like this her eyes appeared to register nothing and her body was quite relaxed; she could be amid pandemonium and remain totally unmoved.

So that she wouldn't be legitimately bored I moved her around with me during the day. This meant she was often in the kitchen, where there was opportunity for all her pleasures. She could wriggle around on the lino floor, burn herself on the radiator, get kicked around by me and, last but not least, there was lots of lovely clattering and banging.

Self-preservation was the one area in which she almost invariably reacted quickly, whether switched on or off, although in the latter state she would deal with the danger as if she were a robot, without changing her expression. She was very funny—and showed more than a spark of genuine intelligence, I think—in the way she dealt with the baby when he learned to crawl. After having her hair pulled and being caterpillared over a couple of times she kept a wary eye open for Dominic when she was lying on the floor, which was most of the time. When she saw him approaching she would twist herself around frantically until her feet were pointing at him and then, when he reached her, would kick him away. Since it was such fun to see her do this I'm afraid we took shameless advantage of the situation. "Cath's bored stiff," I'd say to Ted. "I've tried everything and she just lies there flapping her arm."

"Well, set the baby on her," he would reply. "That never fails." Unfortunately for Catherine, Dominic soon became too fast for her and I was constantly dashing to her rescue until he learned that attacking her wasn't sporting.

By the age of two, Catherine was too long and gangling to continue being fed on my lap. She was a yard long and weighed twenty-five pounds. It would have been fine had she sat up nicely and opened her mouth at the right time but she didn't. She lay sprawled in my arms twisting her head from side to side in an attempt to avoid the spoon, frequently ending up with an earful of mashed potato. So from then on I sat her propped up on cushions in the corner of the sofa or an armchair. She had to be at precisely the right angle, tilted far enough back so that the food didn't fall out of her mouth, but not so far that she choked.

I didn't mind the messiness and the length of time it took to feed her; in fact I never gave them a thought because they were just part of life. What did bother me was that she rarely seemed to enjoy eating, even though I went to endless lengths to make interesting, as well as nutritious, mashed up messes for her. However, I must have got enough food into her because she grew in both directions only slightly more slowly than normal, although it could hardly be said that she was romping through calories.

Using a bottle was the only way I could persuade Catherine to drink. Often, when she had one of the violent chest infections to which she was prone, I had virtually to force-feed her fluids by squeezing a little milk or water into the back of her throat, so that she swallowed it before she had a chance to spit it out. Giving her medicines was a nightmare. I could spend five minutes prying her mouth open and, when I finally got a spoonful in, another five persuading her to swallow. Frequently she brought it up again, together with whatever fluid I had managed to get down her.

Having dealt with the subject of getting food into my daughter, this seems to be the logical moment to turn briefly to a closely related subject—how she got rid of what her body didn't need. Well, the plain fact is that had she been left to deal with this by herself she would soon have been hospitalized. We faced the well-known scourge of all non-ambulatory people, constant constipation. I gave her prunes or Allbran every day plus as much other fruit as possible, but no amount of this type of food could overcome the basic problem of her inactivity. I often had to resort to the drugstore for remedies but disliked doing so because I didn't want a laxative addict on my hands. I can most effectively demonstrate the degree of worry that her constipation caused me by saying that I was actually glad when she had a mild bout of stomach flu. It meant that for a day or two I didn't have to worry about unclogging her.

Another complication resulting from Cath's inactivity was bad circulation, a problem that grew worse as she grew longer. My mother kept her supplied with knitted sweaters and Mary, my aunt, made her woollen leggings. However, even when I put these on her in addition to a normal complement of clothes, her vascular system seemed to stop at her knees, except in midsummer. It was a problem keeping her hands warm, but nothing compared to that of stopping her feet from becoming frigid. I would encase them in a pair of thick cotton socks, Mary's leggings, an extra pair of wool socks and a pair of slippers but they would still, when I unmasked them at night, quite often be red or blue, or mottled in a colourful combination of the two. The odd thing was that this coldness in her extremities never seemed to cause her discomfort or pain. Even so, I acquired the habit of automatically giving her feet a rub between my hands at frequent intervals during the day.

Catherine celebrated the Christmas of 1963, when she was two and a half, by finally mastering the back to front roll. I had been too busy all day to give her as much attention as usual and had left her to have a disgruntled, one-sided conversation with the dining-room radiator while I dealt with the goose.

"I'm coming, Cath," I shouted. "I've just got to sew this thing up. Dominic, that hurts, darling." He was hanging onto my thigh while he stretched up on his toes to see what I was doing. "Here," I handed him a piece of apple and he sat down with a thud to gnaw at it. As the needle squeaked through the goose skin I heard Cath's noise become a series of grunts. When I peered around the corner I saw that she was right over on her stomach but still had one arm under her. She had got this far many times before and been unable to remove the arm by herself. Now she was tugging at it like mad and only had part of her forearm and her hand left to go. I yelled to Ted and we both went in and encouraged her from the sidelines. "You can do it, love—one more big effort—" and with a final snort she made it. We made a huge fuss of her and Dominic came stumping in from the kitchen (he had been walking for a month) to join in the fun and helpfully smeared Cath with apple as he pushed her over and over with us.

As a result of being with Cath twenty-four hours a day I now knew and understood her intuitively and was sensitive to all her moods. Ted, being with her far less, was still uneasy with her unless I was on the spot. He hadn't developed all the tricks I had for amusing her and preventing her screaming fits. However, he and she were now gradually developing a less tentative relationship. It had become his habit to collapse on our bed after supper for a quiet read with Cath lying beside him. She loved this, particularly when he put down his book and picked her up for a game. In fact, we realized after a while that she had formed a timing mechanism for this period of the day. She would lie cooing contentedly for about fifteen minutes, happy just to be beside him and receiving the odd absent-minded tickle. Then she would start to whine a bit and pull at his shirt, letting him know it was time for his undivided attention. After a few minutes of being heaved into the air, balanced on his knees, or sat on his stomach, she would agree to a compromise; he would lie her across his stomach and she would struggle to work her way over and down onto the bed while he continued reading. Then the cycle would start again.

She also regarded Ted as a good person to carry her around or hold on his lap when he had nothing better to do, and often when he had. Being a foot taller than me, he was able to hold her more comfortably than I could. He also had another advantage over me as far as she was concerned; he had a beard and a hairy chest to explore. Catherine found his roars of pain excruciatingly funny.

"She's really developing a character, isn't she?" he said one night. He had been feeding her teaspoonsful of tea from his cup, a practice she loved. Often she would tease him by refusing to unclamp her mouth from the spoon. We were thankful to realize that, if she had nothing else, she did have a sense of humour! Now the tea was finished and she was rummaging in his shirt front. "Rather a warped one—ouch! For God's sake, Cath—but a character nonetheless."

"I know," I said. "I mean I've always thought of her as having a personality but it was pretty difficult spotting it through all her screaming, wasn't it?" The awful memories of Cath's first year of life not being something on which we dwelled, I changed the subject hastily. "Incidentally, one of the mums from the cerebral palsy group phoned today to say she's got a chair Cath might be able to use. It's a special one to 'correct the posture.' Hey, Cath," I said giving her a prod, "you'd better start thinking about getting a posture to correct, hadn't you?"

"I'll get it tomorrow," said Ted. "I think her neck is getting a bit stronger," he added as he tried to sit Cath up.

"Much stronger," I agreed. "Her sense of balance is really developing because she tries to keep her head upright most of the time now." One of the exercises I did with her every day was to pull her up by her hands from a lying position to a sitting position. After months of this she was now usually pulling her head up first instead of hauling it up after I had the rest of her up. She made fearful grimaces while doing it but it appeared to give her a feeling of accomplishment.

When Ted staggered in with the chair the next day I was somewhat dismayed. "But it's massive," I said.

"Cumbersome as hell, too," said Ted giving it a shove in my direction, "and vicious. It's kicked me twice already."

But the chair did have good points. Everything on it was adjustable. The back tilted and had a movable, padded head-rest, the arms could be set at different heights and angles and there was a leg-rest with a ninety-degree choice of position, plus foot-rests that slid up and down to any

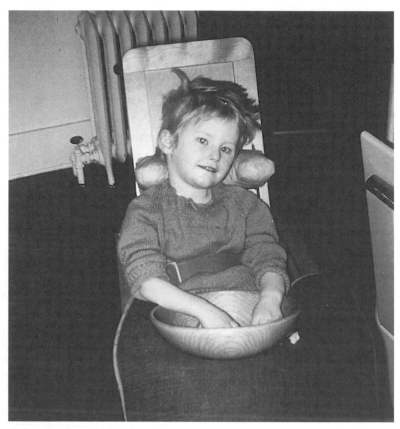

Cath in the adjustable chair.

height. It was set in a tiltable frame on castor wheels and the whole thing was made of solid wood and weighed about eighty pounds.

It was set for its recent occupant, a large twelve-year-old boy, so we started to turn knobs and loosen wingnuts while Dominic watched, fascinated. He may not have learnt much about adjustable chairs in the next half-hour but he got a fantastic groundwork in basic swearing. Everything we tried to move either refused to budge—necessitating hammers and wrenches—or dropped like a guillotine onto stray toes and fingers. When we had at last got it looking approximately right for Catherine I tried to sit her in it. She promptly let out a mighty shriek and did her bent bicycle wheel trick.

I realized that the chair's rigidity alarmed her as she wasn't used to

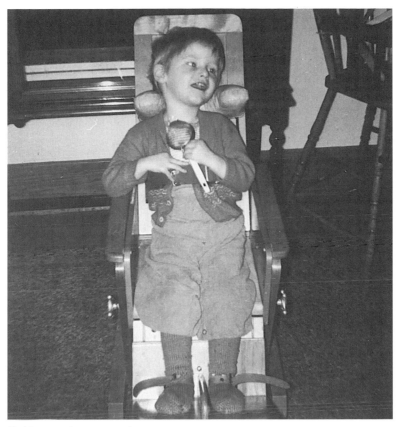

Cath's posture being corrected.

sitting in anything that didn't mold to fit her. It was several days before she would bend in the right places to sit properly. Once she grew accustomed to it, the chair became a boon to us all, but especially to Cath herself. She had a new view of life while she was in it and was also safe from Dominic's attentions. I put a board across the arms so that in theory at least she could play with the toys I piled on it. She, however, thought the point was to shove everything off onto the floor so that I would replace the pile for her to push off again.

I hoped one side effect of the chair might be that the hair on her bald spot would grow, even though she spent only a couple of hours at most each day in the chair. I found her hair difficult to manage quite apart from the bald patch, which was a result of pivoting the back of her head on the floor. Her hair was thick all over but whereas on the right side of her head it was straight, on the left side it was a mass of tight waves. These were usually a frizzy mess because she always lay with that side down. I once jokingly said to Ted that it was probably her brainwaves coming out—it was the deader side of her brain. Some time later I dreamed I'd shaved that side of her head and somehow bandaged it up to stop the hair growing. And suddenly the right side of her body started working normally . . .

We were starting by this time, March, 1964, to prepare for going to England, where Ted was planning to work at the National Physical Laboratory in London. We had already arranged to rent the ground floor of my sister's huge Victorian house in West Hampstead and had sublet our bungalow. With these two major concerns off our minds, all we had to worry about was how we were to get there. We decided the children and I should go by plane and Ted would follow by sea with the car, trunks, Cath's new chair and other essentials.

Ted, I knew, was rather dreading the whole venture, partly because he hated being uprooted from his own laboratory and partly because he was nervous at the prospect of being engulfed by my family.

My enthusiasm, on the other hand, was unbounded, but I tried not to be too blatant about it.

5

In the airport lounge one morning early in June, Ted looked at me and said, "I just don't believe this."

"What do you mean?" I said. We were holding a child each and I was sitting in the midst of my hand luggage.

"Well, look at all this, for God's sake. You'll never be allowed on the bloody plane!"

"Of course I will, it's all been weighed."

"Yes, but for instance did you have to take the pouffe?" He glanced around uneasily as if hoping nobody we knew would appear. "I told you," he said through gritted teeth, "I could bring it in the car."

"I know," I said, "but Cath has to have it. You know that. It's like her old shawl." The pouffe was, admittedly, battered and chewed-looking by now but Cath happened to have chosen it as the inanimate comforter in her life and I wasn't prepared to be without it. Dominic, more conventionally, was trailing a striped blanket knitted by my mother.

"And your basket—" muttered Ted. He jogged Dominic in his arms and looked around desperately.

"Well I can't help that!" I had pared its contents down to absolute essentials for the journey but it was, nevertheless, exploding with disposable diapers, plastic pants, Kleenex, sweaters, bottles, jars of food, toys and apples. And Ding-dong. Tied to one handle of the basket was my handbag which contained, as well as my personal things, a bottle of the ever-necessary Billie Bee honey. Aware that I might need it at any moment, I wanted to know precisely where it was. "You'll be saying I ought to be wearing a suit and hat any minute now," I said crossly.

Ted ignored this. "Catherine's dribbling again," he said, looking at the departure timetable.

This is grim, I thought. Ted was still recovering from having narrowly avoided an accident on the way to the airport and my nerves were taut because I hated flying. I was about to attempt a conciliatory remark when invalids and mothers with small children were called. Ted and I looked at each other and I grinned. He managed a smile and announced in a studiously cheerful voice that he would go and look for some help. He returned with a ground hostess who took the pouffe in one hand and Dominic in the other and set off at a brisk pace with me following. I was so scared of losing sight of her that I only stopped for a second to give Ted a quick peck and a "See you in England, now go and have a drink" before scuttling off.

I had had the wits to book our two seats at the front of the tourist section, where there is nearly twice as much leg space as anywhere else, so I put Cath down there on a rug for as much of the time as possible. Having the pouffe on top of her delighted her, particularly when I shifted it onto her face and thumped on it. Dominic was fascinated by everything. After he had figured out all the buttons and snapped his finger in the ashtray, his main purpose in life became scrambling up me in order to drop in on the people behind us. There was an unfortunate gentleman with a foot condition and crutches in the aisle seat of our row. He told me, as I simultaneously bent to stick Cath's soother in her mouth with one hand and haul Dominic from the back of his seat with the other, that he was returning to England for the first time in thirty years.

He seemed oblivious to the fact that I wasn't hanging on every word and rambled on and on about the royal family, which he seemed to have missed more than his own.

"I do hope my children won't bother you," I said as he paused to suck his pipe alight.

"Children?" he said vaguely. "I've got a scrapbook of newspaper cuttings of our Queen and Princess Margaret Rose when they were babies."

"Have you really? Gosh! Dominic, put that down!" He had found Cath's bottle of juice and was draining it.

"Of course we see much more of Prince Charles and Princess Anne than we did of them."

"Oh, yes. Here's your bottle, Cath." She was winding up for a scream and so was I. After having a swing from the luggage rack and upending my basket, Dominic allowed himself to be settled down for a sleep. Just as everyone else was tucking down with pillows and blankets Catherine started on a serious scream. I picked her up and after negotiating my neighbour's legs and crutches I did a bit of pacing with her along the aisle. My neighbour was dozing when I returned and sprawled across his knees was Dominic. I tried to ease my way around them but Cath chose this moment to do one of her backward flings. As I was bending forward anyway, this threw me right off balance and we tumbled over, landing in an untidy heap half on the floor and half on the seat. It took a while to get sorted out and when I panted my apologies to the poor old man—on one of whose feet I think I trod—he smiled benignly and produced two bars of chocolate. "For the youngsters," he said, as if he'd just noticed them.

"Oh, that is kind," I said, trying to snatch them before they were spotted by Dominic.

The rest of the flight became an endless round of dispensing nourishment and good cheer to the children, changing diapers, nodding agreement to my neighbour's monologue on the monarchy and snatching the odd fifteen winks.

My cousin Julia was working at London airport and was planning to wangle her way onto the plane. Once we had landed I wiped off the children's faces and packed up in a leisurely way. As I was picking up the last apple core from under the seat, Julia's dear and familiar voice came floating down the plane.

"Yoo-hoo darling, I'm just coming. The cart's got stuck." I looked down to the back of the plane but all I could see was an air hostess's neat bum wiggling in the doorway. Then the rest of her appeared plus a supermarket-type cart with Julia, a bit flustered, at the other end.

"Oh Ju, you're marvellous!" I ran down the plane to meet her, Dominic bouncing on my hip. "And this," I said after much hugging, "is my son Dominic!"

"Just like last time. Oh Nix, he's absolutely beautiful!"

"He couldn't be much better, could he?" I said immodestly. "Hey, let's go and collect the rest of my things, including Cath."

"Oh, I'm longing to see her again!" Cath was lying along the seat, looking through the fingers of her left hand as usual. "But she's huge!" said Julia. "How on earth do you manage both of them? Hello, darling."

"Don't expect too much of a response," I said anxiously, and added, "she says she doesn't think much of this flying lark." However, Cath did give me a tired, cross-eyed smile which could have included Julia. "Hello, love," I said, "I'll pick you up when we've got everything else loaded up."

Julia and I filled the cart and sat Dominic on top and Julia pushed while I followed with Cath over my right shoulder. There was a nasty moment as we passed through officialdom when I discovered that Billie Bee had leaked all over my passport. I licked it surreptitiously as we waited in the queue but was still on the back pages when my turn came.

"Just getting some honey off," I said to the officer and he raised his eyebrows and scrutinized me carefully before letting me through.

"Listen, Ju, there's something I've got to do. Where can I send a cable?" I felt awful having left Ted in such a muddle. We found the place and Julia offered to take Cath. When I handed her over and Julia nearly crumpled under her weight I suddenly realized how strong I must have become.

"I thought Mum was coming," I said when I emerged from the booth. "Last time I came over she was down the drains."

Julia giggled. "She's pacing around outside Customs," she said. "Knowing her, she'll break through any moment."

Just then my mother did appear.

"Darling girl! I thought I'd never get to you. How are you? And how's my lovely Cath?" she said going behind me. "Hello, sweetheart. Oh, what a pretty girl you are, I'd almost forgotten! Nix, she's lifting her head up. And reaching out with her hand. Darling, what a change!"

My mother was entranced with Dominic and was happy to be left with him. During the next week I made several expeditions with Cath over to Veronica's house, about six miles away, to sort out our living quarters. Had these trips taken only an hour or two I could have risked leaving Cath as well as Dominic but the silly girl refused to take food from anyone except me. Also, she still had hysterical periods and I was the only person who could calm her down. Ted had told me to take taxis everywhere but, being obstinate, I tried to do it by bus the first time.

Cath was by now too obviously odd-looking for casual passersby to think of her as merely sleepy. I was building up a useful, or rather, essential indifference to the stares and elbow-nudging that were directed towards her when we were in public. So it wasn't the bus conductress saying, "Ahhhhh, poor little thing, it's a bleedin' shame, innit?" which caused me thereafter to follow Ted's instructions; it was Cath's size and awkwardness. She was getting longer by the day and now weighed nearly thirty pounds. I still could, and frequently did, carry her a few hundred yards without any trouble using just my right arm, but it was at least a quarter of a mile from the bus stop to Veronica's house. When I arrived I thought my arm would be rigidly sickle-shaped for the rest of my life. If Cath had stayed in her fireman's lift position I think it would have worked, but she would suddenly stiffen up and kick and get excited and I would have to hang on for all I was worth.

"Catherine looks much brighter than when you were last here," commented Veronica. We had spent the afternoon scrubbing floors and were now having a cup of tea up in her sitting room. "When she's what you called switched on, anyway. Like now." She nodded towards Cath, who was chirping and spitting, pleased because she had wriggled across the floor and found herself under a table. "I don't just mean that she moves more, either. It's a look. To be honest I didn't think she even knew who you were last time but now she obviously knows you. And she's enjoying herself, isn't she?"

"I know," I said. "Whenever I get depressed about her I remind myself that at least ninety per cent of the time she's happy, or at least not unhappy. And that's a better average than most people, isn't it?"

"Bloody sight better than me, anyway," said Veronica. "When do you get depressed about her, incidentally?"

I shrugged. "Hardly ever, in fact," I said. "That just slipped out. No, I really don't. But every now and again I think how small her world is."

"Yes, but if as you say she's happy within that world what do the limitations matter? Any gain in appreciation is a bonus, not something she expects." Veronica gazed abstractedly at Catherine. "It must be restful not to have expectations—one wouldn't constantly be worrying about having them dashed."

"She's beginning to anticipate pleasure now, which is good. I give her a bath every night, for instance, which she loves. It gives her a sense of freedom and movement, and when I take her clothes off she gets very excited. And she didn't used to until she actually hit the water."

"How on earth do you bath her? Do you have to hold her all the time?"

"No. I lie her flat in about four inches of water and she kicks and splashes and has a marvellous time. It looks terribly dangerous—Mum nearly had a fit when she saw her last night—but her self-preservation instinct is intact and she never comes close to drowning, even though her face is in the water half the time. Is there any more tea, by the way? I think she's thirsty."

"Can she drink from a cup?"

"No. She can't seem to get the idea of sucking from anything except a bottle. But if I prop her up I can use a spoon." When Catherine had finished I sat her up to burp.

"She does keep her head up much more now, doesn't she?" said Veronica. "Will her back strengthen with time?"

"I hope so. There's so much of it now, that's the trouble. But look, she can sit supporting herself for a few seconds." Cath obligingly put her left arm down slowly to the floor. I rubbed the palm of her hand on the carpet, and as she let a small part of her weight lean on her arm, I moved my support from her back. She lasted three or four seconds and then tipped over and giggled, refusing to repeat the performance. "But I can't get her to do it on the other side," I said. "I don't think she even understands what I'm trying to do."

As I said this I wondered, as I did so often, whether the exercises I did with her were doing any good. The physiotherapist whom I had been seeing once a month with her in Winnipeg seemed to think Cath was doing well in view of her multiple problems. But I wondered. Despite stretching her legs, pulling them apart, working on her hip joints and so on, the spasticity in her body was, I thought, showing signs of beating me to the losing post. When she lay relaxed on the floor, her legs were both bent to the left instead of being straight. I spent countless hours bicycling her legs and doing knee to chest presses, but she still kicked her legs in unison, rather than seperately, her toes pointed like an over-enthusiastic ballet dancer.

I felt constantly guilty about not working with her every minute I wasn't actually doing something else. Against this I had to weigh the decision I had made two years ago that I wouldn't let her dominate my life.

"Sorry darling, am I asking too many questions?" said Veronica.

"Good God, no! You've always been unusually observant about people's expressions, haven't you? You got mine wrong this time though. I was just having a think. Honest. I like people asking questions."

At that moment Veronica's two children, Richard and Eleanor, aged eleven and nine respectively, exploded into the room.

They stopped dead.

"Hello Nix."

"'Lo Nix." They hadn't seen me for two years and were suddenly shy. This state didn't last long, however.

"How old's Catherine?"

"Will she ever walk?"

"Why's she dribbling?"

"Why are her eyes funny?"

"What's she laughing at? Us?"

"Can she understand us?"

"Can I help you bath her?"

"Does she still wear nappies?"

"Does she know she's there?"

I threw up my hands. "Good heavens, give me a chance!"

My sister burst out laughing. "Good God, no!" she mimicked. "I like people asking questions."

As I whooshed Cath up and down in her bath a few nights later I found myself grinning at one of Eleanor's questions—a strikingly perceptive one, I thought. I repeated it to Cath.

"Hey, you," I said. "Do you know you're there?" The water streamed over her shoulders and ricocheted off the other end of the bath and the resulting tidal wave rushed up her body. She gasped as it reached her mouth. Spitting furiously, she kicked her legs and gave a yelp of laughter, her eyes shining with excitement. "Catherine, do you know you're there? I'm being serious now."

I leaned over the edge of the bath and blew on her to attract her attention. She looked up at me and took a joyful swat at my face. "Now what am I to make of that, you beautiful, silly mermaid?" She laughed again, her eyes still holding mine. "And what does that wicked grin and sideways look mean? Could it be that you don't feel like having philosophical discussions and are waiting for the next whoosh?"

Her smile widened and she tensed up as I cupped my hand under the back of her head. I laughed. "Oh Cath," I said, "I give up."

In Veronica's house, just off the passage outside the kitchen of our quarters, was a door that led to what was originally the coalhole-cum-cellar but to which letters now came addressed to D. Lenton, Basement Flat. And a strange chap called David Lenton did in fact live there off and on.

He was, it seemed, something of a mystery. He was very charming and didn't mind his condemned quarters, even paying a little rent sometimes. His field was music and he seemed to be on close terms with many important people. "Got to go and arrange something with Sir Adrian," he would say, emerging blinking from the coalhole, smartly dressed but smelling musty. Or, "Just popping over to Copenhagen for a few days. Ogden's doing a piece of mine." And there were, in fact, concert programs, letters and photographs lying around his room that suggested the validity of his claims. On the other hand, he could be so vague and disorganized that it was hard to imagine him surviving in any serious way. Whenever he went away Veronica had to deal with irate phone calls because David was supposed to be giving a piano lesson, conducting a church choir, had promised to return ten pounds by yesterday, and so on. On one occasion she had had to placate a tearful French girl who said she and David were supposed to be getting married that afternoon. He apparently lived by taking short-term jobs connected with music and charming scholarships out of various organizations.

When I first met him he had just returned from spending two months studying under a famous French conductor and was busy impressing everyone by accidentally lapsing into French at every opportunity. However, he immediately endeared himself to me by showing an interest in Catherine, deciding he might be able to elicit a response from her through music. I told him I often patted or jogged her to whatever music I happened to have on. David brought some of his records up to Veronica's room and did the same sorts of things with her as I had. As she was in a switched on mood she thoroughly enjoyed it, beaming and laughing and jerking all over. David was delighted. "Alors, elle écoute! Sorry, I mean she's listening!" I didn't like to tell him she was probably responding to being handled rather than to the music. With this in mind I was inclined to disbelieve what I saw when, after being tapped on the head by David for a few bars of a Mozart Divertimento, a dreamy look came into Cath's eyes and she started to wave her left hand very nearly in time.

"Well!" I said. "I've never seen her do that before. She really does seem to be beating time. Oh, she's slowed down. But that was a good three bars, wasn't it? Let's try her with a different tempo, a slow movement of this perhaps." That didn't go down too well, however, and her waving petered out. We experimented all afternoon with different tempi and found that although success was far from constant, she did quite often beat approximately in time for a few bars, particularly when the music was fast and rhythmic, and loud.

"I'd like to try some John Cage on her," said David as we packed up.

"I don't think she'd go for that," I said hastily. "She balked at late Schoenberg, remember? Switched off completely."

"Yes, you can try that downstairs, if you don't mind, dear," said Veronica firmly.

"—or something electronic, just to see what effect the noises have on her. I wonder how much she can hear," continued David, who evidently hadn't heard either Veronica or myself.

"Even I don't know that," I said.

"We ought to try her with feeling music, too—putting her hands on a drum while it's being beaten, that sort of thing. She liked it when Dominic was shaking the floor marching around to that Haydn, didn't she?"

It was the first time anyone besides relations had taken such an active interest in Cath and I decided there could be worse things lurking under the kitchen. Later, we came to an agreeable arrangement whereby David would babysit Cath and Dominic the odd time and I would let him cook in the kitchen (when Ted wasn't around) if he was entertaining a girl in his coalhole and needed more than the single gas ring he usually used. He had an ancient mildewed piano down there but was tactful about playing it. He rumbled and pinged his compositions on it to his heart's content but only when he knew Ted was out. In fact I don't think Ted ever learnt of its existence.

During our year in England it was our unspoken understanding that I would follow my own pursuits as long as they didn't obstruct what work

Ted could do, given the limitations of not being on his own terrain. For this reason it was during the day, when Ted was at work, that most of my social life took place. Because I was somewhat immobilized by the children, this consisted mainly of having my friends over. Quite often, though, I was able to make quick dashes into town. Veronica, who was working on a book, spent her days upstairs writing and didn't mind having Cath on the floor with her; she also kept an ear open in case Dominic woke from his nap early. Occasionally, too, I scurried out to a concert after supper if I thought Cath was in a happy mood. Ted was happy to be left with her, providing I got home in time to change her and give her a goodnight drink.

Eleanor was feeling slightly lost at this time because Richard had just gone off to boarding school, so she spent a lot of time downstairs with us. I loved having her around and Dominic adored her. She played with him and took him for walks and filled the kitchen with hamsters and he thought she was marvellous. Cath benefited from her presence, too, because she was constantly thinking up new ways to amuse her. It was she, I think, who discovered that Cath found it hysterically funny to have cold water sprayed onto her face from a toothbrush while she was in the bath. Eleanor often produced questions and observations far more acute than those of many adults, possibly because as a child she was more interested in what Cath felt than in what I felt. One day she put in a nutshell what I could have spent half an hour trying to explain. "It's odd about Cath," she said. "It's sad, but she isn't."

Apart from the physical care I had to give Catherine, she was an easy girl to have around. She was always grateful for attention but could be left on the floor for an hour or more at a time, amusing herself by rolling around, making faces in her mirror, fighting with a newspaper or playing with her pouffe. Another thing that amused her was having a cardboard box put over her head as she lay on the floor, particularly if someone tapped or banged on it. It looked odd, I suppose, to see a pair of legs kicking energetically from beneath a box labelled "Sunkist Oranges, This End Up" and I had to stop people continually rescuing her. I can see now that she was so easily entertained because her mind was so undeveloped it was quickly satisfied and should have been presented with more stimulating ideas. At the time, though, I was glad Cath was docile and contented because I could give Dominic almost as much attention as if he had been the first child in the family.

His babyish jabbering was gradually being transformed into words. One day he inadvertently sparked off one of my bi-annual weeps when I found him tugging on Cath's arm and saying exasperatedly, "Up, Cath, up." I didn't, thank goodness, frighten him off her when he was tiny by hauling him away from her so often. He loved copying the games I played with her. He seemed to understand her vulnerability instinctively and never, for instance, dropped a rock on her instead of a cushion and it never occurred to me that he might.

I had brought Dominic's stroller from Winnipeg but I had nothing in which to take Cath for walks. The wooden chair was designed for indoor use only and had small castors on it. Ted replaced these with wheels from an old pram. Unfortunately there was no way to spring them, so every time I pushed Cath over even a small bump in the sidewalk she was jolted. Also, getting the chair on and off the sidewalk was almost impossible because the weight and design made it difficult to hitch up on its back wheels as one would a pram. I soon decided she could get her fresh air more comfortably by simply sitting out in the garden.

She was doing just this one day, while I was hanging diapers on the line and Dominic was trying to ride his tricycle up a tree, when it occurred to me there must be something going on for kids like Cath in London.

Mary had suggested taking Catherine to see Dr. McInnes again. I left Dominic with my mother in Hammersmith for a week and took a night train to Edinburgh. Dr. McInnes and I had a long talk about Catherine and the problems she engendered, such as my guilt at not working with her all the time. He reassured me by saying how well he thought I was managing, pointing out that if we hadn't kept her and treated her as normally as possible she would by now probably be a characterless blob with no interest in life whatever.

The area of her physical development with which he was most concerned was her right leg. I had noticed it was slightly shorter than her left and had assumed it wasn't growing as fast. People would ask how tall she was. "Depends on which side you measure her," would be my reply. I felt ashamed of my stupidity when Dr. McInnes said it was happening because the head of her right femur was being pulled out of its socket by her leg muscles; her leg was in fact slipping up outside the socket. He took X-rays that confirmed this and showed me how to pull her leg down. He said, though, that whatever I did, the leg would probably go completely out of joint eventually.

I asked him about the availability of services for children like Cath in London. He advised me to get in touch with the Spastics Society, which would refer me to a clinic in Chelsea. Accordingly, I phoned the Spastics Society when we got back and a social worker came round to the house and fixed up an appointment at the clinic, adding that suitable transportation would be provided. I had visions of roaring through London in an ambulance but it transpired that there was a network of volunteer drivers who drove handicapped people to and from hospitals and clinics.

My volunteer driver was a wizened upper-class lady in brogues and a felt hat who came stumping up the path to meet me.

"Mrs. Schaefer?" she shouted. "Splendid! I'm Mrs. Featherstonehaugh. Nice to meet you. These your children? Come along then, let's get you packed in." This was a most appropriate verb because her car was an Austin Mini and the back was taken up by a box that looked like a coffin. "Pop the boy into the back with the leg—we're dropping it off on the way—and then hop in the front with the girl. That's it." I managed this manoeuvre with some difficulty and almost before I had got Cath, myself and my basket in, Mrs. Featherstonehaugh shot off down the road without warning, causing a passing car to hoot frantically.

"Men drivers," said Mrs. Featherstonehaugh, tucking some wisps of white hair under her hat, "congenitally unobservant, my dear. Now," she continued conversationally, "first stop Ladbroke Grove with the leg. It's going to a young West Indian chappie and it's brown, my dear. *Don't* you think that's considerate?"

"Mmm," I agreed as we skimmed past a bus and burnt our wheels on a traffic island. Cath started to whine and I realized I was clutching her so tightly that I was hurting her. It was a hair-raising drive. At one point Mrs. Featherstonehaugh mentioned she had driven a tank during the war and I had the impression she thought she was still driving one. We were running behind schedule and this bothered her.

"Get you there in time I shall. Aha! Here's one of my favourite shortcuts," she added as she ground into second gear and we spun into an alley.

By the time we got to Chelsea I was in no state for interviews. As had been the case in Edinburgh two years before, Cath was examined by a group of doctors and therapists with one doctor in charge. All the usual questions were asked and I experienced the familiar sense of hopelessness at the paucity of answers there were to be filled in on the Progress Chart. I was told that had I lived in London permanently Cath would have been taken into the nursery school when a vacancy arose. As I was there only for a year the best they could offer would be two afternoons a week of physiotherapy and occupational therapy. I had already tried, and failed, to get Catherine into an excellent program I had heard of run by a woman called Dr. Bobath, but the clinic's offer was certainly better than nothing and I accepted it gratefully. Then we went to have Cath's hearing and sight looked at, two areas about which I was intensely curious.

The tests were not, however, as edifying as I had hoped they might be. The doctor who looked at her eyes said she only used one eye at a time and consequently saw everything flat, two dimensionally. He also said her left eye was, as I thought, the more efficient one, but her vision even in that eye was probably hazy.

"Could anything be done about straightening her eyes?" I asked.

"Yes, probably," the doctor answered, "but it wouldn't help her vision, only her looks. In other words an operation would be purely cosmetic. But I think her eyes may straighten quite a bit by themselves, if you give her a variety of objects and movement to look at." This was, in fact, what happened.

The hearing test was next but was disappointingly primitive and inconclusive. The idea was that Cath should sit with her back to one tester, who would make various types and degrees of noise behind her. A second tester sat facing her and observed her reactions. This might have worked if Cath could have sat by herself but I had to have her on my knee. Since I couldn't see the noisemaker behind me I jumped involuntarily at nearly every noise, particularly if it was a triangle being struck an inch behind my head. When I finally mastered my nerves, Catherine reacted to the noises exactly as I would have predicted. If she was switched on she seemed to hear nearly as much as I did, judging by her smile and the awareness in her eyes. If she was switched off she appeared oblivious, apart from a slight twitch, even to a sudden high-pitched siren noise that gave me a headache.

She had had enough by this time and screamed with rage when I took her down the hall to have her IQ tested.

"This will be hopeless," I said to the woman who was going to test her. "She'll come out minus twenty if you do her now. And actually," I added looking at my watch, "my lift should be here by now." The truth was, I didn't want the IQ test done. I knew that even if it was done at home, where there was at least a chance of Cath being relaxed, the result would be arbitrary, depending on whether she felt like reacting to the stimuli presented her. Luckily my lift did in fact appear just then, so I was spared being told what I already knew: that my child was far from bright. During the year Cath had her IQ tested several times but the results varied so much I didn't even make a note of them.

The occupational therapist who worked on Cath at the centre made little headway with her. I don't think she had had much experience working with a child as dim as Cath. She became frustrated when she found Cath couldn't latch on to the most simple ideas. She persevered but by the end of the year Cath still didn't understand that, when presented with coloured blocks and a bucket on her tray, she was supposed to put the blocks in the bucket. She continued to think it much more fun to knock the whole lot on the floor. The physiotherapist also had trouble at first. Cath started to scream the moment she was put on the rubber gym mat but after a while she began to enjoy the new stretchings and bendings. I usually stayed while she was being worked on because I wanted to see the exercises, but sometimes I took Dominic across the road to the Thames Embankment and we watched the birds and the boats.

One day shortly after Christmas, David was giving Catherine what he called "basic auditory exercise." This meant lying her on a moth-eaten rug on top of his piano while he thumped out the beginnings of concertos; he was very good at beginnings but was apt to fade out after a few bars. She particularly enjoyed Grieg's concerto and the Rachmaninov variations because they made her jump. Just after plunging unsuccessfully into some Bartok, he stopped and said, "Mon Dieu, je viens de souvenir! I've just remembered, Nicola, I was doing the Fauré Requiem at St. Mark's last week and someone told me about an experimental school that's being started in Hampstead for severely handicapped children."

I found out all I could from David and applied instantly. Mrs. Brown, who was to run it, came to see Cath and me. She was qualified both as a teacher and nurse and seemed a warm, capable woman. She was undaunted when I told her about Catherine's screaming fits and refusal to accept food from anyone except myself. She merely said if that was the case then it was time Cath got used to being fed by someone else. Then I worried about transporting Cath but it seemed a special van had been laid on.

The school was to start on a small scale, with nine children attending

Catherine aged four.

on a part-time basis (Cath would go for three half-days a week) so only the ground floor of the house was being prepared. It was freshly decorated and sunny, and toys, therapy mats and cribs were already in place in the main room. It looked terrific and so did Mrs. Brown's assistants, Pat and Sophie. They were bright and eager and Pat soon became a personal friend and even looked after Cath and Dominic sometimes when Ted and I wanted to go out together.

The first few times Cath went to the school I stayed with her. Then Mrs. Brown told me I was being overprotective, which at first I resented and then grudgingly accepted. I posted Cath into the van each school day and bit my nails till she came home. When she wasn't expelled for her screaming, and Pat acquired the art of feeding her, I relaxed and devoted more time to Dominic.

Poor Catherine! She didn't enjoy the school for a while and was withdrawn both there and at home. Then she had another shock to her system. I left her with Veronica for a few minutes one wet day while I lugged the laundry up the road to be dried. When I returned Veronica was looking smug.

"I've chucked out that revolting thing Catherine sucks," she announced.

I gaped at her. "Her soother you mean? But how dare you?" I looked at my watch. "You beast, I haven't got any spares and the chemist's shut—"

"I know," said Veronica more smugly than ever.

"Well! I'll find her pouffe in the dustbin next!"

"Listen, for God's sake stop being so silly about it," said Veronica. "She doesn't need that thing any more and she looks awful with it stuck in the middle of her face. You really must stop treating her like a baby."

"But she is—"

"No, she isn't. She's nearly four. And I don't care what's wrong with her, she's bright enough to have got you right under her thumb. Now darling, let's have a drop of wine," she added, indicating that her harangue was over.

I was very nervous that night but found to my surprise and, I must admit, to my slight chagrin, that an extra pat on the back settled Cath almost as quickly as her soother had in the past.

"Watch this," I said to Ted the next morning. And I threw Billie Bee into the garbage with a flourish.

"Well, Veronica was right, wasn't she?" he said maddeningly.

"Oh, shut up."

"OK. Anyway, no more sticky messes everywhere. Thank God for that. We should celebrate. How about having Veronica down for a nice boozy supper?"

The people at the Chelsea clinic suggested I try to toilet train Cath and lent me a chair rather like her wooden one but with a hole in the bottom and a pot underneath. I had frequently sat her on the lavatory in the past but it frightened her and she could never relax. It was also exhausting for me because I had to hold her up under her arms. The chair was better but it was rigid and unpadded and she stiffened uncomfortably when I put her on it. What I did was to leave her dry for as long as I dared and then sit her on the chair with the hole padded with a diaper and wait. And wait. I ran taps, hissed at her and tickled her tummy but in all the weeks I sat her on that damned thing she peed into it exactly three times. On these occasions I leapt around, clapped, cheered and gave her hugs and ice cream but her face remained blank and I felt she had no idea what she had done. So I gave up. I now think I should have persevered but at the time the returns didn't seem to justify her discomfort and my effort.

I continued to take Cath for therapy at the clinic but she missed many appointments because of respiratory infections. She missed a lot of school for the same reason but despite this she began to enjoy the program there. Most of the children were not as badly handicapped as she was and the staff had almost immediate success with them. There was, for instance, a six-year-old girl, Jane, with Down's syndrome who was quite bright but had never been disciplined in any way at home. As a result, she threw temper tantrums that disrupted the whole class at first. Mrs. Brown was firm with her, and soon Jane would greet one with a handshake, instead of a prolonged and sometimes embarrassing hugging session, and then settle down to some activity instead of rushing around hysterically and upsetting the other children.

There were also two children who were more handicapped both physically and mentally than Catherine, a situation I had only been able to assume existed until now. My shocked reaction to seeing them brought home some of the feelings people must have had when they first encountered Cath. One of the children was a pathetically tiny, skeletal boy with an extreme degree of Down's syndrome. At the age of nine he was still fed entirely on fluids from a bottle. He was almost lifeless; he just lay still in a crib, blowing bubbles as he breathed, and nothing seemed to rouse him. Somehow the saddest thing about him was his wardrobe. Every time I saw him he was dressed in a different set of immaculate clothes and his feet were always laced up neatly in shiny brown boots. When Pat first took me over to see him I swallowed and said, "Oh, what lovely clothes," because it was the only positive thing that occurred to me. I then realized why so many people, when seeing Cath for the first time, said, "Oh, what a lovely complexion she's got."

The other child was quite different. To begin with, he was one of the most startlingly beautiful children I have ever seen, with sunbleached hair, enormous blue eyes and a quizzical half-smile. At first glance he looked like a physically perfect four-year-old, as if he might get up the next moment and run into the garden. But then I realized his eyes saw little or nothing as he sat quite still, propped up against cushions. Except for a vague flapping of his limbs he remained without moving in whatever position he was placed. Every now and again tears would roll from his eyes as he quietly wept. More rarely, he would laugh, but it was a quiet and private laugh, not one that one could enjoy and share, like Cath's. I think that had he been my child, and if he had always been like that, I would have felt the same way about him as I did about Cath. The tragedy in his case was that until the age of two he had been completely normal but had then contracted meningitis. He was incorrectly diagnosed and treated and was, as a result, even more blocked out mentally than Catherine. His parents had been told that his brain was so badly damaged there was no hope he would ever progress at all. Now they were planning to take him to the Institute for Human Potential in Philadelphia. I heard later from Pat that the Institute had been unable to give any hope or help.

The main purpose the school served as far as Cath was concerned was that it accustomed her to being looked after by someone other than myself. According to Pat she rarely emerged from her shell enough to have the rip-roaring sort of fun we had with her at home, though she did start to return smiles more often and respond to cushion-shoving and block-throwing games. She also showed a real interest in lying on the floor with the other children at rest time, just as she always enjoyed it when Ted or I lay down and played with her. I suppose it made her feel that someone was getting down to her level for once.

Watching the daffodils and crocuses pop up in the garden a few months before had given me ideas about babies. Waiting one day until Cath was pivoting happily on the kitchen floor and Dominic was sitting on his potty and being cute with a picture book, I mentioned the idea to Ted.

"Sure. If you think you can manage, why not?" Ted looked up briefly from a page of equations as he said this. "They're not bad, are they?" he added as he put down his pen and had a good look at his children. "Hey, Dominic, would you like to come with me to put gas in the car when you've finished there?" Dominic clearly fancied the idea; he loved private outings with Ted.

So I duly became pregnant and was rather annoyed when I found that more people reacted to the joyful news with worried frowns than with the lit-up faces I had anticipated. How, they said, will you cope? I knew myself that I could not only manage but would enjoy another baby. However, I found it hard to convince some people of this. Time would tell, I hoped.

Now, though, about two months later, a frightening thing happened, something that had never happened during my first two pregnancies. I had a spate of severe cramps and bleeding and was terrified I was about to miscarry. Virtually paralysed with fear, I didn't so much rush to the doctor as creep, taking very small steps and shallow breaths. Once in his waiting room I sat stiff and still and tried to concentrate on a crumpled copy of last year's *What's On In London This Week*. The room was full of West Hampstead feeling poorly, including two women who were comparing varicose veins. They had just graduated to miscarriages and "The Big One" when fortunately I was called. Dr. Field knew me well by now; he was an old-fashioned family doctor and had come to the house many times to see Catherine during her violent attacks of bronchitis. When I told him my problems he said that under the circumstances all I could do was rest as much as possible and do a minimum of lifting.

I smiled wanly at these words.

"How badly do you want this baby?" he asked. "Would it be a real blow if you lost it?"

I was alarmed. "I want it very badly and yes, it would be a real blow if I lost it. I want Dominic to have a normal sibling as soon as possible. I think it'd be tough on him just to have Cath. Why, do you think—?"

Dr. Field shrugged. "I just wondered how important it was to you. Having looked you over I don't think you will miscarry but it won't help if you sit and worry about it. Incidentally, you don't expect me to offer you any pills, do you?"

"God, no!" The appalling effects of thalidomide were coming to light at that time and nothing would have persuaded me to take anything more potent than National Health orange juice.

That night I had a thought that was to cast a shadow of worry and doubt over the rest of my pregnancy. What if my body was trying to get rid of the foetus because there was something wrong with it? I recalled a cousin telling me a short while earlier how grateful she was to have miscarried at three months because she had been told the baby would have been deformed. Maybe I should be helping nature along by dosing myself with gin and castor oil and falling down stairs. I didn't do any of these things, of course, but I found myself mentally preparing for trouble. Sometimes I even wondered whether I was being reasonable to hope for another normal baby after having been so lucky with Dominic. At no point did I tell anyone of my worries. They were too alarming to share, and besides, nobody could have helped. I continued to have cramps and bleeding every now and again but they weren't as severe as that first time. After a few weeks the bleeding stopped and I assured myself the cramps were psychological.

Ted was returning to Winnipeg at the end of July and suggested I stay in England with the children until September. It seemed a bit rude of me to agree too eagerly but after some polite expostulation I did. This meant I could spend some time with my family at Greatham, which Ted always found rather overwhelming.

6

I can't pretend it was anything but a wrench to leave England at the end of the summer. Back in Winnipeg I was once more virtually chained to the house because of the children. I missed the hubbub of Veronica's house where friends were always dropping in and there was constant activity. Five months pregnant now, I was extremely uncomfortable and still worried stiff about the baby I was carrying. To alleviate my restlessness I devoured potato chips and indifferent novels until I felt I was going into a stupor, physically and mentally.

For some time I had been plaguing Ted about buying a house but he had resisted the idea. One day at supper, though, he announced he had changed his mind and suggested I start looking. Two days later I had found a lovely old house in a pleasant neighbourhood and twenty-four hours after that we had signed on the dotted line. Ted was dazed. He hadn't counted on my actually finding a house; he had hoped that hunting for one would entertain me until the baby was born. Although by his own admission he is not a person to adjust to new ideas with alacrity, eleven years later he is glad we bought the house when we did and would be reluctant to leave it.

There was no question this time that I would have to find somewhere for Catherine to go while I had the baby. Wilf and Ann offered to take Dominic and I set the bureaucratic wheels in motion for Cath to stay for a month in the St. Amant Ward, part of a Catholic hospital set aside for mentally and physically handicapped children. Most of the children were in there on a long-term basis, until the age of about six when they had to go to the major institution fifty miles outside Winnipeg. But if one booked well enough in advance one could place a child there for a short time. Ted drove me out one day to have a look at it and when I got back to the car he asked me what was the matter.

"Nothing," I said, "nothing. Just a bit gruelling, that's all." I settled myself into the back with Catherine. "God," I whispered, "I've never seen such deformities. I nearly passed out at one point." I shivered, and tried to blow the smell of disinfectant and sickness from my nose. "Ted, do you think I'm awful to say that?"

"Good God, no. It's a perfectly natural reaction. I'm sure I couldn't have taken it. I mean we're used to Cath, after all, but I'm sure people get a shock when they first see her. One instinctively recoils from the unnatural."

"I still feel vaguely that I've sinned reacting like that, though," I said.

A kindly nun had taken me on a tour of the wards where the "worst" children were. This was where Cath would be staying. I suppose what had shaken me most was seeing so many of nature's cruelest mistakes all together. Some were sprawled in special chairs in the corridors but most of them were just lying in cribs, many with their hands strapped to the sides so they couldn't mutilate themselves. Nearly all the children were deformed. Very few of them were moving or reacting much to what was going on around them. Several appeared to be alive only because they were hooked up to bottles of fluid over their cribs. The place itself wasn't at all gloomy. It was bright and sunny, there were plentiful toys and pretty pictures, and the nuns and nurses bustled around chattering to each other and to the children. Everything was cheerful, in fact, except the children. One boy scared me so much that I turned away sharply and had to dare myself to look at him a second time to make sure I wasn't imagining things. He looked like Humpty Dumpty in Dominic's nursery rhyme book. He had a grotesquely blown up head with a tiny limp body attached; and his head, even his face, was covered with a network of bulging veins. The misplaced eyes, nose and mouth and the ginger fuzz on top seemed a mockery. The nun asked me if anything was the matter. Trying to hide the horror I felt, I stammered that I'd never seen that degree of hydrocephalus. She said they had an even bigger one in the next room and would I like to see him? She made him sound like a prize vegetable marrow. I shook my head numbly and she looked at my stomach and nodded. I departed soon afterwards.

"Will Cath be all right in there?" asked Ted.

"What? Oh, yes, I think so," I said. "Sure. Sure. The nuns are really super and they're always stopping to hug the kids and talk to them. It's just—well, she won't know what's hit her, will she?" My eyes started pricking as I said this so I added hastily, "There's a nice little playroom at the end of the ward with a few kids like Cath wriggling around on the floor. The nun said Cath would be there for part of the day and not left in a crib all the time. That she should enjoy, at least. And she can have her Ding-dong and mirror in there too."

I couldn't sleep that night. I lay on my back and watched the blankets undulating over my stomach as the baby churned around. My mind was a mess of muddled worries. I worried about the bewilderment Cath would feel at being dumped into a strange environment, about whether she would eat and drink, about whether the nuns would know when she needed suppositories and about whether they would be able to comfort her when she was unhappy. My worries about the baby's normality got completely out of hand and I began to see no reason why I shouldn't have another like Cath. Only a few days ago an acquaintance had taken it upon herself to inform me, with the requisite shock and tongue-clucking, about a young couple she knew who had *two* children with cerebral palsy. But the worst worry, the most persistent and yet most intangible, was the sense of guilt I felt about my reaction to seeing all those wretched children earlier in the day. Ted's pronouncement about this reaction being normal made sense. Still, I was caught in the familiar intellectual versus emotional dilemma; I realized he was right but I felt awful.

When I finally fell asleep I had exceedingly nasty dreams.

The baby was due on January 1st. To relieve the tension I felt as the day for Catherine's admission to St. Amant approached, I wrote out a list of her likes and dislikes to give to the nuns. On the day itself I put on my sunglasses and a fixed smile and off we went.

"I'm coming back, darling," I said as I arranged her in her crib.

Even when I was just dashing up to the store I always said this. And when I returned I said, "See, I've come back." I think the idea was beginning to lodge in her mind but I suspected that even she would be able to tell the difference between ten minutes and a month. My misery, as I kissed her and walked quickly away, was indescribable. And so silly, I thought as I bared my teeth and ducked my head at the nun in charge who was reassuring me and seeing me out. I flicked away the tears that were splashing onto my stomach from behind my glasses. She'll be beautifully looked after, I told myself, and I can phone and ask how she is whenever I want to. And it's only for a month, not a lifetime. I blew my nose and made my exit.

Not having Catherine around was very strange at first and created frequent voids during the day. People were always saying, "I don't know how you manage with Catherine!" But I found myself wondering what they did all day without a Catherine. Once I had established, through frequent and no doubt irritating phone calls, that she was settling in and apparently contented at the hospital, I adjusted myself gratefully to my additional time and freedom. I did all sorts of exciting things like getting my teeth fixed and darning Ted's socks. However, I had too many pains and discomforts to do the one thing I desperately wanted to do—sleep.

New Year's day came and went and a couple of days later I went to see Dr. Friesen. Two weeks earlier he had said any day now, making me wonder whether we would get Cath into St. Amant in time.

"Couldn't you induce it?" I asked. "It's using my bladder as a trampoline now, and that's not funny. And Ted's sleeping on the sofa because he says the baby keeps kicking him."

Dr. Friesen smiled in his calm way. "I know it's fashionable to induce, Mrs. Schaefer," he said, "but I don't like to unless it's absolutely necessary. Don't worry though," he added. "I won't let you go on like this for more than another week."

"Another week! My God!"

Finally, early in the morning of January 8th, I scrawled a note to Ted, "Have gone to have baby, back soon," and as quietly as possible called a taxi. I wasn't at all as excited as I had been at this point with Dominic; I was scared. Soon I would know whether the last seven months of silent worry had been justified.

I was close to hysteria by the time Dr. Friesen appeared. "I don't want this baby," I greeted the poor man. "I'm frightened."

"It's a bit late to say that, Mrs. Schaefer," he said after a minute or two. "It's a boy, and he looks even bigger than Dominic and just as strong."

The baby was held up. He was utterly lovely, pink and puzzled. And he looked perfect.

My next sentence might be expected to start "Relief flooded over me—!" Such was not the case, however. I had prepared myself too well for disaster. He may look super, I thought guardedly, but Cath's peculiarities didn't show up at once. We're not out of the woods yet; the next few weeks will tell. Still, I must do the sensible thing now, be grateful it's over and sleep while I can. Never have I slept as I did during the next five days. I awoke, or rather was woken, only to wash and feed myself and the baby.

Benjy, as we called the baby, gradually convinced me of his normality. After a week or so he was holding up his head steadily, though Dominic had done this literally from the moment he was born. He cried rather a lot, but it was a normal baby's cry and not, I told myself, the terrifying inhuman scream that Cath had had. He was adorable, and I treasured him.

When we went to get Cath I anticipated keenly her pleasure at seeing us.

"She probably won't remember you," said Ted. "Be prepared for that."

"Of course she will!" Nevertheless, I took his advice and it was a good thing I did. There wasn't a flicker of recognition in Cath's eyes as I walked up to her crib and kissed her. My God, I thought, she's turned into a zombie like all the others. She's lost weight too, and she smells icky.

"Cath, sweetheart. Cath, it's me, your mum. I'm back. I said I would be, remember?" But her eyes avoided mine. When I picked her up she remained immobile and limp in my arms. Maybe she's full of drugs, I thought. I called one of the nuns and asked her but no, Cath had only been having her Ospolot and her quarter grain of phenobarb at night. How had she slept? Very well, it seemed, straight off to sleep at seven and not a peep out of her till she was woken up in the morning. I couldn't believe it! Maybe it was the high temperature at which the hospital was kept. She'd probably liven up when we got out.

"She looks drugged," was Ted's first comment when I got out to the car.

"I know, she looks completely blanked out, doesn't she? Cath darling, please!" I was holding her on my knee and tried once again to get her to look at me. "That's it—" She had given me a furtive sidelong glance. Then she made the tiniest gurgling noise in her throat and turned one side of her mouth up in a faint smile. By the time we got home she was smiling more freely and beginning to laugh and jerk excitedly. It was as though she had been awoken from a long sleep and couldn't believe she was back in the world. The first thing I did was to give her a bath, partly because it was one of her favourite things and partly to make her smell like herself again. I felt rather like a mother cat licking strange smells from her kitten when it has been away from her.

By the beginning of March, I was feeling somewhat housebound. My only outings since sometime before Benjy's birth had been early morning dashes uptown for medical checkups. Ted didn't have early lectures on these days and could stay at home with whichever children I wasn't taking. It was an unsatisfactory arrangement for both of us so I began to cast around for someone who would be prepared to babysit for me regularly one afternoon a week. I was lucky enough to find the perfect person. A Mennonite whose family, like Ted's parents, had come from Russia, Mrs. Bock was one of the most gentle, conscientious and self-effacing women I've ever met. Right from the start she was far more than just a babysitter. She regarded my children as her grandchildren, although she had several of her own, and soon became an invaluable friend to all of us. When she first came over to meet us I was afraid she might justifiably be overwhelmed at the prospect of coping with Catherine in addition to a three-year-old and a small baby. Far from it. She said Cath seemed to be less odd and difficult to understand than a lot of people she knew and was anxious to know the best way to care for and amuse her.

Family outings were quite a business these days. We often saw Wilf and his family, and Ted's sister Lily and hers, but they lived locally and it wasn't too complicated. When a family get-together was being held at Ted's parents' home in Gretna, on the other hand, it involved mountains of diapers, baby food and hours of sitting in the car, hoping that all three children wouldn't need attention at once. These visits were enormously enjoyable, though, and the Schaefers were always thrilled to see their grandchildren. Ted's father's attempts to communicate with Cath as a baby had made us all uneasy. Now it gave me great pleasure to watch him in animated conversation with Ted, breaking off every now and again to tickle Cath, chat with Dominic or wholeheartedly admire Benjy.

Cath was now too big and awkward for her wooden chair, so we passed it on to the St. Amant Ward. Ted built up the back of a child's rocking chair and she enjoyed sitting in that for ten minutes or so at a time. She couldn't be left in it alone, however, as she could only remain steady for a few seconds without either flopping sideways or forwards or sliding down until her chin was on the tray we had put across the arms. There are photos in our album showing her looking very happy in the chair, but they are excellent examples of how pictures can lie, or at least exaggerate. Looking at them, one could get the impression that she spent hours sitting neatly in the chair playing with the toys on the tray. But in fact we hovered with a camera for ages before catching the right moment. It was the same with a photo of her sitting by herself on the floor. Her head control was pretty good by this time. She could sit completely unaided, with a very curved back, for a few seconds; but then she would lose her balance and crash over. If I wedged a cushion behind her bottom, she could sit for longer and was learning to fall curled up so that she didn't bang her head when she landed.

It may seem odd that I hadn't considered getting a wheelchair for her. There were two reasons why I hadn't. First, we had got along so far without one. My strength had increased with Cath's growth. It didn't bother me to carry her over my shoulder the length of a block to see a friend, though it shocked people to see me do it. When I wanted to go further afield with her, I took a taxi. Second, there is something so uncompromising about a wheelchair. To me, the act of getting one would be a symbol of defeat; not in the sense that I had failed to get Catherine to walk, but in a more subtle way. I had always strived to make her appear as much like any other child as possible and to use my wits to accomplish this rather than special equipment. Getting a wheelchair would be crossing the boundary into the world where the handicapped are instantly recognizable.

There was no ordinary vehicle that could be adapted for Catherine's use and now that it was spring I wanted to join other Winnipeggers who were cautiously emerging from hibernation. Like them, I wanted to go out for walks with all my children. So I took the plunge and made enquiries about children's wheelchairs. I was staggered at the cost and difficulty of obtaining one and ended up renting one from the Society for Crippled Children.

It was the smallest available but was still too big and I had to put padding on either side of Cath's hips. There was also the problem of her sliding down because of the spastic way she shoved her middle forward all the time. I stabilized her hips with a cumbersome but effective strap, but keeping her upright was impossible. When she was feeling energetic she would shoot up straight and look marvellous, but most of the time she slumped forward over the tray or hung sideways over one of the arms. When she did this she could usually pull herself up again and it made her hoot with laughter. At first I didn't worry when I saw her in this peculiar position, but on one dreadful occasion she got stuck there and when I went to check her she was unconscious. I rushed her indoors, put her on the sofa and rubbed her all over until she gradually turned from blue to white and opened her eyes blearily. After half an hour or so she was pink and cheerful again. I checked her more frequently after that.

The wheelchair also made it easier to entertain Catherine indoors. She loved being pushed from room to room in it, preferably at high speed with lots of banging into door frames en route. She also liked being tilted backwards and forwards in it, which produced predictable shrieks of bright-eyed pleasure-cum-terror. She could sit in the chair comfortably for longer than in any previous seating arrangement so she now spent much less time on the floor and presumably appreciated life at a higher level. The chair fitted neatly under the cutlery drawer in the kitchen. She liked rattling around amongst the wooden spoons and nut-crackers, delighting herself every now and again by managing to extract something and drop it on the floor. I had hoped she would enjoy the piano we had recently bought, but once she had landed on a clump of keys with her elbows a couple of times she tended just to sit and dribble over the keyboard. I persevered and tried playing tunes with her fingers, but she was surprisingly and discouragingly uninspired by the idea. On the other hand she did seem to like sitting by me as I crept painfully back to the level at which I had stopped taking lessons ten years before.

By the summer of 1966 I felt truly happy in Winnipeg. Ted had recovered from his year's absence from the chemistry department and had stopped groaning so loudly about mortgage payments. Benjy was patently normal—a beautiful baby with wicked blue eyes and masses of white hair that stuck out all over his head like a dandelion clock. We were all, including Cath, well. And last but not least I had made many friends on our street. This, combined with having our own house, gave me a sense of security and belonging that I hadn't felt before.

Soon after we had moved in, a bouncy girl called Mary appeared at my door with her two small children and a lopsided cake. She hoped I would agree that it was the thought that counted. I said yes and asked her if she didn't mind this morning's coffee heated up. We were off to a friendly start. Through her I met other neighbours. Directly opposite us were Ann and Harold who, like Mary and her husband, were home-grown Canadians; they were a serenely chaotic couple of musicians and lived in a huge house with two baby grand pianos and one baby daughter. Down the road were Nancy, a tiny but explosive Irish girl, and her Canadian husband, Christopher, a theatre critic and columnist; Ted and I frequently exchanged books, records and opinions with them. Then there was Mia, a mercurial Yugoslavian girl married to a calm, handsome Englishman; we acquired our cat, Dido, from them. There was also Piroska, an outspoken Hungarian refugee and one of the brightest lights for miles around; clever, witty and unfailingly kind she was also—unfairly, some felt—beautiful.

Between us we had a variety of backgrounds and interests and we developed close but easy relationships, helping each other out and spending much time in each other's company. Our children, too, became friends and often virtually lived in one another's houses. Cath was accepted by everybody simply as a child with more peculiarities than most. It wasn't long before I felt safe parking her with someone if I had to dash off somewhere.

Meeting a number of new people in a short space of time made me aware that I had developed a rough formula for introducing Catherine that I hoped would quickly dispel as much embarrassment as possible. "This is my daughter Catherine," I would say. Then I would explain her problems as briefly and as succinctly as possible, indicating that it didn't cause me, or Cath, so far as I knew, any discomfort to talk about her and answer questions if someone wanted to know more. I never consciously thought about it but I suppose I acted in the way I would appreciate being treated if I were to meet someone like Cath for the first time.

Towards the end of the summer I had a shock. I was forced to conclude I was going to have another baby the following spring. I was devastated. I knew, without a shadow of a doubt, that going through another pregnancy at this point would tear me apart physically and mentally. But what could I do? I spent many bleak days thinking about abortion and finally presented my problem to Dr. Friesen. He surprised me by saying that, despite my evidence, he didn't think I was pregnant. He told me to try not to think about it for two weeks and report back then. I thought about it not only all day but evidently for large chunks of the night because I had vivid dreams from which I awoke sweating and rapid-pulsed. I was trying to keep up a good front but Ted asked me one day what was wrong.

"Nothing," I said.

"Yes there is. You've broken three plates in the last week."

"Have you kept count?"

"Yes. And why is my only pair of white underpants now pink?"

"Well, they got in with my red jeans and the colour ran." I never bothered to separate white things from the rest of the daily wash because I liked suddenly having a row of pink or blue diapers flapping on the line. It made a change. But I did usually remember to extract Ted's undies and do them separately. "Sorry," I said. "I'll Javex them."

"OK." Ted opened the fridge door and peered in. He always heads for the fridge when he's uneasy about something. "What the hell's this doing in here, may I ask?" He held up my miniature score of Mozart's flute and harp concerto.

"Must have been Dominic," I said.

"Hm." Ted banged around in the fridge. "Where's the cheese? I thought we had some." Something clicked in my mind and while he continued to hunt I crept into the dining room and opened up the piano stool. There was the cheese, of course.

"Dominic indeed!" said Ted behind me. He couldn't help laughing but added, "Look, why are you being so absent-minded?"

I took a deep breath. "I seem to be pregnant."

"God almighty." He swivelled around and yanked at the fridge door again.

A few days later, however, I found that my fears were, as Dr. Friesen had predicted, unfounded. My relief was instant and profound but it had been a bad scare. I was soon back in the office and this time emerged with a grin and a prescription for "the pill."

Shortly after my pregnancy scare something else cropped up to plague me with worry. But this was on a long-term basis.

Once the snow came I had to use two sleighs when taking the children out for walks. Cath still just fitted into one Ted had built up for her last year and I put Benjy in a cardboard box on Dominic's old one, pulling one sleigh with each arm. I felt a bit like a dray horse but it worked. Quite often I dropped in on someone, if only to make a point to the walk; I disliked walking under such cumbersome circumstances for no reason other than getting fresh air into us all.

One day I did the block and stopped at Piroska's house on the way back. I handed Benjy to her and then bent down to pick Cath up to take her in. But something had happened to my left leg.

"Piroska!" I yelled. "Buck up! Quick, can you take one end of Cath?" Piroska came and grabbed Cath's legs and somehow we got up the steps with Cath between us.

"What is it, darling?" said Piroska when we had shuffled in and dumped Cath, who was hysterical with laughter, on the floor. "How you carry that child I can't imagine. I could barely cope with her legs."

"My leg went numb," I said. "It's all right now, but it felt as if it wasn't there, sort of paralysed." I waggled it around. "It was scary."

"Well, sit down and have some coffee. I'll spike it. Don't be silly darling, the coffee."

"Piroska, has that ever happened to you?"

"Frequently, darling. When I'm plastered. Only it's usually both legs. Don't worry for Chrissake. Take that idiotic look off your face. You probably got a nerve caught or something. Here, drink this and forget about it. When did you last have a checkup, by the way?"

I was surprised. "I never have them as such," I said. "In fact the only doctor I've ever been to here is the obstetrician. I've never had anything wrong with me. Do you mean you go to a doctor regularly?"

"Vaguely, yeah."

"Did you get him out of the yellow pages or what?"

"No, no, he's a friend from Hungary. Benjy darling, stop eating my toes will you? Only I wouldn't advise going to a friend. It's kind of embarrassing when he's got his finger up your bottom one minute and you're chatting over drinks the next."

"Mm, quite. I'll see if Dr. Friesen can suggest one." I hauled Benjy up from under the table. "Here sweetheart, have one of Piroska's homemade cookies. They're even more delicious than her toes."

My leg was perfectly all right. But the incident, however insignificant, sowed in me the seed of an obsession with my health that rapidly bloomed and has flourished ever since.

I had always brushed aside the question of what we would do with Catherine eventually. Ever since she was a baby, people had been asking this and it annoyed me. Not only, I felt, was it ignoring the fact that we were currently functioning quite well as a family despite Catherine, but it was looking for bogies. My reaction was always, "We'll deal with that one when we come to it. I'm young and strong. I'll be able to manage her for years yet."

But now, suddenly, I started to think about my mortality, particularly in relation to Catherine. What would happen to her if I dropped dead tomorrow? One reason why I hadn't worried about this before was that I knew she could be admitted to the St. Amant Ward if necessary. I hated the idea but presumably she would get used to it in time. She had just had her fifth birthday. After the age of six children were usually moved from the hospital to the unspeakable-sounding institution for "retardates" fifty miles from Winnipeg. I had never been there but I knew people whose children had had to be put in there. Their stories were so horrific that I had shut the place out of my mind. I knew I should go and check for myself but what if it was as bad as I'd heard? I would then be worse off than if I hadn't gone. So I didn't go.

Instead I took out a term insurance. The idea was that if I died Ted would receive a lump sum to be used specifically for the extra help he would have to hire for Catherine's care. This was assuming that his salary would cover a housekeeper for him and the boys. I hoped and imagined that by the time the insurance money had run out the government would come up with a solution for the care of people like Catherine within the community rather than in institutions.

I also took myself to be checked up; I had to anyway for insurance purposes. I was apparently in good health, despite a violent and painful lurch I had experienced in the region of my heart that morning. But the damage was done and thenceforth I became a dreadful hypochondriac.

I didn't take to my bed in a pink bedjacket and fill myself with patent medicines; I carried on quite normally. But I became ultra-aware of my body and its functions and was always on the lookout for signs of trouble. Unfortunately, I had acquired a certain amount of medical knowledge both because of my general interest in the subject and because I had done a year and a half of nursing as a teenager. But, as the adage goes, "a little learning is a dangerous thing," particularly to an overimaginative person like myself. During my third visit to the doctor before Christmas, with a mole I had inspected through Dominic's magnifying glass and had decided was becoming a melanoma, I was told that if I reappeared before February I would be sent to a psychiatrist. Fair enough, as far as the overworked doctor was concerned, but I knew why I was neurotic, and unless a marvellous home for people like Catherine suddenly materialized, there was no cure.

At first I kept Ted informed of my latest discoveries of imminent disaster but his patience was limited. It made him wonder what would happen if I really did get ill. After that I prudently used my friends, rather than him, as confidants. Even they found me difficult to cope with on occasion—like the time I realized I had indisputable signs of leprosy.

Four years later, when I told Dominic and Benjy I had to go into hospital for a few days, they naturally wanted to know why.

"Well," I said, "you remember when we took Dido down to the vet for an operation to stop her having more kittens?" They nodded. Choosing my words carefully, I thought, I went on, "I'm going to have the same thing done—"

"But Mum," said Dominic, "you haven't had any kittens yet!"

Benjy looked at him in astonishment. "People," he said, "have babies." A flash of alarm crossed his face and he looked back to me for confirmation. I laughed as I hugged him.

Dominic's eyes shot heavenward and then back to me.

"OK Mum," he continued seriously, "so you're going to get fixed. How come?" Ted and I had always encouraged forthrightness in our family so I could hardly complain at this somewhat indelicate turn of phrase.

"All right, I'll tell you—"

Although I put it less bluntly to the boys, my reason for deciding to have a tubal ligation was that despite sometimes wanting another baby, I knew myself well enough to realize that having one would probably wreck me physically and certainly mentally. Not only would I be worried about the baby's development during my pregnancy but, being constantly at death's door, I felt it would be irresponsible to have a baby only to leave it motherless. And I hated the idea of being on "the pill" for another fifteen years or so.

Cath was nearly ten at this time, strictly speaking far too old for St. Amant, but the kind nuns there agreed to take her for a week. Because of her size she was put into a cheerful ward where most of the children were either ambulatory or semi-independent in wheelchairs. After I said goodbye and promised I was coming back, she was pushed off grinning by an enthusiastic girl with pebble lenses and a large teddy bear, which she plonked on Cath's tray. Ted was able to stay at home for the few days I would be in hospital, so I didn't have to farm out the boys. They looked forward to him being in charge. For one thing, he didn't make them wash, and for another they knew they would eat out most of the time.

Dr. Friesen asked me recently whether I had ever regretted having that operation. "No," I said, "not for a single instant. I love looking at other people's babies, and cuddling them and playing with them, but I never wish they were mine."

But the instinct to produce babies is a hard one to stifle, in me, anyway. Sometimes, just before waking, I dream that I'm pregnant or that I have a new-born baby, and I experience the most intense and singular happiness.

7

At Christmas a friend working at the Argonne National Laboratories near Chicago had suggested to Ted that he might like to spend the summer working there as a visiting scientist. My immediate reaction had been, oh no, not another upheaval, but the more I heard about it, the more attractive it sounded. What really decided me in favour of the idea was that Ted appeared to be winding himself up to a state of genuine enthusiasm. However, he was awaiting my response before saying yes.

Chicago, Chicago, pompiddy pom pom, pom pompiddy pom—I was humming as I whacked rugs on the clothesline. I wondered if the children and I would ever get there. Ted had already left with the car and I was clearing up the house in preparation for friends who were moving in for the summer. Cath was watching me from her wheelchair and was laughing so energetically that she was nearly tipping it over; she evidently found my banging and sneezing wildly entertaining. Dominic was doing gymnastics on the swing set and Benjy was temporarily captive in his playpen beside the wheelchair. He was nearly eighteen months now, a fiendishly active and inquisitive baby, and I didn't dare have him on the loose unless he had my undivided attention.

Flying down separately with the children had seemed a less awful choice than driving a thousand miles in our small station wagon all together. Cath took up the entire back section of the car and we would

Catherine at six. TOM SAUNDERS PHOTO

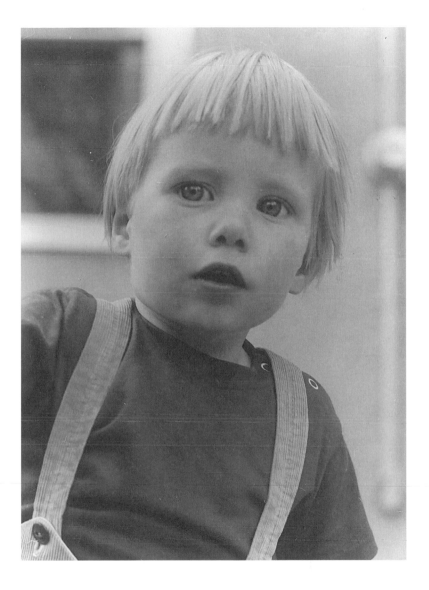

ABOVE. *Benjy aged eighteen months.* TOM SAUNDERS PHOTO

FACING PAGE. *Dominic aged four and a half.* TOM SAUNDERS PHOTO

have had to fit in the wheelchair and Benjy's stroller in addition to suit-cases. This way, too, Ted could take extras such as Dominic's bike and Cath's pouffe, which was now tattered and torn beyond repair and recognition but still much loved. Now that the flight was a bare twenty-four hours away I began to despair of being ready to go, although I had been working furiously for the last week.

Mary appeared and helped me drag the rugs indoors. "Now look," she said, "why don't I come and do the final spit and polish after you've gone? I know what it's like trying to leave a place decent when you've got kids underfoot."

I chewed my nails and wondered whether to let my pride take a beat-ing. I had been so determined to manage this tricky exodus single-handed and efficiently. I said as much to Mary.

"You idiot," she laughed, "as if you have to invent challenges."

"Mum!" yelled Dominic from the back door, "Benjy's got out again and he won't come away from the lawn mower!"

When I returned with Benjy under my arm Piroska had appeared.

"Wow!" I said, "You've gone and blonded yourself—"

"Yes, yes. Now look darling, will you give up trying to do all this yourself. We all think you're wonderful but this is ridiculous. Come here, Benjy. I'm taking you for the rest of the day." She whisked him away from me. "You too, Dominic darling. We've got the paddling pool out so bring your trunks."

Having only Catherine to think about was a tremendous help and I was soon back on schedule.

The journey to Chicago would have gone smoothly, I think, had our plane left Winnipeg on time. But it left late and we missed our connec-tion in Minneapolis, which meant a two-hour wait on standby. It was ninety-four degrees in Minneapolis and those two hours were gruesome. A ground hostess dragged us from queue to queue every time she found a plane going to Chicago. But we always arrived just as it was announced that the last seats had been taken. We were all drooping with heat and the boys wanted drinks constantly. I kept mislaying Benjy and we missed one plane because Dominic was in the Gents. After that I ruled out drinks and washrooms entirely but I knew that unless we got moving soon I would have to change Catherine; though how, I hadn't a clue. I took her out of her wheelchair at one point because she was getting uncomfortable. Just as I got her over my shoulder for a walk our hostess rushed up with news of yet another possible flight, so I had to throw her back in. When we should have been arriving in Chicago, I phoned O'Hare Airport and tried to get Ted paged. I knew he would be wondering why we hadn't appeared. I had no luck but left a message.

Eventually we were squeezed into the back seats of a plane. By now I had to change Cath because she was drenched and I didn't fancy leaving wet patches on the seat. I put the boys in the gangway and laid her full-length on our row of seats, giving myself optimum operating space. She always enjoyed being changed. It provided a diversion, and this occasion was particularly amusing to her because I tried to keep her decent by doing it under a towel. When I had got us all seated again, I felt quite pleased with myself. Benjy, however, sitting on my knee, ruined my sense of self-satisfaction by leaning back suddenly and bashing his head into my face. The result was an egg on the back of his head, to say nothing of my nosebleed, a cut, swollen mouth and two loose teeth.

My message to Ted had gone astray at O'Hare. He had spent two hours getting increasingly worried and wasn't in the best of tempers when I finally found him.

"What happened?" he said as he surveyed us. "And what's the matter with your face, for God's sake? You look as though you've been mugged!" Poor man, I think he still dreamed, as I did, that I would one day manage to leave or arrive somewhere looking fresh, organized and composed like other people. "Well, at least you've arrived—" I tried to detect a note of enthusiasm in this last comment.

"What's this?" I asked Ted. We had turned off the expressway out of Chicago and were driving through what looked like a beautiful national park.

"This is Argonne," he said. "It's lovely, isn't it? There are twelve hundred acres of this." He pointed. "The labs are way over that hill behind a wood."

"But this is fantastic! Look at all these trees everywhere—they're magnificent! And that lake down there—and all these hills—gosh, it's all so lusciously green, isn't it?"

"There are some rare white Chinese deer in the grounds, too," said Ted. "I think they've been put here to breed."

"I'd love to see them sometime. What's our accommodation like, by the way?"

"It's good. Motel-like places. Four of them dotted around under the trees, about ten units in each. Lovely view every way you look. We've got a sitting-room-cum-kitchen and two bedrooms plus a bathroom. It's not enormous, but everything's provided so I should think you'll manage."

I did manage very well. The living quarters for visiting scientists at Argonne were excellent. The kitchen was much better equipped with utensils than mine at home, and each block had a maid who dealt out clean linen every week. A short distance across the grass was a utility building with a laundry room with enough washers and dryers so one didn't have to queue. There was a huge sandbox, shaded by trees, near every block and a short walk away was a swimming pool and tennis courts. No pets were allowed, so there were numerous rabbits bounding around and many species of birds. The place was dominated by massive trees in which cicadas whirred and a man with a machine cut the grass every week, adding to the park-like effect.

There were scientists and their families from many different countries. Our block alone had representatives from Norway, Israel, Canada, the States, Germany and England. A number of us made friends very quickly but one didn't have to mix.

Dominic, who had gone through several moves in his life, was conveniently scared of getting lost. He always stayed within screaming distance, either cycling around the paths or playing with the other children. Benjy, on the other hand, was in seventh heaven at finding so much to explore and so many opportunities to vanish. I lost him on average three times a day. Quite often he was only a few feet away in someone else's place but he could have been in the pond. He figured out the locks and chains on the doors almost instantly. The only time I could relax my guard with him was when he was asleep, and not completely even then. His urge to explore struck early in the day. The man in the office phoned at seven one morning to ask if a fair-haired baby in blue pyjamas holding a bunch of keys might belong to us. He had already, it seemed, disconnected the coke machine and was now concentrating his efforts on dismantling the cigarette machine. Would it, perhaps, be his breakfast time? The man was very cordial.

Usually it was hot during the day and the boys and I spent hours in the pool, with Cath in her chair watching. If it was too hot for her I left her back in our air-conditioned living quarters, with some kind person periodically checking up on her. I longed to take her into the pool but after two attempts I had to give up. The water was too cold and she went rigid and purple. We spent a lot of time that summer sitting or lying under the trees, but in the evening, when it had sometimes cooled off, she and I went for long walks. Ted was enjoying his work set-up. For the first time since I had known him, he was sticking more or less to regular nine-to-five hours. Quite often we would go for long drives after supper, exploring the surrounding countryside. We returned from these expeditions with bunches of wild flowers collected from the roadside to decorate our quarters. I particularly loved the orangy-red tiger lilies, which abounded in much the same way as poppies in England.

I became friendly with a girl who lived a few units down from us. Anne-Marie was of Norwegian origin, married to an American and living in Arizona. One thing we had in common was an interest in music. Anne-Marie often came to listen to my portable record player which, with ten or so of my most indispensable albums, I had sneaked into the car under a pile of rugs before Ted left Winnipeg. One day Anne-Marie showed me a brochure for the Ravinia Festival. I had heard of this open-air music festival but had purposely neglected to investigate it. I knew how impossible it would be to get to any of the concerts as Ravinia was about sixty miles from Argonne. Now, with names like Barenboim and Ashkenazy jumping out from the list in front of me, I was sunk.

"Anne-Marie, there are a couple here we *have* to get to. Let's try approaching our husbands."

Neither of our husbands would be interested in going, we knew, but I was hesitant to land Ted with the children for what would be at least five hours. I must have been very tactful because soon he was insisting that I go, saying it was far too good a chance to miss.

The main barrier to my going out for a long late evening was, of course, Catherine. Dominic was no problem and Benjy wasn't either, really, except that he had a tendency to strip and escape out of doors if he felt he was being put to bed too early, which was nearly always. Cath though, had a complicated diapering arrangement and also still refused to let anyone but myself give her a drink. She needed both these ministrations before going to sleep. Also, she still had occasional screaming sessions that were extremely alarming and difficult to stop, unless you happened to be me.

The evening of the concert I fed the rest of the family and, just before leaving, gave Cath a double dose of phenobarb, fed her, put six diapers on her, and just hoped she would last. Anyway, I reasoned, if she really needed a drink before I returned she would surely take one from Ted.

Anne-Marie and I had a wonderful evening. Quite apart from any-thing else it was, frankly, pleasant to be out on a jaunt by ourselves. For once, we were able to talk without our children needing attention. The weather was perfect and a lovely golden light had settled on Ravinia Park when we arrived. The concert itself was everything I had hoped it would be, although I felt sorry for the performers. Judging by the amount of dis-creet slapping and scratching being done between movements they must have been bombarded by mosquitos. Afterwards Anne-Marie and I impulsively bought tickets for the next concert, hoping that our hus-bands were surviving the evening and wouldn't mind being left holding the babies a second time.

When I crept in late that night, imagining Ted pacing around with Cath, he looked up from his light reading—*The Origins of Totalitarianism*, by Hannah Arendt—and said he had had no trouble. I went in to see Cath and found her wide awake, drenched and thirsty but perfectly happy. Anne-Marie's husband had coped too. She and I not only went to hear Ashkenazy, but also went into Chicago a couple of times to hear Julius Katchen play both Brahms' piano concertos in Grant Park. Not only that, we saw Margot Fonteyn and Rudolph Nureyev in *Les Sylphides*. I wished Ted enjoyed this sort of thing but he has always insisted that his idea of pleasure is being at home with a drink, a packet of French cigarettes and an absorbing book. "Music is taken far too seriously these days," he main-tains. "It's like a religion. I'd have enjoyed it in the eighteenth century, I think. I like to be able to wander around, stretch my legs, smoke, drink, read while I listen to music. You go ahead, but I'll listen to the radio and records at home." We're considered odd by most people but we've been far happier since coming to terms with the fact that I like going out and he doesn't. It's better than pretending to enjoy each other's leisure pur-suits. Also, as babysitters go, Ted is good and cheap.

Before leaving for Chicago I had arranged for Cath to go into the St. Amant Ward for six weeks at the end of the summer while I took the boys to England. When the idea of this holiday had first arisen it hadn't occurred to me that I might leave Catherine behind. Ted's arguments against my taking her had been inescapably sensible, however. She wouldn't enjoy it for one thing. To her it would be nothing more than a series of uncomfortable journeys and constant changes; far better for her to be in the calm environment of the hospital even if she was homesick for a while. Anyway, she would probably realize she didn't have to resign herself to it forever this time, as I suspected had happened before. Secondly, he said, I would be able to do far more without her, and besides that I needed a break from having her constantly around my neck. I objected at that. Did I ever seriously complain? She was just part of my life, as far as I was concerned. In fact I found it hard to imagine life without her. He said he hadn't meant it like that and was I being purposely obtuse? Thirdly, he said, we would save hundreds of dollars by not taking her.

And so I had been convinced, but I still felt horrible as I handed her over to the nuns. This time, in addition to her mirror and pouffe, I took along the electric fan we had bought her some time before; she always suffered more from the heat than from the cold and the ward was as hot as a greenhouse.

"Goodbye, exotic flower," I said hugging her, "and remember, I'm coming back." I turned the fan on. "There you are, that'll cool you down." She had been lying in the crib looking withdrawn and suspicious till that moment but when the wind hit her face and blew her hair streaming back she shut her eyes and laughed. I retreated and didn't look back. As I walked down the corridor past the other children I was pleased to find I was much less sensitive to their deformities and oddnesses this time.

My cousin Julia had a boyfriend who drove a minicab. She had borrowed both of them to meet the boys and myself at the airport and take us down to my mother's cottage.

"Julia!"

"Darling!"

Much hugging and then, ceremoniously, I said, "And this is my other son Benjy."

Delighted exclamations from Julia, who then said, "This is getting very unfair—I've decided to do something about it."

"Goodness, are you pregnant?"

"No, but I'm getting married tomorrow."

"Julia Fisher! To whom, may I ask?"

"Jeremy, of course."

"Oh good." He was the boyfriend waiting for us outside and had been my favourite for a long time.

The boys and I had the most wonderful six weeks. By making short trips to Oxford and other places, and a longer one to London, I managed to see everybody I wanted to see and to pack in an extraordinary number of activities. The house in Hammersmith had been sold and my mother and my brother Edgar had moved permanently to the cottage, with Harry appearing between acting jobs. We spent the greater part of the time there, of course. An old friend and her new husband offered us a room in their basement in London whenever we wanted it so we stayed there for a couple of hectic weeks. Chloe, as welcoming as ever, automatically expected us to appear at her house in Oxford for a few days and of course appear we did.

Apart from missing Catherine, which naturally I did, I can't pretend that it was anything but a relief not to have her with us. I felt wonderfully free with just the boys, and consciously enjoyed every minute of it. How complicated, if not impossible, most of our activities would have become had Cath been around! Hopping onto a bus to go to the zoo or to see friends would have been impossible. It would have involved a taxi each way, plus folding and unfolding the wheelchair and heaving it in and out of the trunk. Whizzing down to Oxford with a friend in his sports car, the boys sat snugly in the back, but where would Cath and the wheelchair have gone? Bonfire picnics in the woods at Greatham with the clan would have been out. I could just imagine how tricky and exhausting it would have been to get Cath over the bumpy ground and through all that bracken. I would have had to cart a blanket along because the ground would have been so uncomfortable for her to lie on with all those pine needles. And yet I would have managed all these things even with Catherine. It was just so nice not to have to.

Front doorsteps, flights of stairs, the steep bumpy path from the road down to the cottage I didn't think twice about. Normally they would have represented obstacles that I would have had to hump the wheelchair up and down and over. It was also such a luxury to be able to stay out late, late, late with friends after a concert, knowing there would be no Cath to give a drink to and otherwise deal with when I got back. And for six whole weeks I didn't have to wonder continually, as we travelled around, what and where I was going to feed her, and how I was going to change her diapers in privacy.

However, once the boys and I returned home I looked forward immensely to having Cath back with us. As I walked down the ward to her room in St. Amant I braced myself for a repeat performance of the last time I had gone to fetch her—a total blank. But an unexpected and beautiful thing happened. The moment she saw me, a good thirty feet away, she went absolutely wild with excitement, shouting and whooping and making her wheelchair rock as she kicked her legs and waved her arms. I went and hugged her and as I did so a nun came swooping into the room followed by a concerned-looking nurse.

"Well!" said the nun when she saw what was going on. "You'll jump right out of there in a minute, Catherine!"

"I wondered what could be the matter with her," said the nurse. "We've never seen her do that before. Who'd have guessed she had it in her!" Several more staff members came to view the phenomenon, all of them exclaiming in surprise.

By the time I got her out to the car she had calmed down somewhat but the moment she saw Ted she started up again.

"Wow, Cath! That's what I call a greeting!" he said as he swung her around in his arms. He shot me a look. "The first thing your mother did when she saw me was to throw your brother at me." He hugged her and she pulled off his glasses.

"Beast," I said. "Anyway I made up for it later on."

While we were driving home Ted turned to me. "I'll bet you never thought she'd give you a present," he said. (I'd brought Cath back a new pouffe.)

"True," I said, "and it was one of the best presents I've ever had."

Ted was asked to return to Argonne the next summer. Since the American economy appeared to be sliding into a recession we took the chance to go while we could. Knowing the ropes made that second summer even more enjoyable than the first. We met up with old friends, including Anne-Marie and her family, and made new ones. Anne-Marie and I sneaked off on several trips together, including one to Ravinia to hear Yehudi Menuhin and the Bath Festival Orchestra. When I found a nice teenage girl on campus who would babysit, even Ted allowed himself to be persuaded to go out to the odd supper party.

The boys were happy to be back in pleasantly familiar surroundings and settled down at once to their old activities. It was incredibly hot and they spent almost the entire summer in their bathing suits, even when it rained. I left Cath out in a rainstorm by mistake once and she enjoyed it so much that thereafter I often did it intentionally. At other times I took her for walks, both of us clad in bathing suits. Another of the elements' tricks that she enjoyed were the windstorms. To her it must have seemed as though a giant fan was playing on her. I had to be careful, though. These windstorms were sometimes so fierce and sudden that one minute you could be lying on the grass with not so much as a breeze ruffling your hair and the next you were dashing out from beneath the trees to avoid falling branches.

It was a good three months for all of us. We returned to Winnipeg cheerful and well, except for my psychosomatic diseases, which were as rampant as ever.

That summer was rounded off by a six-week visit from my mother. She was a marvellous guest, fascinated by everything, enthusiastic and enormous fun to have around. It was lovely being able to show her all the things I had been writing to her about for years, introducing her to my friends and watching her hit it off with them, as I had known she would.

It was three years since she had seen Cath and despite the photos and descriptions I had sent she was amazed at her size. What struck her more, though, was Cath's increased awareness of, and response to, life. This had happened over the years at such an infinitesimally slow rate that I could only see it by comparing her to a few years ago. This, of course, was exactly what my mother was doing.

"She's so much more of a person now, darling," she said. "Aren't you, precious?" she added to Catherine, who giggled and grabbed a fistful of her curly black hair. "And she never seems to cry now. I mean not those awful hysterical bouts. I used to be scared witless being left with her in case she got one of those. Goodness, she's a happy creature. No, darling, let go. You're pulling my hair out. Nix, help!"

"Cath, for heaven's sake show a little respect," I said uncurling her fingers, "or your grandmother will think you haven't been properly brought up." She responded with a raspberry.

"Well said, darling!" exclaimed my mother.

What she had said was true. Cath really was a very contented child and if she did cry it was nearly always for an identifiable reason, usually boredom or pain. By keeping her in the midst of things and periodically giving her specific attention, boredom was mostly kept at bay. Sometimes when she was left unnoticed for longer than she felt was reasonable

Ted and Cath enjoying the evening. BARBARA ZUCHOWICZ PHOTO

she would whine, or if things got really bad, burst into a storm of tears. And Cath felt she had certain rights. She and Ted had long ago established an evening routine. He would give her a hug or tickle or some other form of greeting when he came in from work and then, at some point after supper, he would take her on his lap while he alternately read and played with her or lay by her on the floor, for anywhere up to two hours. If he missed either of these customs, Cath would be very grumpy with him; he would have to woo her back to a happy frame of mind, usually by having a romp on the floor with her and the boys, which they all loved. He figured she had him absolutely under her thumb and I think he was right. If he wasn't around in the evening she never tried to blackmail me into such undivided attention.

Inevitably Cath got hurt physically sometimes. Our house was often full of small children charging around and although they were extraordinarily careful about avoiding her as she lay on the floor in the middle of the commotion, they would sometimes trip over her feet or bang into one of her arms. This often convulsed her with laughter but if she was really hurt one could cheer her up with a rub and a hug just like any other child.

I often wondered to what extent, if any, she suffered from frustration. Was she bright enough to know that she wasn't talking, feeding herself, walking? I didn't know then any more than I do now but I would have thought that if these things did bother her she would have shown her feelings in some way. As it was, she was so contented and so easily amused that she really did seem to live in a world of her own, delightedly and delightfully accepting anything nice that came her way but not relying on it happening.

Because Catherine was so easy to have around, apart from the total physical care she needed, she didn't hamper our lives nearly as much as people often assumed. None of us was prevented from doing anything we would have done had she not existed or been normal. It just took a little organization. Dominic and Benjy participated in all the activities of their peers. Whenever I wanted to take them out to places I couldn't possibly take Cath, swimming lessons at the Y, for example, I would get a babysitter. Mrs. Bock came whenever possible; otherwise there were several teenagers in the neighbourhood who were very good at being with Cath for an hour or two. Or I could leave her with friends on the street. Ted often took the boys out for trips on the weekends—tobogganing and so on. And, as I thought it important that he and I should sometimes go out together with the boys, we did this too, again getting a sitter for Cath.

The one thing we rarely did was to go on expeditions as a complete family. A visit to Ted's parents or to friends, a drive, a picnic, yes; but anything more ambitious, particularly if it involved rough terrain, was tricky. There is a picture in our photo album of Ted and myself, the boys and my mother standing on the beach at Lake Winnipeg with our friends Chris and Nancy and their two children. We are a smiling, relaxed group. But where is Cath? Well, no, she's not taking the picture; she's lying in the back of the car up on the road and as soon as the picture was taken either Ted or myself would have gone to check that she was OK. Why was she in the car? Because it's impossible to get a wheelchair over sand and pebbles. When Catherine was with us on an expedition— which she had to be if it was longer than two or three hours because of feeding and changing her—our activities were restricted.

Some of the problems we had to cope with in raising Cath would probably never occur to anyone who had no experience with such children. The question of finding suitable presents, for example. Had Cath been either just mentally retarded or just physically disabled this would

have been relatively easy, but trying to find things that were both stimulating to her tiny mind and manageable for her feeble, spastic hands was
tough. I suppose I could have said she doesn't understand the concept of
Christmas, birthdays or presents, so why bother? Had Cath been our
only child I might well have done this and simply bought her appropriate
things when I chanced to see them. Dominic and Benjy, though, being
very fair-minded children, would have been shocked had Cath not
received her quota of parcels and treats whenever they did. I did my best
but must admit I cheated sometimes. When I ran out of ideas for squeaky,
squeezy, rattling and ringing objects, I would find myself in a record shop
buying a Beethoven quartet for Cath on the flimsy pretext she would
enjoy listening to it with me. I also bought her jazz records . . . and those
she really did enjoy. She would thump on the floor or her wheelchair tray
with her arms, roughly in time to the beat, her eyes alight with pleasure.
She particularly loved it when the boys and I danced around to the
record, and if we swung her in circles in her chair she was ecstatic.

Another problem was getting Cath out for some fresh air during the
winter. Have you ever wondered how a person in a wheelchair gets out
when there is snow on the ground, how he or she gets further than from
the house to the car, I mean? I doubt whether I would ever have given it a
thought had I not been faced with the situation myself. By the time
Catherine was six years old, she was far too big and awkward to fit into
any conventional child's sleigh, however cleverly Ted built it up. By late
fall that year, when the sky was heavy with snow, I wondered how I
would get her out once winter was under way. I thought of locking the
wheels on the wheelchair and attaching skis to them but couldn't quite
see myself pushing Cath and, at the same time, pulling Benjy in his sleigh.

I decided the answer was to have a sleigh custom built and I asked
friends if they had ever come across a good carpenter who didn't charge
the earth. All that that raised at first was a laugh, until a friend produced
the genuine article literally out of her basement. A one-man business
called Mr. Victor had just finished building her a bathroom down there.
An individual of immense industry and few words, Mr. Victor's only reaction when I drew him a diagram of what I wanted was a nod. Two days
later he delivered the sleigh, looked at his boots and muttered a price that
sounded so low that I asked him to repeat it. He seemed embarrassed and
produced a crumpled piece of paper on which he had written the cost of
the materials he had used. He pointed these out apologetically and I

realized that he thought my astonishment had been because I thought the bill too large, rather than the opposite.

The sleigh was exactly as I had visualized it—basically a long box on steel runners. Mr. Victor had devised a way of making the back of it 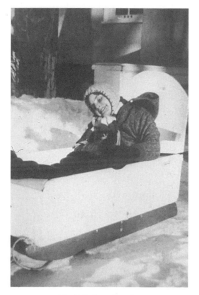 adjustable so that it could be upright or slanted, depending on how strong Cath was feeling. I had wondered how to keep her from slipping down in the sleigh and had asked him to drill a hole in the floor in front of where I judged her bottom would land. I made some Velcro-edged straps and nailed them on the underside of the sleigh and, bringing them up through the hole, drew them over her groins and attached them around the back. It worked perfectly and the thought passed through my mind for the thousandth time what a resourceful person Cath was forcing me to become. I painted the sleigh white, with red runners. The finished product was really super and became known as Cath's chariot. I lined it with foam rubber and once she was tucked in with a pillow and a rug, she was very snug.

Cath in her chariot.

Two afternoons a week the ice rink at the community centre, about a quarter of a mile away, was earmarked for pre-schoolers and mothers. Mary persuaded the gang on our street that it would be fun to join up. It was quite a business getting down there, but Cath's chariot was a handy repository for all the skates, and for Benjy. Rather than taking a separate sleigh for him, I found it easier to bundle him in with Cath when he got tired of walking. Thus loaded, the whole caboodle weighed roughly a hundred pounds, the sleigh itself being about thirty-five. I kept the runners well waxed and it ran smoothly. When I got tired of being the horse, there were always a number of children willing to take over. Cath loved this, as two of them went faster than one of me. She screeched with pleasure when they got behind the rope and raced off down the sidewalk.

Dominic and his friends learned to move quite efficiently on the ice almost immediately. My efforts, and those of some of my beginner friends, however, were disastrous. We crawled around the edge of the rink, arms reaching forward ready to clutch at the boards, our mouths open, whimpering with terror. Mary, who skated with grace and expertise, would pull us around in turn. Whimpers would turn to screams, and we didn't dare let go because we were unable to stop.

I spent quite a lot of time pushing Cath around the ice in her chariot. Not only was this enjoyable for her, it also helped me get the feel of being on skates. Often Cath was joined by Benjy and other toddlers too young for skates, and I would find myself giving rides to four or five kids at once. When I left Cath alone to trundle around by myself, someone else would take her for a spin every now and again. Several children learned to skate by pushing Catherine from behind.

It was about this time I suddenly had the urge to learn to play the cello. I had listened to music long enough. Now I wanted to play.

I brought up the subject one day after supper. Ted was reading in the rocking chair with Cath, I was playing gin rummy with Dominic, and Benjy was training a kitten to jump backwards.

"Oh, yes," said Ted. "Why?" He was apt to be cautious when I made startling announcements.

"Because I think it's the most beautiful instrument in the world. I've thought so for ages. Also I need what's known as an outside interest. My brain's beginning to doze off. And I don't want to take an evening course in paper flowers or French philosophy. I want to learn the cello."

"Hm. How would you find time? You've got your hands full with the kids and everything. You're always busy—"

"I may be but my mind isn't. And anyway a lot of my wife-and-mother activity could be telescoped. Having a challenge might spur me to even greater efficiency than I exhibit at the moment!"

I looked around and cursed myself. I have a talent for picking the wrong moment to make such pronouncements. The boys had fashioned a fort from the sofa cushions. A colony of spiders had moved onto the window ledge. I still hadn't sanded and stained the table leg on which Cath had chewed a bare patch, and the room was littered with bits of toys plus the entrails of an old radio Benjy was dissecting. Ted stopped rocking and looked around.

"Hm." He can charge that noise with more cynicism than anyone else I know.

"Well, did I or did I not completely transform the basement this winter?" I asked defensively. I had spent all my spare time scraping and painting every inch of it and felt that this endeavour might at least temporarily compensate for my superficial sluttishness upstairs.

"Yes, yes, yes, agreed. Cath's just leaked through to my trousers—" I leaped up conscientiously and took her off to be changed.

"I think it's a good idea, the cello," Ted said later on. "Much less painful than the violin. Go ahead and do whatever you have to do to get going." From Ted, these were enthusiastic and encouraging words.

I mentioned my idea casually to Harold across the street, and was not a little disconcerted when within hours he was on our doorstep with a cello borrowed from a student at the university school of music, where he taught.

"Play around with it during the weekend," he said. "See how you like it."

"But Harold—" I'd literally never touched one before and was terrified even of holding it.

"Oh, and it's for sale," Harold shouted as he reached his front door. "I should grab it while you can—there aren't many around."

"What's that?" asked Benjy when I had carefully removed the cello from its cloth case. "Snormous. Dominic! Come and look!"

"Hey, it's a cello," said Dominic. "It looks as though it's going to have a litter of violins!" He screamed with laughter. "I know who the father is. It's a double bass!"

I bought the instrument and embarked on lessons with Mrs. Vallentyne, a lovely teacher who lived only four blocks away. Since then I've had more fun with my cello, one way and another, than I could have possibly imagined.

8

Over the years with Cath I've both appreciated and been heartened by the praise and encouragement that friends and strangers have given me (except when words like "martyr" and "saint" are thrown around). When she was young it was only occasionally that my reluctance to institutionalize her caused unease and resentment in people. Dr. Hall was the prime example of this but I recall another time when a professional was upset by my attitude and tried to bully me out of it. The professional involved was a social worker.

When she was in her sixth year, I realized it was two and a half years since I had last taken Cath to see a doctor. She and I were not going back to Dr. Hall, but I felt that some doctor in the field should take an interest in her. After a good deal of phoning around I discovered that a cerebral palsy clinic was held periodically at the Society for Crippled Children, the agency that had provided me with the wheelchair. I made an appointment for Catherine. Although the new doctor was unable to do anything more than Dr. Hall, he asked me if I wanted Catherine's care co-ordinated at the Society. My interest quickened. Care? I said. What do you mean? I thought maybe he had unearthed a special school or a proper therapy centre. He was apologetic. No, he said, he hadn't meant that, unfortunately. Winnipeg was lagging in that area. But he could arrange for a social worker to come and visit me. A social worker, I said, defensively, what on earth for? He shrugged. Someone to talk over my problems with perhaps? I didn't want to appear ungrateful, so I agreed.

A few days later a man appeared on the doorstep.

"Mrs. Schaefer? I'm Mr. Lynch. I'm the social worker from the Society and I've been sent to see you."

I sat him down with a cup of coffee and tried to answer politely the impertinent questions he snapped out at me. Any siblings? Did they react unfavourably to Catherine? What was my husband's work? Did he resent Catherine? Did Catherine affect our marriage? I started to bristle with suppressed rage and finally told him that really, we were managing quite well and perhaps I shouldn't be taking up his time. He changed his line of questioning at that point. What about the future, he asked aggressively. Had I thought about that? Yes, of course, I said, and told him that I had always accepted that if Catherine became detrimental to our family at any point she would have to be institutionalized somewhere. But so far she had caused no problems, I added.

With the air of a prosecutor triumphantly producing a question that will at last make the witness's defences crumble, he leaned over towards me and stuck out his chin.

"Great," he rasped. "You seem to think you're doing just great, right? She's only five now but—" he leaned further over and glared at me "—

what are you going to do when she starts to have sex feelings? Huh? Have you thought about that one?"

To give the Society due credit I don't think Mr. Lynch lasted long with them and I was put on the list of a pleasant lady who was careful not to ruffle my feathers. In terms of actually helping me, as opposed to providing an ear, she was little use. It wasn't her fault, though, and she at least recognized the inadequacies of the system and didn't try to make me feel stupid or guilty. I was also visited by an occupational therapist. She, too, was kind and concerned but had clearly never seen anyone as badly handicapped as Catherine. I was able to give her rather more ideas than she could give me.

Anyone with an obvious problem is bound to receive unsolicited advice and I was no exception where Cath was concerned. Often I was grateful for the advice because not only was it well-meant, but useful, too. Once a woman spotted me rubbing Cath's feet and told me about some woolly, zippered slippers she'd seen in Eatons which might be just the thing for my daughter. At other times, though, advice did not go down so well. Sometimes it sprang not so much from a desire to help as from a desire to ignore Cath's existence by wishing her away into an institution.

One day skating at the community centre I was having a cup of coffee to revive myself after a particularly heavy crash onto my knees. A woman suddenly came and parked herself beside me on the bench. Cath was in her sleigh at my feet and I was giving her sips of coffee from the spoon I always carried with me.

"What's the matter with—uh—her?" asked this woman. She had a pale I-have-to-watch-my-health look and was wearing the sort of fur coat I wouldn't have worn even if I could have afforded it.

"She's my daughter," I said. "Her name is Catherine." I reeled off my short set piece. She opened her eyes wider and wider as I spoke and, knowing what she was going to say, I emphasized my finale. The bit about not having to feel sorry for Cath because she was probably happier than most people.

My ruse failed. "Oh, but it's so sad, isn't it?" She tut-tutted away and then asked me how old Cath was.

"Six and a half," I said shortly. This woman was a bore.

"Oh, my!" She shook her beauty-parloured curls and looked sorrowfully at Cath who was happily chewing at the rug covering her. "Poor wee girl, six and a half and she's never walked or talked. Oh, boy! Tell me," she said suddenly, "what will you do when she gets her periods?"

What? It really threw me. Not that I'd never thought of it, but it just seemed such an irrelevant question, and impertinent. It reminded me of Mr. Lynch, the ludicrous social worker.

"I'll worry about that when it happens." I sought to change the subject. "Have you got a child skating here?"

"Oh, yes, my little Craigie. He's out there on the ice. And you'll never guess what." The woman snuggled down into her fur and smiled confidingly at me. "For the longest time I thought he might be retarded! But of course it turned out he wasn't, thank goodness."

Wow! I stared at her. "No kidding," I said. I prepared to leave.

"Oh, yes. You see I had the most awful [she pronounced it 'offal'] the most offal time delivering him and the doctor said he was surprised I ever got through it, let alone Craigie. It all started when Craigie decided to come early—" She launched into a tedious monologue as I collected myself together and tested my knees for strength. "—to watch the baby's colour for weeks afterwards and of course I was as sick as a dog," I heard her finish.

"But little Craigie wasn't brain-damaged after all?" I said sweetly.

"Oh, no. You should see him. He's just the brightest boy imaginable!" The woman's smug expression changed to one of sickening pity. "But of course I do realize I'm so lucky," she said. "I mean when I think what could have happened. Oh, it must be terrible for you, just terrible."

"Yes," I said. I gave her a hard look. "Sometimes it is. Sometimes it's just offal." I turned around and bent down to pick up the rope on Cath's chariot. I felt my sleeve being tugged. The woman's face was unpleasantly close to mine and I moved back.

"Why don't you," she said slowly, as if trying to talk reason to a child, "put your daughter away? Like into an institution?" She didn't say it nastily; rather, her tone implied that she really felt it was her duty to give me the benefit of her advice. "Surely she would be happier with—well, you know—her own sort? I mean, you've got to think of the rest of your family, haven't you?"

"Look," I said, "thank you for your concern, but no, she wouldn't be happier in an institution. And actually I do give the odd thought to the rest of my family. In fact I must go and see what two other members of it are doing right now." I steamed towards the rink in a furious temper, hauling Cath behind me.

"Hey, Nicky, what's wrong?" Mary scrunched to a halt when she saw me. "Knees still hurting?"

"No, they're OK. I'm in a rage, that's all." I told her what had happened.

"What a bitch," she said, "Why didn't you tell her to mind her own bloody business?"

"I couldn't, somehow," I said, "I think it was stupidity on her part rather than bitchery."

I tried not to dwell on the incident. The insensitivity she showed was so unusual that it didn't seem worth getting worked up about. But it rankled nonetheless. I was aware that when she had suggested that I "put Catherine away" she was merely voicing what many people, particularly casual acquaintances, secretly thought. And why not, come to think of it? If I had never had anything to do with very disabled children, and saw a young woman struggling to drag a hulking great helpless baby in an outsize toboggan onto a skating rink, might I not have thought the same? Might I not have thought that life with such a child must be very gruelling and unrewarding?

But then I wouldn't have known that the other side of the coin was surprisingly shiny. I began to regret my reaction to the woman at the skating rink. She had doubtless gone off with her negative feelings reinforced. Maybe if I had been less huffy I might have been able to make her understand that it really wasn't so difficult having a child like Cath at home, that she really was one of the happiest and most delightful people to have around, that our family life was in many ways richer for her presence, and that all these benefits compensated for the practical problems she posed. And, most important of all, that by virtue of being so terribly handicapped, she could at times cause more intense happiness than any normal child.

Little Craigie's mother had struck me as a particularly hard nut to crack. I doubted whether she could ever have truly understood why, for instance, Cath's astonishing greeting at St. Amant, when I had picked her up after having been in England, had caused me such piercing joy that I had wept.

That small but profoundly significant incident raises the question of Catherine's own point of view. Wouldn't she be happier in an institution, with her own sort? I could have expanded my curt response, telling the woman that if surrounded by children physically and mentally worse off than herself, Cath would become one of them, withdrawn and unresponsive. The very thing that kept her going was receiving the stimulation provided by being a member of a comparatively normal, active family, who had always known and loved her.

"Why don't you put her in an institution?" The obvious solution perhaps—to the judgemental doctors, glib social workers and unthinking strangers. But would they, and others, be so quick to suggest it if they knew our family better? I knew that many parents did in fact institutionalize their handicapped children but it was usually from necessity rather than choice. For one reason or another, they were unable to keep their children at home. Others, like ourselves, were lucky enough to find that we could surmount our problems, at least for the time being. Why couldn't people accept this?

But there was no getting away from it. Catherine was definitely an unusual six-year-old: narrow-headed, long and thin, one leg two inches shorter than the other, stiff jerking limbs, dribbling and making weird noises, no speech, eyes crossing sometimes, unable to feed herself, incontinent, often not responding to the call of her name, apparently understanding virtually nothing.

Yet despite all this there was something positive about her. There was some elusive quality that engendered more than mere pity in people. All but a few responded to it once they had recovered from their initial shock and had come to know her. I hesitate to put a word to it, but it was Cath's innocence that was attractive. Less elusive to pinpoint in her list of attractions was that, despite her physical oddness, she often looked really pretty, even beautiful sometimes, especially when she was relaxed and happy.

There was her ability to make people laugh, too; not at, but with her. When she was amused by something, which was frequently, her laughter was animated and infectious. People could feel a sense of communication with her if they made her laugh. Her capacity to tease delighted Ted and myself and could be appreciated by other people too. Often when she saw me coming with a cup and dessert spoon her eyes would light up and her mouth spread in a wide smile. She would then wait, still grinning and trying desperately not to collapse into a laugh, until I got the spoon to within a quarter of an inch of her mouth. Whereupon she would turn sharply away with a shriek of pent-up laughter. Her enjoyment was doubled when I pretended to be cross. If, as often happened, I

Cath removing her mother's sunglasses. BRUCE GOODWIN PHOTO

shot the drink down her neck, she became hysterical with delight. Again and again I would approach her with a spoon, always with the same result—a mischievous grin, the sharp turn and the burst of laughter; followed, of course, by a sidelong glance to see if I was going to keep the game going. I loved my mother's comment when I wrote and told her about this teasing.

"How splendid, darling, that Cath can be naughty!"

A strict progress chart of Catherine's achievements at that time would only have had one item on it: "Can feed herself cookie or banana with left hand." Even this would have had to be qualified with "but doesn't hang onto object between bites." Still, we were delighted with this new skill. The curious and irritating thing about it was that she would only feed herself in this way while she was lying flat on the floor, or at most with her head on a cushion; she showed no interest if she was propped in a sitting position. Her physical appearance had changed little. She was longer, of course. We had to be careful not to catch her toes when going round narrow corners because her legs tended to stiffen and stick out when she was being carried. One positive effect of having the wheelchair was that the bald spot at the back of her head was at last growing in. Although the hair was as bristly as a scrubbing brush, it would presumably soften up in time.

Periodically during Catherine's life I have found myself looking at her objectively, putting myself in the place of someone seeing or meeting her for the first time. This sometimes happens when we are suddenly amongst strangers, but more often when someone is noticeably put off by her, as happened one day soon after we first arrived at Argonne. I was collecting our mail in the office when a new family came in to get their keys. The parents were snapping in undertones at each other and their child, a girl of about five, so I assumed they had had a long hot journey. I was sympathetic until the wife grabbed her husband's arm and nodded across to where Cath was sitting in her chair by the sandpit.

"Oh, jeez, Phil, just take a look at that. A kid in a wheelchair. That's all we need. Debbie'll flip."

I was rather alarmed then. Since I was inevitably going to be seeing more of this family, I decided to say something quickly to prevent the woman embarrassing herself when she discovered who I was.

I cleared my throat. "Is Debbie scared of wheelchairs?" I said.

The woman, who was pretty but vacant-looking, turned round. "Is she ever! And I can't figure out why! She's never had anything to do with them but she only has to see one and she's grabbing onto my hand and then she has these nightmares for weeks afterwards. Jeez!"

"That must be very difficult for you," I said, "but look, maybe there's an answer." I hurried on. "That's my daughter Catherine out there and I'm sure that if we introduced Debbie to her and the wheelchair gradually she wouldn't be frightened." I laughed nervously. "I used to be scared of wheelchairs, and the people in them, when I was a kid. I used to run a mile to avoid them!" I continued in this vein for a while and ended up inviting the woman over to coffee when she had settled in. She had been nonplussed when I first started talking to her but now she had relaxed a bit. She said she'd be over tomorrow, and thanks very much for speaking up. I felt I had gambled; perhaps the child would land up with a psychiatrist after being confronted with Cath. But I had done it on the spur of the moment and could hardly retract.

As it happened, my plan was a success, although I began to think it wouldn't stand a chance because Roxy, Debbie's mother, kept saying, in front of the child, how scared Debbie was and how difficult it had been to get her to come over. As I was pouring some juice out for her, Debbie herself asked in a perfectly straightforward way why Catherine was in a wheelchair. Roxy tensed up and looked at me uneasily.

"Well," I said handing her the juice, "she can't walk, you see."

"How come?"

"Because her legs aren't strong like yours and mine and most people's."

"How come?"

"Well, it's your brain that tells your arms and legs to work and Catherine's brain wasn't made quite right—the bit that tells you how to move."

"How come?"

"That's the trouble. Nobody really knows, even the clever scientists and doctors. But a lot of them are trying to find out, so that other babies won't be born with brains that don't work properly."

"Mind that juice, honey. Don't spill it," Roxy interrupted.

A little while later Debbie asked, "How come she can't talk?"

"Because the part of her brain that should make her talk isn't working yet."

"Like the legs bit?"

"Exactly."

"Mm. How come she dribbles and spits all the time like that? It's not nice."

"I'm afraid she can't help it—"

"Just like you can't help asking questions!" Roxy again.

"But she's quite right," I said. "It's rather disgusting. We just have to put up with it, Debbie. I mop her chin with a Kleenex when she does it, see? Like this."

"Can she see us?"

"Yes, she can, but not very well."

"And hear us?"

I nodded. "Yes."

"So," said Debbie, "the seeing bits and the hearing bits of her brain work all right. Maybe the other bits will work soon."

"That'd be nice, wouldn't it?" I agreed. "Now could you be a kind girl and go and tell Dominic to come in for a minute. Look—he's just out there in the sandpit." When Dominic came in I gave him a squeaky toy and asked him to put it on Cath's tray. He did so, and Debbie watched with interest. Within days she was casually picking up Cath's toys for her just as the other children did and she even sat in the wheelchair and pulled herself around in it, which was something Dominic enjoyed doing.

The children on our street treated Catherine with a casual friendliness, even though she rarely noticed it. Almost all of them shouted a greeting to her when they saw her out on the lawn and often chucked a fallen toy back onto her tray. Sometimes, too, they would stop in passing and ask her how she was. There were one or two girls who would even take the omnipresent Kleenex from her sleeve and wipe the dribble off her chin. When several kids were playing baseball or football on the road they would tell each other to watch out for Cath, and there was consternation if a ball sailed by too close to her. They were good watchdogs, too; if I was busy in the house and Cath was out in the front I knew that if she was unhappy someone would ring the bell and shout, "Cath's crying, Mrs. Schaefer, and I can't cheer her up."

There was one child who took a particular interest in her, though, and this was Andrew, the youngest son of a family who had recently moved in next door. He was a nice friendly boy and was frequently in or around our house playing with Dominic and Benjy. Right from the start he had not just wanted to know all about why Cath was wonky but often sat in the kitchen discussing her problems with me and thinking up games to amuse her. A number of children had done this in the past but their enthusiasm had understandably waned when there was so little immediate response from Cath. But Andrew persevered and now when he came up and hugged her and chattered to her, she obviously recognized him. Catherine responded to his attentions in much the same way as she did to those of Dominic and Benjy. She made pleased noises, gave him a big cross-eyed smile, jerked her body in stiff, excited movements, and often there was also an inordinate amount of joyful spitting. Today, nearly ten years later, he continues to be just as interested and friendly.

Another of her most devoted friends was Mr. Behr. He and his wife lived two houses down from us and they gave the street a touch of dignity. An elderly Viennese couple, she in her seventies and he nearly ninety, they had for years been a familiar and endearing sight as they took their daily constitutional up and down the sidewalk. They walked arm in arm and very slowly, Mr. Behr almost invariably in a black Homburg and his wife, tiny and frail, in an impeccable suit or dress.

They enjoyed stopping for a chat and liked to be kept informed about the neighbourhood. They stopped to pat all the dogs and talk to the children they encountered on their walks and frequently beckoned the latter into the house for treats. Whenever Dominic or Benjy were given something by the Behrs they would come back with a bar of chocolate "for Cath, Mr. Behr says."

The first time I had caught sight of Mr. Behr bending over Cath as she sat in her wheelchair on the front lawn I had gone out to say hello. He lifted his hat when he saw me and said he hoped I didn't mind his talking to her. I made the usual introduction but he waved aside my ensuing explanation.

"She is a lovely child," he said simply, "and she knows I am her friend. She knows," he repeated. "Look, you will see her smile—" And Cath promptly fixed an eye on him and smiled a great drooly smile. I was amazed.

"She hardly ever acknowledges people she doesn't know," I said, "let alone smiles at them."

After that he and his wife never failed to come over to Cath if she was out. "How is my friend?" he would say, and she really did respond, smiling and gurgling as he talked to her and even letting him hold and kiss her precious left hand. Sometimes, too, and this was really extraordinary, she would see him and his wife approaching from several houses away and work herself into a state of great excitement by the time they reached her. She had never done this with anyone else except Ted and myself and the boys. Maybe it was the singular shape and motion of the Behrs as they walked along that attracted her attention and stuck in her mind.

The Behrs had a much-loved cat that caused them great anguish. It was forever disappearing for days at a time and coming home suffering from exhaustion and chewed-up ears. "Where can she be?" poor Mrs. Behr would wail. "Why doesn't she come home? Such a worry she is!" and a group of children would be dispatched to look for it. "She" was in fact a lecher of a male, king of the neighbourhood, who swaggered around fathering kittens galore, including four that our cat, Dido, produced one spring.

As far as the children on the street were concerned the birth of kittens ranked higher in terms of drama than a new baby, and Dominic's and Benjy's prestige soared when the news was announced. Dido had the kittens on Dominic's bed in the middle of the night. He had a marvellous time holding his friends spellbound as he described the event. We all enjoyed the kittens and even Ted found himself spending a ridiculous amount of time playing with them. Catherine regarded them with mixed feelings. She hooted and kicked with excitement when she saw one or more of them bouncing up to her, but when they ran up her legs or climbed up on her chest, a look of alarm would flash into her eyes. She knew that trouble could follow. One day I heard her laughing and thumping her heels on the floor but after a while these happy noises were replaced by urgent squawks. I dashed in and couldn't help laughing when I saw what was happening. Cath was on her back on the floor as usual; one kitten was on her chest playing with her shirt collar. She was trying to rub off another which was clinging to her like a burr, and the other two were tugging at either end of a length of wool they had somehow stretched over her stomach. Poor girl, she must have felt like Gulliver when the Lilliputians had him at their mercy.

Even though she spent more time upright as she got older, Cath continued to get numerous respiratory infections. I tried to see her through them without antibiotics and often they were mild and cleared up quickly. Once, though, I let things get out of hand and by the time I called the doctor she had a raging ear infection. I felt awful, and for a while after that the doctor was summoned every time she sneezed. (This was our original pediatrician. He was a good and conscientious doctor and a kind man, and apart from Cath's special problems, looked after all our children.) One difficulty with Cath was that often I could only guess where and to what extent she was hurting, and when she cried with pain for no detectable reason, it really bothered me.

It occurred to me that one undetected trouble she might suffer from was toothache. Outwardly, at least, her teeth were her best point and, having come in and fallen out at the right times, would have been the one aspect of her that would have rated high on a developmental chart. They were white and even and certainly not noticeably decayed. But she had always ground them, sometimes really fiercely, and I thought this might have worn away the enamel and exposed the nerves or had some other detrimental effect.

I discovered that a dental clinic for problematic children had recently opened so I made an appointment for her. From the moment we entered the building, Cath became very quiet and seemed to sense that something nasty was ahead. As soon as I had arranged her in the seat, her eyes began to dart nervously from side to side. When she was approached by the dentist she went scarlet and started to scream at the highest pitch she could manage. He looked alarmed and I apologized and explained that she didn't understand what was going on. I suggested that he try to sneak a quick look every time she was in mid-scream. After being bitten a couple of times he decided it wasn't such a good idea and gave up.

"I'm awfully sorry," I shouted. "Cath, darling, do pipe down. It's all over now. Come on sweetheart." I hauled her out of the chair and put her over my shoulder. After thumping her on the back and jogging her around for a while she quietened down. "Were you able to form any sort of opinion?" I asked.

"As far as I can see," he said nursing his finger, "her teeth look remarkably healthy. But the only way we can really find out what's happening in her mouth is to give her a general anaesthetic." He looked at his finger surreptitiously. "Then we can X-ray and clean her teeth and do any necessary fillings."

"A general!" I said. "Goodness, that seems a bit extreme." Still, I could quite see that unless she was unconscious, he'd never get his pickaxe into her mouth, let alone a drill.

It turned out to be quite a business, involving hospitalization. First of all a public health nurse appeared at the house with a raft of forms to fill out on Cath's history and a request for a urine sample. Canadian medical people have an unreasonable passion for urine samples and I asked her why she needed one now, when Cath wasn't going to be done for ages. She had no idea, but was adamant on the point. She produced an intricately designed plastic bag with lots of sticky tapes on it and suggested that I put it on Cath.

"She won't go," I warned her. "You'll be here all day." Much to Cath's indignation I did make an attempt to put the beastly thing on her, however. After a while the nurse admitted defeat and took off with a sample I had squeezed from Cath's diaper. "Tell the lab to disregard the Tide," I said. I was fed up. Cath was still screaming from the effects of having had the sticky tapes ripped off her, and the whole exercise was pointless as far as I could see.

Next, I received two more forms, one to be filled out when I took Cath to the hospital and the other to be completed by my pediatrician, who was required to state that Cath was fit to have a general anaesthetic. This had to be done "within twenty-four hours prior to admittance." I stared.

That meant I had to take her to the doctor's office to be looked at the day before I took her into the hospital. Why? She could easily be fine then but ill by the next day. In which case, obviously, I wouldn't take her to be done. And besides, surely a person's respiratory system was given a check before a general anaesthetic anyway? The trip to the doctor would, on two counts, be a waste of everyone's time. I phoned the admitting office to see if I could get an explanation for this odd procedure. "It's regulations," the lady told me and no, she didn't really know why, and no, I certainly could not skip it. It was obviously useless to argue so I switched to another subject that had been puzzling me. Why was Cath required to spend a day in hospital before being operated on? The answer came promptly: orientation. I explained that while this might be sensible in the case of a normal child it would not be in Catherine's. Far from orientating her, it would muddle and upset her. She would also be difficult to handle, probably necessitating my staying with her the whole time. Might it not be possible for me to starve her from midnight on and bring her down on the day itself? I would also be saving public money this way, I pointed out. My pleas were to no avail, even though the woman was more sympathetic by the time I had finished.

Early one morning in October the hospital phoned me. There had been a cancellation and could I by any chance bring Cath down to be done that day? It said on her file that she didn't require an orientation day. That's right, I said. Had she eaten since midnight? No, I was just about to give her breakfast, poor girl. Fine. Could I run her down to my doctor to be checked before bringing her down? Well, I supposed so, but couldn't a doctor at the hospital do that? Sorry, there wouldn't be time.

The pediatrician pronounced Catherine to be in good health and I took a taxi directly from his office to the hospital. Considering it was mid-morning and she had had nothing to eat or drink since the night before, she was being remarkably uncomplaining, although she was beginning to lick her lips and look worried. Once at the hospital she became increasingly restless and, after having her finger pricked for a blood sample, regarded everyone who came near her with the gravest suspicion. A urine sample was required, of course, and a plastic bag proffered. Luckily the nurse who was dealing with us took my point when I said that Cath would suffer this indignity even less gladly than she had the blood sampling. I got her undressed and into a hospital gown and held her tightly while she was given her pre-medication needle. I hoped it would make her drowsy and after an hour of carrying her around she did at last stop crying. The dentist and the anaesthetist came and had a chat, and the latter checked her respiratory system, which made me laugh. Then Cath was wheeled off on a trolley by a porter and taken to watch TV in the waiting room by the operating theatre. The porter sat down too and watched the puppet show with deep interest. Cath was quite relaxed now and I stayed and talked to her until she was taken behind the swing doors.

Until this moment I had been practical and calm. Now I was suddenly consumed with the anxiety I suppose most mothers feel when their child is taken away to be put into an unnatural sleep. I walked slowly away with burning eyes and a constricted throat. She had looked so diminished and vulnerable somehow, lying placidly beneath the white honeycomb blanket, her left arm raised as always so that she could study her hand. I told myself not to be mawkish and headed for the cafeteria. I had to do something for the next two hours. "I'm sorry Mrs. Schaefer, she just never came out of the anaesthetic—" Oh, shut up. Let's see now. Soup of the day, green pea. They could keep it. A hamburger and french fries? Veal croquette and mashed potatoes? "We tried everything—" Shut up. Egg salad. Yes, an egg salad might be OK. I took one and instantly realized I couldn't eat it so I replaced it. I ought to have something sweet. I hadn't eaten so far today. Fruit salad? Blueberry pie and shaving cream? "We think it may have been a congenital heart condition—" Now really. A couple of nurses behind me were getting impatient so I went forward, my tray still empty. "Would you sign here for permission for a—" For God's sake. I grabbed two cups of coffee and a doughnut and sat down at an unoccupied table.

Afterwards I wandered downstairs to Casualty, where I had been told to wait. I phoned the boys, who were being given lunch by Mary. Dominic was upset that he hadn't had a chance to say goodbye to Cath and wanted to know exactly what was happening to her. Benjy said he missed me and wanted to know whether Cath was going to die. I said no, and he responded casually, "Oh, that's good." Next I phoned Ted and told him about Benjy and we had a rather strained giggle. Then I sat and smoked furiously and read two chapters of my book before realizing I hadn't assimilated a single word.

The nurse who had admitted Cath was very friendly and sat down to chat with me for a while.

"I know how you feel," she said. "It's a worry the first time, isn't it? She should be back in the recovery room soon though." She wanted to know more about Catherine and was indignant when she heard there were no schools or programs for children as badly handicapped as she was. "You mean you look after her twenty-four hours a day? With no help from anyone?" she asked.

"Oh, no," I said. "I have a good husband and a babysitter one afternoon a week and my neighbours help out if there's an emergency."

"No dear, I didn't mean that. I mean doesn't the government give you any support?"

"You mean money?" I laughed. "Good grief, no! What an amazing idea! But we've never expected it—I mean she's our responsibility, isn't she? It's not as if we can't manage. Anyway, you must realize she's very little bother. She's very happy most of the time and we all get a big kick out of having her around. She's fun!"

"That's as may be but you ought at least be paid for not having put her in an institution. Think of the money you're saving them!"

"That's a thought I suppose," I said. "But I've always felt very lucky that we've been able to keep her."

"Well, it just burns me up when I realize you're managing all by yourselves and at the same time there are hundreds of able-bodied so-and-sos in this city living on welfare!"

"They've probably got other problems," I said. "I really don't think we're so badly off. People always tend to be shocked when they find out about our situation but it's not nearly as grim as it looks. We've had eight years to get used to it, don't forget. It'd be quite different if we'd suddenly been landed with Cath."

"Mm. I guess. Still—oh, excuse me, dear—" She broke off to answer her phone. "She's in the recovery room, dear, if you want to go up."

"Oh, thanks! It was nice talking to you. Bye." I shot off.

Apart from a slightly swollen mouth, Cath looked fine. She was back in the ward already, which meant she was no longer being watched for signs of choking. She grunted when she saw me and held out her hand limply. "All the worry I've gone through on your silly behalf," I muttered as I gave her a hug.

"Are we ever glad to see you!" said a nurse squidging into the room.

"It says on her chart cerebral palsy, severely retarded, no speech and we had no idea what to do. Would you like to give her some apple juice?"

"Thanks, yes. Do you think I could take her home today?" I asked. I had been told that she would have to stay in for the night but it seemed unnecessary.

"It wouldn't be the usual thing," said the nurse doubtfully.

"Catherine isn't the usual thing either," I pointed out.

"I'll ask—"

She returned with the anaesthetist. He scratched his head and frowned and looked from Cath to me and back again. I gave him what I hoped was a winning smile.

"Why on earth not?" he said suddenly. "As long as she shows no signs of distress in the next couple of hours—nausea and so on—sure, she can go home. Of course it's very irregular," he added dutifully.

"I know," I said, "and I am grateful." Rule-bending was becoming an essential part of life with Catherine.

I was talking to a particularly lonely-looking boy in the room next to Cath's—he had both legs in traction—when the dentist appeared.

"How have you kept your daughter's teeth in such good order?" he asked.

"Were they good? Oh, that's marvellous! Probably by having complete control over her diet," I said, "and it's easier to keep them clean than with the other children because she doesn't gobble garbage between meals. What did you do?"

"Two small fillings—otherwise they're perfect."

"And the grinding?"

"No damage done. In fact it's probably compensated for the lack of chewing."

"That's good to hear. What a relief. When should I bring her back?"

"Oh, in about a year, I should think. You've done an excellent job. I wish all mothers were as conscientious about their children's teeth." He wandered off.

"It's probably because she's inherited my husband's teeth," I said to his back.

A year later I became really worried about Cath's legs. Her adductors, or inside thigh muscles, were increasing in strength and causing her legs to scissor tightly. It was not only difficult to change and dress her, but also impossible, however meticulous I was about keeping her clean and dry, to prevent sores from developing in her pelvic area and on the insides of her thighs.

I took her to the clinic at the Society for Crippled Children and it was suggested that releasing or cutting the adductor tendons in her groins would improve the situation. This wasn't the most pleasant thought, but I was assured that it was a tiny operation, involving just a snip on each side and not even any stitches. It would help me a great deal and give her more kicking freedom, so she was scheduled to be done.

The Children's Hospital had recently devised a more sensible system for small operations, like the one Cath was having. Rather than being hospitalized for two days, children were now admitted in the morning, done, and allowed home in the evening. I couldn't help feeling that Cath had given the authorities the idea a year ago. It was far simpler for everybody, but I still had to take her to be checked at the doctor's office a day beforehand.

What with one thing and another, I was by now very familiar with the people in Outpatients and Emergency, and they with the children and myself. Cath had had her teeth done again a few weeks before and she and I were greeted as old friends. After all the usual preparations, except for the urine sample, which they had given up on, Cath went off with the porter. "You again?" he said to me and, with heavy hospital humour, "You must like this place!" I headed for the cafeteria for a cup of coffee, a cigarette and a think.

Having a bath had always been one of the joys of Catherine's life. Without clothes and with the buoyancy of the water, I think it was the only time she experienced a sensation of freedom. She gave every indication that she would be happy to stay there all night. Kicking and bouncing and rolling around, she gulped down so much air that I had to sit her up frequently for a burp, which made her laugh so much that of course she swallowed more water and air the moment I let her down. She always hoped there might be extra excitement. Sometimes Dominic, Benjy or myself would put a finger under the running tap and squirt her, or blow soap bubbles for her. Best of all, she enjoyed the boys flipping toothbrushfuls of cold water over her. The very sight of a toothbrush caused every muscle in her body to tense and her face to shine and smile with anticipatory pleasure.

Regrettably, Cath's baths had had to be cut from every night to twice a week. She weighed over fifty pounds now and was about four feet long and I simply hadn't the physical stamina to carry on as I had before.

I was thinking about this during my first cup of coffee. While sipping my second, something occurred to me which, if I could wangle it, might compensate for fewer baths. There was a heated therapy pool in the basement of the hospital. How Cath would enjoy being taken into it! I could never take her into ordinary pools or lakes because they were too cold, but this pool would be perfect. As I embarked on my third cup of coffee, I looked up and spotted the doctor who had arranged Cath's surgery. With him was the developmental specialist to whom I had taken her when I removed her from Dr. Hall's "care." The very people, I thought, to discuss this with, and impulsively went over to their table. They readily agreed to prescribe hydrotherapy on a weekly basis for Cath as soon as she had recovered from surgery. A very good idea, they said. I was delighted but I couldn't help wondering why it had been left to me to think of it. Why had it never been suggested by any of the doctors who had seen Cath over the years? I could only conclude, as so often before, that the prevailing attitude towards parents who chose to care for seriously handicapped children at home was that they were expected to bear the full responsibility of management. Oh well, things would presumably change eventually. Meanwhile we were coping and I didn't want to be a nuisance.

That night, with Cath safely home and not, it seemed, in too much pain, I had an odd experience. I dreamed I saw her walking towards me. It was the first time I ever remember dreaming about her unrealistically. Until now she had appeared in my dreams as regularly as the rest of the family but always as her normal self. I was upset when I woke up. Wish fulfillment, I told myself sharply. I was still shaken but I couldn't help smiling at the touch of reality my practical nature had insisted upon in the dream—Cath was limping heavily as she walked because of her dislocated hip.

The slits in Cath's groins were so small that they looked like mere punctures, and fortunately they didn't become infected as I had thought they might. The inside cuts must have been bigger because the tension in her adductors was greatly reduced. Once everything had healed, her legs stayed quite neatly apart even when she kicked.

The first therapist to be given the job of doing Cath's hydrotherapy was very pleasant and willing. Unfortunately, I don't think the poor girl had seen many kids like Cath and didn't know what to make of the situation. Next, Cath was passed on to Therese, a delightful Irish girl who had worked with many Caths in Dublin and was unflustered by Catherine's difficulties.

After a couple of sessions Therese had not only figured out a set of exercises for Cath but had discovered how to make them the greatest fun for her. Cath regarded the pool as an unbelievably wonderful bath, I think, and soon knew what being wheeled into the therapy room meant. I pointed this out to Therese, who hugged Cath and said cheekily, "Ah, you're a brilliant girl, aren't you Katie?" whereupon Cath grinned and made a grab for her ponytail.

Despite the considerable energy I had to summon up for these weekly hospital visits, the effort was well worth it. Winter day swims, in particular, involved a total of at least an hour of dressing Cath, undressing her and dressing her again, never mind heaving her in and out of taxis and dealing with her chair. But it was a joy to watch her limbs moving around so freely under the water and to see the excited, happy expression on her face. I often got into the pool too because then Therese and I could give Cath some terrific stretches between us. Benjy got in as well and lunged around, as did Dominic when he could accompany us.

9

In 1971, Ted was due for another sabbatical, and as soon as Chloe heard we were planning to spend it in Oxford she offered to look out for a suitable house. The only essentials, I told her, were an adequate heating system and a large study for Ted. I was prepared to live in a slum just for the pleasure of being in Oxford but Ted, understandably, wasn't. He had spent three years in digs crouched over a gas fire and he didn't fancy such a Spartan existence again. He had been promised half a desk—a generous offer, considering the lack of space—in Lincoln College, where he had done his D. Phil. work, plus use of the labs. I knew he would be working at home a lot and would therefore need a study as a retreat from my family and friends.

Spring, 1971, burst upon Winnipeg with its usual long-awaited suddenness and our street shook off its winter coat gratefully. Crews of city employees raked the winter debris on the boulevards into neat heaps that blew away before the next crew rattled down in trucks to collect them; the street was alive with kids swooping around on their bikes or squeezing their creaky baseball mitts into shape; babies and grandparents were put out in the first warm sun; at least one member of each household was out scratching at the lawns with rakes and spreading the bald spots with seed and topsoil; flowerbeds were closely inspected and poked at for the hardy perennials planted last year; jubilant shouts were called to neighbours if any were found to have survived the winter; Mr. and Mrs. Behr set out cautiously for their first shaky walk of the season together; new neighbours were discovered; across the road the children left the front door open and the music of Brahms rolled out into the street as Harold and Ann practised for their next recital; storm windows were replaced with screens; Ted was to be seen, and heard, scraping up with a shovel what one refined lady down the road referred to as "doggies' visiting cards;" parents flocked to the community centre to register their children and bikes for summer activities; hoses were connected to outside taps and sprinklers shot rusty water fitfully over lawns onto surprised cats crouched ready to pounce on bumblebees; our front porch shuddered as myriad children pounded up and down the steps; walking around the block with Cath took an hour because there were so many people to chat to; and when darkness fell the neighbourhood rang with stentorian commands to "Come in, right now!" and the invisible, whooping games continued as offspring elected not to hear.

As summer approached, everybody started talking about upcoming holidays and trips to be taken. The children and I spent odd weeks with Chris and Nancy and other friends at the lake but we hadn't been anywhere as a family since our second working summer in Chicago in 1968. The boys had been embarrassed about this so I pointed out that when we went away we did it in style—we went for a whole year.

I had little success with my house-renting ad until I omitted the final three words, "Added attraction cat." Then four Catholic priests appeared and agreed to care for Dido in return for use of our stereo. They proved terrific tenants, and when we returned at the end of the year, we passed them on to friends. Their fame spread, and to this day people phone me and say, "About those priests who rented your house—are they still available?"

At my cheerful and optimistic insistence we undertook to drive to Montreal and cross the Atlantic by boat. Like the boys, I felt we should do something as a family and this seemed the ideal opportunity. I thought we did very well, but Ted now claims that his scientific decline dates from the day we ventured forth.

In the car we were, it was true, somewhat cloistered, but it was better on the boat. Ted spent most of the time reading in the cabin or otherwise amusing himself in the casino, while the kids and I explored and made friends. It was a good thing we had brought adequate reading material with us. The ship's library, which Ted and I remembered as being a whole room of books, plus several writing tables, had shrunk to one half-empty bookcase and a couple of cubicles equipped with pock-marked tables and empty ballpoint pens.

One day Dominic started making one lousy excuse after another for not coming on deck with Benjy, Cath and myself. After a little prodding he told me, in unhappy lurches, what was wrong. The day before, I had left him alone up there with Cath while I did something with Benjy. A girl had spotted Catherine and stared at her.

"She stared and stared and stared, Mum. It's not fair, I mean Cath can't help being like she is—"

"Well, at least she doesn't mind the staring," I tried. "Imagine what it would be like if she realized people stared at her, and why. Always remember that—she doesn't mind."

"But I do," he said. "I mind for her." And for you, I thought. People had stared before, of course, but it had never bothered him. I suppose it had suddenly disconcerted him because we were in alien surroundings. He had lost the security he always felt at home, where Cath was simply Cath, an accepted member of the neighbourhood.

"Look darling," I said, "I know it's annoying and rude, but people do stare at anyone who isn't normal. I noticed you taking a good look at that lady with a moustache, for instance, and even I couldn't help—"

"Why doesn't she shave it off?" asked Dominic with momentary interest.

"I can't imagine. OK, bad example. But—"

"It's all right. I know what you're getting at. But we don't go on staring, like that girl."

"Listen Dominic, you've explained to lots of kids what's wrong with Cath, haven't you? So let's go and talk to her. And I'll talk to her mother."

"Nope. I hate that girl. She stinks." He kicked the cabin wall.

I decided, though it wasn't easy, that I'd better be casually tough.

"Don't be ridiculous," I said briskly. "You've got to build up an immunity to stares and comments. I'm very rarely bothered by that sort of thing these days, but I've had to work at it. You can't go around hating people just because they're ignorant."

Sniff.

"Come on, love. It won't be nearly as grisly as you think. Imagine you're building armour around yourself—"

"Like a knight?"

"Yes, except that it's your feelings you want to protect."

"I know." He cast a naughty glance in Catherine's direction. "*I'm* not stoopid, Mum." Cath, who had been lying contemplatively on her bunk, stuck out her tongue and blew a terrific raspberry. Dominic and I burst out laughing. It was amazing how well she timed her rude noises on occasion.

"I'll come," said Dominic.

"You're a good kid," I said.

Chloe had found us a house in North Oxford but we couldn't move in at once so we headed for the cottage in Sussex. It was already full, what with my mother, Harry, Edgar, Richard and Eleanor, but Mum had written to say that the boys had put up a tent on the lawn. "And I've dealt with some of the dry rot in the cottage beams, darling," she added, "and Harry has whitewashed all the bedrooms and the cesspool is all right *at the moment.*"

Perhaps anticipating the effect on his nerves of a month with my family, Ted had cleverly found himself a two-week conference in Norway. He took off shortly after the first rapturous reunion scenes.

Dominic and Benjy were ecstatic to be at the cottage and did all the countryish things I had promised them they would. They also drove Edgar, Richard and Eleanor nuts with incessant demands for games. My brother, nephew and niece had all undergone a startling metamorphosis since I had last seen them. It took me a while to stop thinking of them as children. The boys were at the university, dirty-limerick, motorbike stage and Eleanor, beautiful and sweet, drifted pensively around in long, flowing clothes and talked about vegetarianism and Morocco.

Cath spent many tranquil hours in the garden either in her chair parked by a bush so she could pull at the branches, or on an air mattress on the lawn. She missed Ted, and loved it when Harry acted as surrogate father, cuddling her on his knee and making funny faces and noises.

"You're better at her noises than she is," commented Benjy.

"We're having a serious discussion," said Harry with dignity. He blew noisily at Cath. "Aren't we, darling?" She yelped with laughter and blew back.

Oxford, 1972. Dominic with camera, Cath amused at Benjy's face-pulling.

Greatham was at its summer height, with over forty members of four generations of family staying there. The Fishers, Mary and David, plus my cousins and their children, occupied one house, so we had a base where we could dump swimming things and food and make pots of tea.

"Darling," said Julia when we flung our arms around each other at our first meeting, "how funny we're not at the airport! Oh," she added as a small naked boy appeared behind her, "my turn. This is my son Oliver!"

"At last! Oh, Ju, what a gorgeous boy!"

Julia's twin sister, Rosalind, had four children. She's an exceptionally good and calm mother and instantly offered to take care of Cath whenever I wanted to take off. Not only that, she went to great lengths to get to know Cath and find ways of amusing and stimulating her.

Dominic and Benjy were soon enveloped in games and activities with their numerous cousins—croquet, tentative tennis, swimming, getting lost in the woods or just screaming around being happy. Meanwhile, Cath and I ambled from kitchen to kitchen and lawn to lawn getting caught up with four years' worth of gossip from different branches of the family. We all joined in the mass bonfire picnics in the woods near Greatham. Ploughing the wheelchair through the undergrowth was arduous and I sometimes employed a more primitive method of getting Cath over this rough terrain; I took her out of her chair and two of us carried her slung in a blanket. She preferred this method as she didn't get jolted so much. When, I wondered, will someone invent a well-sprung wheelchair?

Ted returned from Norway in good spirits and laden with Norwegian goodies for everyone, including a pair of fur boots for Cath, which she wears in the winter to this day. While my husband appreciated the aesthetic qualities of the cottage, he found it a hard place to work, partly because it was inevitably noisy and partly because Ted is not a small man. Most of the doors only came up to his chin, and only in one room upstairs could he move around without bumping into beams. Even creeping around with a permanent stoop didn't prevent him from thunking his head with awful regularity. After a couple of days his scalp was a scabby mess of dents and contusions, and clumps of hair are probably still decorating the door frames and beams in the cottage. "This place was built for bloody dwarfs," was the constant muttered refrain we heard as the poor man nursed excruciating headaches. "It was built for ordinary fifteenth-century farmers," I would counter, "not twentieth-century giants." But I hoped the house in Oxford would coincide more with his proportions.

It did. The house belonged to an archaeological couple who were digging in Greece for the year. It was big and bright and comfortable, with just enough chips in the paintwork and blotches on the carpets to make one feel at home but not enough to cause Ted to make rude comments about the domestic habits of English academics. The garden was huge and pleasantly shambolic, with apple and pear trees, fruit bushes galore, a fishpond in which there were reputed to be fish, and a great variety of flowers and shrubs. Realizing that maintaining it could occupy most of my time, we kept on the regular gardener. Apart from anything else, he knew what to pull up and what to leave and also what to do about pruning things. He was a charming old man and wheezed up the driveway once a week laden with magnificent dahlias and chrysanthemums from his allotment. "Just a few spares," he would say as I opened my arms wide to receive them. "Thought you might like them." And off he would lumber to mow the lawn and clip the hedges.

Ted installed himself at his half desk in Lincoln College and in his study. I was glad of the latter because there was an almost constant flow of my friends and relatives through the house during the year, with visitations lasting anywhere from an hour to a fortnight. Ted surprised himself by enjoying this far more than he had thought he would, but when things did get too much for him he simply shut himself in the study. If the pandemonium penetrated that sanctuary he took off and recovered his equilibrium in the Radcliffe Science Library. "The menagerie you create around yourself does at least have the redeeming quality of forcing me to work sometimes," he said once.

The boys settled down in the state elementary school around the corner and soon made a number of friends. They were horrified at first when they found they had to wear a uniform, but I rather enjoyed the novelty of white(ish) shirts, grey trousers and eggy ties. Oxford offered many things to interest them, including an eccentric museum full of mummies and skeletons and shrunken heads, the sort of thing boys really want to see.

Chloe lived only a few miles away and dropped in frequently between delivering babies. I dug the old bike out of her cellar and, after I replaced a rusted-through wheel, used it to do all the shopping and travelling to my cello lessons, a hilly nine-mile ride away. The bike had no gears, so I thought this showed great dedication on my part. Ted thought I was bonkers, but was amiable about staying with Cath while I was out. And not just for lessons, but also when I wanted to attend the numerous local concerts.

Chloe, who was well acquainted with Oxford's medical world, contacted the local day-care centre for spastics. Shortly afterwards, the lady who ran it asked me to bring Cath up so the staff could meet her and I could see the place. After years in Winnipeg of being told that Cath was too difficult and too generally hopeless to be included in any program, my enthusiasm was guarded.

"I'd love to come, Mrs. Andrews," I said, "but first I think you should know that Catherine's not what is known as educable."

"Miss Fisher has told me all about Catherine," came the response, "and she sounds just our sort."

There were two classes at the centre, both with eight or ten children. One was for the smaller, usually not so severely handicapped kids and the other for Caths in the higher age range. The atmosphere was friendly and positive. It was evident that considerable thought was being put into helping each individual develop his or her potential for learning and gaining pleasure from life. The staff, apart from the overseeing therapists, weren't specifically trained to work with the severely handicapped. They did, however, have another equally important qualification—they liked the children and were determined to see them make progress, even if progress meant something as small as a child learning to hold a toy.

Due to lack of space, attendance at the centre was part-time. Cath was allotted three days a week one week, and two the next. Mrs. Andrews was apologetic about this but I thought it was marvellous. For the first few days I took Cath up myself and stayed with her, but after a while volunteer drivers picked her up and brought her home. She left right after breakfast and didn't return till teatime. This meant that if I bribed the boys to stay at school for lunch I could manage a quick spree to London. This involved biking like mad to the station, catching a fast train up and cramming as many activities as possible into the time. Then I would catch a fast train back with the bowler hat and *Times* crowd, leap on my bike and pelt home to arrive dry-mouthed and trembling to greet everyone back for tea. I only did this trip about once a fortnight. Nevertheless, it meant I was able to see a number of friends whom I might otherwise not have seen. I could also saunter around art galleries or go to noon-hour concerts.

I don't think people who are used to having freedom of movement could understand what it meant to me to have, for the first time in ten years, six or seven hours during a day when I could pursue my own interests without neglecting any member of my family. Ted was more than happy to have a quiet house to himself as long as there was food around, the radio was working properly and the *Times* had arrived. Radio Three and the papers were the best aspects of living in England as far as he was concerned.

One of the things we were hoping to do while on the other side of the Atlantic was to get over to the Continent. Ted considers holidays frivolous and hadn't taken one, as such, since our disastrous trip to the Rockies ten years before when Cath was a tiny baby. I was determined that now, when there was something he actually wanted to do, we should do it. The idea of having Cath with us was daunting; even I, with my perennial optimism, had to admit that. Travelling from motel to motel across Canada with her was one thing but exploring Europe quite another.

I was looking up "brain damage," "minced beef," "suppositories" and other such relevant words in the dictionary one day when Chloe blew in.

"Hi," I said. "How would you say brain damage in French?"

"Well, you could say 'bad in the head,' couldn't you?" she offered. "Mal de tête."

"Don't be soppy. That means headache. I suspect I might be given some funny looks if I explained Cath by saying, 'My daughter has a headache.'"

Ted looked up from the RAC guide to France. "I wouldn't mind seeing the Roman Theatre in Orange," he said. "I wonder if one can park close to things like that."

"I'm sure one can," I said. "France won't be teeming with tourists in mid-winter, I shouldn't think. Anyway, I could probably pay a passing kid to stay by Cath in the car while we're looking round."

Ted turned the page. "She's hardly likely to be kidnapped," he said.

"Very funny. I meant so there'd be someone to tell us if she was crying."

Ted snapped the book shut. "Oh hell, we may as well give up the whole idea," he said. "I'd be in a filthy temper all the time. It wouldn't be a holiday at all."

I was trying to think of something encouraging to say when Chloe, with masterly timing, said quietly, "You don't have to take Cath."

Ted and I stared at her.

"That's what I came to tell you," she went on. "There's a home near the hospital that will take her for a couple of weeks. It's a super place, only about twenty kids, not a bit institutional. There's a nice chap running it and several nurses and motherly types helping. The kids are always kept occupied, never just left. It's really homey. There are even a couple of stray dogs running around. Mr. Williams says you can make arrangements any time."

"Chloe," said Ted, "are there any problems you can't solve? You're the most incredible woman!"

"This was pure luck," she said with typical modesty.

The home was just as she had described it and I had no qualms about leaving Cath there. Apart from a boy who attended the day-care centre with Cath, most of the children were much less handicapped than she was. All the children went to school away from the home during the day, but I gathered the staff was prepared to cope with two or three severely handicapped children when parents needed relief from caring for them.

Chloe said she would drop in periodically to see Cath while we were away and I gratefully accepted her offer.

"It's not an offer, darling," she said. "I want to see her."

Our holiday was marvellous, full of new sights and experiences for all of us. At first Ted and I commented to one another frequently on how restricting Cath would have been. "Imagine carrying her up these," said Ted as we puffed up three flights of spiralling steps to our room in Reims. We liked the smaller hotels and *pensions* but few boasted elevators. "And," I said, when later the four of us strolled towards the cathedral down a street lined with linden trees twittering with sparrows, "down again and up again every time we wanted to go out." These comments soon ceased because we could have made them a hundred times a day.

I was so happy to see Ted relaxing and enjoying himself. He fell in love with the south of France. For him, unless he ruins the illusion by returning during the summer, it will always be a land of gentle sun and countryside, ancient fortressed towns, picnics on the edges of dormant vineyards, no tourists, little traffic and delicious habits. One evening in a sleepy bistro in Avignon as he chased down his sixth cognac of the day with black coffee, he said, "Maybe we should go on holiday again sometime." A remark, for him, of unbridled enthusiasm that I stored for future reference.

A part from the times when I treated myself to the local laundromat, that year I did all the washing every day in the double kitchen sinks. It wasn't as irksome a job as it sounds. For one thing there was a lovely view of the garden from the window, and for another we had an electric spin dryer that eliminated all the hand wringing. Cath was usually with me when I did the washing, and the spinner was a constant source of entertainment to her. It had several nasty habits, one of which was to pump water all over the ceiling when the pipe into the sink disconnected itself from the outlet on top of the machine. Being suddenly drenched and watching me crashing and skidding around as I tried to turn the machine off caused her to go into gales of laughter. More constructively, I found that if I put her in the right position she could, with her left arm, push down the lid of the machine to activate the spinner.

I was delighted to find that after a while she seemed to understand that she should only push down the lid when I'd finished stuffing things into the machine and said, "OK, now, Cath." I was even more pleased when she confirmed this supposition by teasing me about it. I told her to push the lid down one day and she put her hand on it and then started to laugh. "Go on, darling," I said. "Push it." But she would only give it a pretend shove and then giggle. The more stern I became the more she enjoyed it. Thereafter we both enjoyed the game enormously, but it took hours to do the washing.

The far end of the garden became a mass of daffodils in the spring and soon everything else started sprouting too. Years of coaxing along every blade of grass and individual flower in the garden at home sharpened my appreciation of this horticultural wonder; until, that is, the day our invaluable gardener phoned to say he'd "done" his back and couldn't even manage his own garden and allotment, let alone ours.

I was snapping at a hedge with the shears one afternoon when I was interrupted by Ted. "I'll take over," he said.

"Oh, thanks, darling. It's just those bits up there—"

"Take over completely I mean. The garden."

"What?"

"Why not? I might enjoy it."

I looked at him with astonishment and mounting fury. "You mean to say," I exploded, "that I've sweated and slaved year after year at home spreading yards of earth, sowing grass, digging, planting flowers, mowing, watering, weeding, while all you do is snicker and say 'why don't you concrete the whole lot and paint it green and stick some plastic flowers in?' and all this time you've been a *latent gardener?*"

He shrugged. "Take your hands off your hips," he said, "and for God's sake stop ranting. I just thought I might have a go, that's all."

He did indeed take over completely, although the boys and I were allowed to weed the odd bed. The only advice he would accept was from Chloe, who knew about gardening, particularly pruning rose trees. He ignored me when I observed that he should pull out the exotic things he was carefully cultivating in one of the beds, and the result was the biggest thistle patch in Oxford.

The garden wasn't the only thing sprouting in all directions. Cath, getting on for eleven now, was shooting up and out and looking increasingly ungainly and uncomfortable in her wheelchair. I was wondering what I could do about this when the answer came from the day-care centre. Mrs. Andrews phoned me in great excitement one day to say that Cath had just drunk a cup of tea from an ordinary cup.

To appreciate the drama of this statement it should be understood that although she had graduated from a spoon to a spouted cup for drinking, Cath didn't seem able to apply the sucking motion to an ordinary cup. She would either put her head back and wait for me to pour the drink into her mouth or, if she was feeling silly, lean forward and bite the edge of the cup and blow bubbles. But she would never suck.

So as soon as I'd put down the phone I called Janet, a friend whose two boys were classmates of Dominic and Benjy, and asked her to look out for the boys. Then I dashed up to the centre to see how the miracle had been accomplished. The secret was in a special chair. It belonged to one of the other children and, unlike a wheelchair, had been designed specifically for children with lack of head and trunk control and with general muscular weakness. It was similar to the old wooden chair we had had when Cath was small in that it gave support where it was needed and was adjustable everywhere, but it was far less cumbersome and rigid. It also had a tray with an alterable height, a luxury I had never before encountered. The moment I saw Cath in the chair I decided it was just what she needed. She looked very comfortable and well-supported and if she could be given drinks in it she could probably be fed in it, too.

It happened to be lunch time when I was there so I tried feeding her in it. It worked beautifully. Cath and I were both delighted and so were Mrs. Andrews and the rest of the staff. And when I gave her a drink she did indeed take it like anyone else. She sucked and swallowed without choking.

The only drawback to the chair was that it was designed for indoor rather than outdoor use, with two small wheels at the back and a steel bar to rest on the ground at the front. I contacted the people who designed and made the chair to see if they could make one for us with bigger wheels at the back and swivel ones at the front, like a wheelchair. In a short time they produced exactly what we wanted and after that we rarely used the old wheelchair.

Soon after Cath started having her meals in her chair up at the table with us a remarkable change occurred in her attitude towards food. Until now she had accepted and usually enjoyed eating but had never shown what one might call a consuming interest in it. Now, however, when I pushed her up to the table for a meal, she would start thumping on her tray and chirrupping excitedly. I'm sure she enjoyed the conviviality of eating with the rest of us, but what really changed her attitude was that she gradually learned to chew. This meant I could introduce her palate to whole new range of tastes and textures—fresh fruit, a variety of salads, delicatessen goodies like salami, and even plebian fish and chips. As long as I chopped the food up she could manage nearly everything we ate.

I'll never forget the climax of this new-found pleasure in Cath's life. We were having steak and salad for supper. Solid meat was one of the few things she still didn't have the chewing power to cope with so I had made her some minced beef. She finished that and then started watching me with obvious interest and envy as I lifted chunks of dripping steak to my mouth. "You've had yours," I said firmly, but she equally firmly reached out and tried to pull my fork towards her. I felt such initiative should be rewarded and gave her the mouthful, praying she wouldn't choke to death. She chewed and gurgled and dripped and grinned for about five minutes; this was clearly the best new taste to date. Just before the moment I judged she would try to swallow it, I hoiked out the lump of grey, matted felt which had been the steak. Whenever we had steak after that I chopped her up a portion she could chew and swallow without choking and I think to this day it's her favourite food, especially when combined with a garlicky salad.

What a godsend that chair was! I hadn't realized, until I no longer had to do it, how taxing to my imagination it had been always to have to prepare a separate diet for Cath. This concern had now been eliminated. Not only that, but never again would I have to carry around prepared meals in little pots when we were travelling or visiting friends.

Another benefit was that the increase in her diet of things like lettuce, cabbage and raw fruit helped Cath's digestive system to function, if not regularly, at least more normally.

One of the advantages of Catherine attending the day-care centre was that I was able to spend much more time with the boys. Best of all, the centre continued functioning after their school had finished. Janet and I often went on joint expeditions with Dominic and Benjy and her two boys, Duncan and Willie. There were things we could do locally, like going to the museum or fishing in the nearby river, but sometimes we ventured further afield, to the London Zoo, for instance. Janet was one of several good friends I made during the year, and our families, husbands included, had many good times together.

Oxford is a city people want to visit, so quite a few Canadian friends arrived on the doorstep. During the summer, Chris and Nancy and their children, and Mia and her boys arrived with sleeping bags. Both these families had moved away from Winnipeg, so it was splendid to see them. With Cath at the day-care centre, we could make longer and more complicated excursions with them than would have been possible had she been with us.

As the end of our sabbatical approached, I continued to go to every concert in sight, almost developing musical indigestion at one point after hearing John Ogden, George Malcolm, Alfred Brendel, Paul Esswood and the English Chamber Orchestra all within a couple of weeks. The Allegri Quartet was in residence at the university for part of the year and I attended all their open rehearsals, as well as the recitals themselves. I found myself infused with fresh inspiration as I pedalled to my cello lessons. One day, perhaps, I might be able to make some sort of music with other people. At the rate I was going, though, they would have to be charitable.

When we had picked up Cath from the home after our French holiday, Mr. Williams had offered to take her for another fortnight if we wanted to go away again. We did so in July, and once again put Cath into his and his staff's capable and friendly hands as we toured the Lake District. It was an enormously enjoyable trip and, as with our French holiday, there was no doubt that it was to no small extent the absence of Cath that made it so.

I found this disquieting, especially when I linked it to the realization that all of us had been able to do so much more during our time in Oxford than we would have been able to had Cath not been at the centre.

To reassure myself that I could still lead a relatively normal life *with* Catherine, I accepted when an old friend of mine in London invited me to a party. But, I said, although I could leave the boys with Janet, I would have to bring Cath with me and could she sleep on the floor somewhere? Sure, said Judy, there was a spare mattress knocking around the house and she'd fix it up. Everyone thought I was mad but I went ahead undaunted. Knowing the train I was planning to take would be packed, I phoned the stationmaster and had a chat with him and he promised to help me onto it. Then I piled Cath and the wheelchair (the new chair didn't fold) into a taxi, waved goodbye to everyone and said see you tomorrow at lunch time.

The stationmaster was marvellous. He picked a compartment for me and wouldn't let anyone else into it until he had got Cath and myself settled. She sat by the window and I wedged myself next to her, keeping her upright. The wheelchair was parked at the end of the corridor. Our compartment companions, all men, buried their faces in papers or books. They were so determinedly English about not noticing Cath that I began to feel we didn't exist, and certainly didn't feel the need or inclination to do any explaining. As the train slowed to a halt at Paddington, however, one of them suddenly stood up, straightened his tie and took charge. "Now chaps," he said to the others in turn, "you and I will take the chair out, you take the lady's basket and brolly, you carry the little girl and you see that nothing's left behind." They all jumped to attention and performed their duties like a well-trained team, while I stood by saying, "Thanks—gosh, thanks awfully." Then, as if dismissed, they evaporated into the crowds on the platform. The commanding officer stayed with us and saw us safely into a taxi.

It was a terrific party and having Cath there was no problem at all. In fact she thoroughly enjoyed herself on her mattress in the corner of the coats room. People were constantly banging in and out and everyone stopped to chat to her. Judy came with us to the station the next day because I was a bit tired, having stayed up all night talking with her after the party. We both got a dreadful attack of the giggles as we struggled to get Cath onto the train with no handy stationmaster around to help. The trouble was, the chair wouldn't fit through the carriage door with her in it so in the end I said, "I know, we'll go in the baggage compartment. That's got big doors and there's a ramp into it." Judy's last sight of us was as we sat parked happily amongst trunks and crates and a couple of caged dogs. Mine of her was as she stood on the platform with her hands to her mouth and tears of laughter streaming down her face.

In going to the party I had thumbed my nose at the future. I was being an ostrich, though, and knew it. The future, the day I needed help with keeping Catherine, was almost upon me. Our year in England had shown me that day centres and holiday care for children like her greatly enhanced the lives of the family and the child. When we returned to Winnipeg she would be bored and I would be "de-liberated".

And what if I dropped dead or became incapacitated? Till now I had always taken comfort in the thought of the term insurance I had taken out years before. Now I had to face the fact that the money Ted would get if I died wouldn't last long and Cath would end up in the dreaded institution, the big one fifty miles out of Winnipeg that I had never dared go to see.

I determined that the first thing I would do when I got back would be to see this institution. Next, I would find out what was going on in Winnipeg and what plans there were for severely handicapped children. And finally, since I suspected that these enquiries would result in a zero, I would get in touch with other parents in my own situation and we would do something.

10

The whole place smelled of excrement ineffectively masked by a pungent disinfectant, but the smell became a stink as I approached the room to which I had been directed. It wasn't very encouraging. My nose pinched itself in and I tried not to breathe too deeply. I could hear moans and garglings and ahhhs as I got nearer so I tried to block off my ears, too. And I half-closed my eyes, as I do when I know something ghastly is about to appear in a film.

Thus partially desensitized I walked stiffly into the place where my daughter would spend her days if ever she had to be committed to an institution.

I have a fairly vivid imagination and I thought I'd prepared myself for the worst. The outside had been roughly what I had expected—a drab collection of long, two-story buildings, interspersed with the odd factory-like chimney—but I did think the inside might be less utilitarian and more cheerful. Maybe parts of it were, but it took all my courage not to turn sharply and run away from the part that now faced me.

It was a ghetto of rejects. Not so much rejects of parents, because placing their children here had been a sickening necessity for many people, but, rather, rejects of the institution itself. For other less handicapped "residents" there were, I gathered, training programs of sorts, but not for this lot. This lot, the Caths, the severely physically and mentally handicapped children and adolescents, had been given up on. They were no good to anyone and there was no point in doing anything with them.

So there they were, packed together in a couple of featureless rooms, euphemistically known as a play area, hanging and lolling and drooling in wheelchairs with nothing to do and nothing to look at except each other. Some of them were making noises but many were totally withdrawn and silent. Some looked around vacantly, others had their eyes flickering or shut. One boy, jammed and strapped into an ill-fitting wheelchair, stared at the dingy ceiling with a look of secret terror in his eyes. The reason I noticed him particularly was that he started to emit a high, thin scream.

Not all the people were in wheelchairs. At the far side of the first room was a row of mats on which lay twisted and inert forms, heads pointed to the chipped wall and feet to the centre of the room. At least that seemed to be the pattern, but one child was so contorted that it was hard to tell which way round he was. A few grubby toys were scattered around but they appeared to be there for effect rather than use.

Through to the second crowded room I could see a nurse making conversation with a relatively happy looking young man in a wheelchair. But a few feet away a skeletal, crooked boy in a football helmet stood repeatedly hurling his head against the wall. He did it with such force that he appeared bent on demolishing either the wall or his head. With each awful thunk he uttered what sounded like a war cry. High above him, just below the ceiling, a TV was showing a non-stop electrical storm.

Today was Open House, when presumably the institution was at its best.

Not wanting to stand mesmerized with horror in the doorway forever, I started to edge my way through the wheelchairs towards the end of the first room. A man in a white jacket, who looked like the head nurse, stood there. On my way I tried to smile in a natural way at the crew-cropped teenage boy whose mouth, with no teeth save two rotting stumps, was wide open in an unenchanting but engaging smile. When I paused and said hello his smile vanished. He grunted urgently and grabbed my arm, trying to pull me towards him.

With my free hand I flicked a fly away from a sore on his scalp. "These flies must be an awful nuisance," I said. I was keeping my cool admirably, I thought.

" . . . Aaaaaaaaah . . . " He tugged at me convulsively, one eye holding mine.

"Will you be having tea soon? That's something to look forward to I expect—" I was getting agitated.

"Aaaaaaaaaah . . . aaaaah . . . " Still he clasped my arm, his fingers wet and slippery but hanging on like mad. I had no idea if he understood me.

"I wish I could understand what you're saying. I know you're trying to tell me something."

"AAAAAAAAAH!"

Suddenly I was filled with rage. The thought that a prosperous society like ours could allow its most unfortunate members to be shut away in this place, without joy or hope until the day they died, infuriated me.

But what could I do for this boy right now? Or about the whole obscene situation? I wished I had never come, could make my escape and obliterate it all from my mind.

As if he sensed what I was thinking, the boy smiled ingratiatingly again, so widely that I could see down his throat. And his grip became painful.

In my despair I was curt. "I'm sorry, I have to go now," I said. I pried my arm loose.

God almighty!

I had a stilted chat with the head nurse. I could see that he was a compassionate man and liked working with these people but was clearly frustrated by the appalling conditions with which he had to contend. All the staff in the institution did their best, he said, but the odds were against them. The place was ill-funded and under-staffed. How could he provide anything but minimal care to his forty patients when he only had at the most eighteen staff, who were spaced over three shifts? Still, he said, here at least an effort was made to take everyone out into the fresh air whenever possible. In a similar situation in which he had worked in England, the patients got out of the building only about twice a year.

I asked why some of the children were in chairs and the rest on the floor. He said that the routine was one day a chair and the next on the floor, adding, when he saw my expression, that there just wasn't time to change them more frequently. I thought of the number of times Cath was moved into different positions during the day and of the contractures she was developing nonetheless. No wonder these kids were so hideously deformed. I asked about physiotherapy and was surprised to be shown a fair-sized room, though with hardly any equipment. But then I was told that it served the entire institution of eleven hundred people, of whom at least six hundred desperately needed physiotherapy. And there wasn't even a trained physiotherapist on the staff. However, added the nurse while I searched for words to respond to this information, a volunteer physiotherapist came in from town once a week. I said what a wonderful woman she must be. I said it sincerely but my mind was still occupied with the enormity of his previous statement.

Another staff member, a warm and charming lady, showed me one of the dormitories. It was one of the most offensively dreary rooms I have ever seen; mesh-covered windows, thick with dirt and darkening the whole cavernous place; acres of black-flecked, but beautifully shiny, grey stone floor; rows of chipped iron bedsteads, all with identical two-tone brown covers. Everything was very neat, but there wasn't a personal possession in sight. The only spark of colour in the whole nightmare was a huge pink elephant dangling incongruously from the ceiling at the far end.

I stared silently.

"We're hoping for a paint job soon," said the lady.

And to think that there was a long waiting list for this place. . . .

I hurried out past the baskets of gaudy plastic flowers in the entrance hall and went to the car where Ted was waiting with Cath. How beautiful she looked as she kicked with pleasure at seeing me and reached out to remove my sunglasses!

"Well?" Ted looked up at me. I tried, but failed, to muster a reassuring smile.

"I'd sooner feed her a bottle of phenobarb," I said. "At least my trial might raise some publicity."

"Here—" Ted handed me a cigarette. "You're being melodramatic."

"No," I said, "I'm not."

Would I really have done anything so drastic? If at that time I had discovered I was dying, and knew that Cath would soon be institutionalized, would I in fact have done anything to terminate her life? Which of my convictions would have been the stronger? Would I be guided by the certainty that if I did nothing I would in effect have failed her utterly— given her eleven years of love and happiness and family life and then doomed her to a terrible non-life where she would abruptly be deprived of all this and where she would know only the bewilderment and pain of being abandoned? Or would my natural respect for life assert itself?

This hypothetical, but not inconceivable, problem remained unresolved but I think my subconscious produced an interesting indication of how I really felt when, after days of worrying, I had an exceptionally vivid and realistic dream.

When the dream started, for some unknown but quite definite reason

Cath had to be put permanently in the institution. At the moment, though, she was lying in her bed deathly sick with a chest infection. I was about to call the doctor but I knew, as one does in dreams, that if she didn't receive any antibiotic she would die within hours.

With complete serenity and a feeling of inevitability I made the decision not to call him. I gave Cath a regular dose of phenobarb to calm the seizures her fever was causing. I tried to persuade her to drink. I crooned to her. I stroked her. In other words, I did all the things I would normally do if she was ill—except call the doctor. Eventually she fell asleep and I lay beside her on the bed, and, holding one limp hand in mine, waited. The dream faded but I already knew how it would end. I felt the lightness and tranquillity one feels when an enormous burden has been lifted.

So that was it. I would probably never have the courage, or wickedness, to snuff out her life but given the set of circumstances of the dream I might allow her to die. I realize, naturally, that Cath's instinct for survival is strong. She wouldn't give up her life without a fearful struggle. But that wasn't the point.

My visit to the institution had frightened me very much indeed. During the next few days I spent so much time on the telephone that I had a permanently red ear and a sore nerve in my elbow from resting it on the table as I talked. I was convinced I had multiple sclerosis because my arm kept going numb.

First I called every school for the handicapped in the city. As soon as I launched into a description of Cath's defects, I was regretfully told that "she wouldn't fit into our program but have you tried such-and-such?" The closest I got to success was when the principal of a school for the multiply handicapped evidently decided I was being unduly modest about Cath's mental capabilities. He sent a psychologist to test her IQ, but the poor woman was embarrassed when she saw Cath. She wrote some perfunctory notes on a form and left before she had finished her coffee. I didn't hear from the school again.

Next I tried all the agencies and societies for the retarded, the crippled, and so on, but it was much the same story. Catherine didn't fit in anywhere; she had too many disabilities to be eligible for any sort of program. "There are very few children as badly handicapped as your daughter living at home," I was told more than once. On occasion there was a touch of asperity in the comment that made me feel as if I had no right to bring her existence to anyone's attention.

Finally, and most important to me at the time, I made enquiries about residential services for children like Cath; that is, small local homes for handicapped children, like the one in Oxford, that would cater to a few extreme cases. But all I could establish was that there weren't any.

So the picture seemed as black as I had feared. My multiple sclerosis spread; two of my toes kept going numb and I spent hours sticking pins into myself to see if I had lost my feeling elsewhere. I was lucky enough to find an extremely kind and understanding general practitioner who was willing to add a self-confessed hypochondriac to his list of patients. When, for a while, I crawled into his office almost weekly with symptoms of yet another deadly disease, he assured me I was merely taking sensible precautions, not being neurotic at all.

Meanwhile we were all settling back into life in Winnipeg. The boys returned to school with hybrid accents. Ted put on a determined look and a tie and went out to the university to get into a lecture-giving mood. And Cath and I, forced once again into each other's company twenty-four hours a day, went for extensive walks through the leaves and tried not to be too bored with one another. I reinstated her weekly hydrotherapy sessions at the Children's Hospital with Therese. Judging by the way Cath gazed around when I wheeled her into the pool room, looked surreptitiously at Therese and then burst into laughter, she must have remembered it all. She also remembered a game we had played in the physio room on swim days—rolling a huge beach ball to each other along parallel bars. As soon as Cath was positioned at one end in her chair, she looked around for the ball, clenched her fists and shouted when she saw me bringing it. She even remembered her habitual joke of refusing to hit it back to me until I threw it in a corner and announced I wasn't playing.

I had hoped, during my recent phoning spate, to find someone who was not just concerned about the lack of services for children like Cath but was actually doing something about it. So far my quest had been fruitless. I was beginning to think I might have to conjure up two non-existent ingredients of my character—initiative and organization—and do something myself. One day, however, I was plodding through a Bach gigue on my cello, with Cath, a captive if not captivated audience, responding with hoots of laughter, when the phone rang. Cursing, I answered it. It was one of the many social workers I had talked to. She was calling to give me the number a woman who had recently moved to Winnipeg and who had a severely handicapped daughter. She had this last summer helped in setting up an innovative and very successful program in Winnipeg for such children. Would I be interested in meeting her? Interested was hardly the word. I phoned at once.

Alice Rothney was a warm and intelligent lady. That was evident just from talking to her. Equally important, she seemed to be extremely knowledgeable, not just about severely handicapped children themselves but also about what was and wasn't being done for them, both locally and elsewhere. And she had a clear idea of what should be done, and how to do it. By the end of our conversation, I was hopeful that I had found someone whose leadership I could respect and follow. I was anxious to become involved so she suggested bringing Cath to a fortnightly winter recreation program she had created—an off-shoot of the summer one.

As I had anticipated, I gained more from our initial visit to the program than Cath. She was alarmed at suddenly finding herself in the vastness of a school gym full of strangers, noise and activity. She reacted predictably, appearing to be oblivious to everything except her left hand, to which she paid inordinate attention. I knew, though, that she would gradually take more of an interest on future occasions.

I was immediately struck by the general atmosphere of fun and enjoyment. Most of the thirty or so participants were severely handicapped in one way or another, but they were having a good time within the confines of their disabilities. They were being taken for runs and races in their wheelchairs, rolled around on mats and exercised or being entertained in some other way. The more mobile ones were loping around trying to push and bounce balls, practicing extraordinary dance steps over by the record player, and so on. And all this was accompanied by wide smiles and excited noises and gestures.

Alice had it organized so that there were enough volunteer helpers, mostly high-school and university students, for everyone to be worked with on a one-to-one basis. Looking around, a number of good relationships were visible between handicapped child and helper. I gathered these had evolved during the more concentrated summer program. For many of the handicapped people this had been the first time anyone outside their families had worked with them on an individual basis. This, together with exposure to other new experiences, had resulted in progress, often marked, for all of them, in terms of increased enjoyment of life and awareness of themselves and others.

"I didn't know what to make of Alex when Mrs. Rothney assigned him to me," a psychology student told me as he deftly fielded a sandwich dropped by a big boy similar to Cath. "He was terrified when I first took him into the pool this summer but by the end of it he was so excited every time I got him into his trunks that I could hardly handle him. He trusts me now and I figure we're pretty good for each other. Hey Alex, here's a Kleenex. Mop up that mess on your chin—that's the way—feels better, doesn't it? See," he said, turning to me again, "that's really great progress for him. We started on it four months ago and he can do quite a decent job now."

There were group, as well as individual, activities. Someone had donated the silk part of a parachute and everyone was stationed more or less evenly around the thing, holding and pulling it towards them, with help where necessary. A huge waist-high circle was formed and all sorts of things could then be done by heaving the 'chute up and down. Waves and winds could be created, a ball tossed back and forth or, best of all, turns could be taken to be rushed across underneath it as everyone raised and lowered it. Even Cath, when her turn for this came, gave a hint of the pleasure she would eventually show, especially when we got trapped and were suddenly enveloped in red and white silk. There were numerous ways in which this simple idea benefited the children. For one thing the group aspect of it was novel to most of them and helped to lure the more introspective of them from their isolation. It encouraged movement and co-ordination in the arms and hands. It demonstrated the cause and effect principle. But above all it was fun.

Family involvement was very important to the program and there were many parents, brothers and sisters, and friends present to provide help, enthusiasm and refreshments. When I demonstrated to a high-school student that Cath wouldn't snap in half if I slithered her around on the floor by her feet (as long as I didn't actually cause a whiplash effect), I was suddenly struck by the difference between this scene and the dismal one I had witnessed at the institution. The protagonists were similar. There was a boy with a huge hydrocephalic head, laughing as someone wiggled a hand puppet for him; a twisted girl in a cushion-padded wheelchair shouting approval as her bracelet was admired; a psychotic, retarded boy being encouraged to wrestle playfully with his helper rather than to claw his own face to ribbons; a lanky, cross-eyed boy jerking in all directions as he struggled to make his grunts understood, and splitting his face with pleasure when he accomplished it. I had seen them all before, but here I could see them as the interesting and diverse individuals they were, not as pitiful objects to be "dealt with."

One of the most interesting aspects of the program was the interaction not just between participants and the helpers but between the participants themselves. People of all ages and with all types and degrees of handicap were finding happiness and fun by entertaining each other. Working the hand puppet for the boy with the hydrocephalic head was a girl of about twelve who could move around by herself but was very retarded. Still, she was enjoying the game just as much as the boy was. At one point a woman asked me if her daughter, Judy, could push Cath around in her chair. I said of course and together we supervised the operation. Apparently Judy was thirty-two but had the mentality of a two-year-old baby. When she saw she was allowed to push someone she stamped her foot and made Cath-like noises of delight. "It's so lovely to see her enjoying herself," said her mother. "She and I live alone and she's so bored hanging around me day in and day out."

When, for a few moments, Alice wasn't busy, I went to tell her how terrific I thought the program was.

"But it's so hopelessly inadequate," she said. "Except for this one afternoon a fortnight many of these people are stuck at home with their families all the time, and vice versa. Well, I don't have to tell you that! Some families are still managing to cope but many have reached breaking point."

"I can imagine," I said. "But why couldn't the summer program have continued? Become permanent?"

"That sounds like the obvious answer, doesn't it? Whoops! Careful Jeanie," she turned to her daughter who was threatening to mow us down with a wheelchair. The passenger, a girl, was screeching with laughter. "But you see the program was financed by a short-term government grant; which we got, I may say, not because we were providing a program for disadvantaged children, but because we were providing students with summer jobs!"

"That program was the best thing that ever happened to Philip," said a mother who had wheeled her son up to us. "And to me, come to that. Best break we'd had in nineteen years. I just don't understand why nobody would support Alice in continuing it." Alice told me later that this woman had been widowed soon after her son was born. He was even more handicapped than Cath and she had coped singlehanded ever since, and on the most meagre income as she obviously couldn't go out to work.

"The main problem is one of basic attitudes," said Alice. "Most people are conditioned to think that nothing can be done with these severely handicapped individuals, that they can't progress, that they're not worth spending time and money on."

"But don't you think that's understandable," I said, "if they've never had anything to do with children like Cath and Philip? I mean just to look at them, anyone might think, good God, nothing much to be done there."

Alice agreed, but said what really upset her was that often this negative and ignorant opinion was held even by professionals in the field of mental retardation. This included the top people in the institutions, the most powerful people in CAMR (Canadian Association for the Mentally Retarded) and people in the mental health department in the government. And when it was proved to them, as it had been in the summer program, that even children with the very lowest levels of intelligence can and do respond to stimulation and interesting activities, they turned a blind eye and a deaf ear. They simply didn't want to know.

I gathered that the students working on the summer program had written a full report on the progress of the handicapped kids they were working with, and that the progress of some of the children had been really significant. One was feeding himself by the end of the summer, another had added three words to his original vocabulary of four, and even Philip, his mother said, had shown a remarkable degree of intelligence by trying to unbuckle his belt at swimming time.

Alice felt she had let everyone down when the program ended. Parents were still phoning her to say how marvellous it had been and asking when a regular program was to start. A number of students had become really interested in working with multiply handicapped children and wanted to know if any permanent jobs were available in the community. Most of all, she felt it was unfair to the children themselves to have given them just a tantalizing taste of a different life.

"But surely," I said, "the report the students did must have impressed loads of professionals. Surely they were excited by it?"

"That's what I expected, I must say, but people don't like having their minds changed. Oh dear, excuse me, I must go to Jeanie—"

From that day on I attached myself to Alice, avidly listening and questioning. I tried to absorb not only some of her knowledge but also her ideas about what could and should be done for people like Cath and Jeanie and all the others who were so badly handicapped that nobody had thought about providing help for them and their families.

Alice's daughter Jeanie had been born fourteen years ago with brain damage, resulting in severe retardation and epilepsy. She was a delightful girl but in many ways was far more of a handful than Cath. Alice had squeezed Jeanie into a school for the retarded on a part-time basis during term time but she was at home most of the time. Sometimes she was, of necessity, loaded with anti-seizure drugs and quite docile, but Alice felt strongly that physical activity was good for Jeanie and she never tried to restrain her. This meant that Jeanie was usually moving about and, with the enquiring and mischievous mind of a two-year-old and her tendency to frequent seizures, she had to be watched continuously. She would have five or six seizures a day. Since these occurred at any time Jeanie was forever damaging herself, falling through windows, crashing downstairs and so on. However, between Alice, her historian husband and older children, they managed to cope, though it was becoming an increasing strain. They were desperate for a good "home" where Jeanie could go for short periods just to give everyone a rest.

Somehow, despite all this, Alice was one of the most active, determined and persistent crusaders I've ever met, working harder and more productively in the field of retardation than many paid professionals.

If I lived that sort of life I'm sure I would look and feel a total wreck. The extraordinary thing about Alice was that although she was often exhausted and worried, she nevertheless invariably managed to look fresh, dignified and cheerful. She put her own problems in the background and was an attentive and sympathetic listener to the many people who needed the hope and encouragement she provided.

When I first met her she had only been in Winnipeg for two years but was already well-known, and in reactionary quarters strongly resented, as a torchbearer for bottom-of-the-barrellers like Cath and Jeanie. She knew, often personally, more than sixty families in and around Winnipeg who were caring for a multiply handicapped child or adult at home and it was safe to assume that this was only a fraction of the true number. She worked in two main directions: first, pushing school divisions into instituting good daytime programs for multiply handicapped children, rather than posting them into existing but unsuitable programs or leaving them out altogether; and second, starting small "homes" for the multiply handicapped. She was doing the latter in her capacity as chairman of the community residences committee in the local branch of CAMR. I had always been told that CAMR wasn't exactly falling over itself to take an interest in people like Cath. Alice admitted this was true but urged me to join the association, saying that one could only change attitudes and exert pressure from within. She was excited about the progress she and her colleagues were making. They had already bought an old house and were fixing it up. Although this one was to be strictly for retarded adults, the bigwigs in CAMR had promised her that children under eighteen would be included in the next project—not children as complicated as Cath and Jeanie, but it would be a start.

The message Alice had been gently but firmly transmitting since I had met her was clear. Services for our children would only materialize if we parents made them do so, and this required determination and hard work, a great deal more of each than I had imagined. I had wanted to become involved but now I wasn't so sure. I've got enough to cope with, I told myself, I'll just stay on the periphery and help at the recreation program and so on. Alice is obviously doing a great job representing wonky kids and she doesn't need an ignoramus like me trailing along behind her.

There was something else, too. I found myself in a moral quandary. Over the years I had been obliged to accept that many people, particularly professionals, saw my refusal to institutionalize Cath as an act of defiance against the system. I had been too cowed by their disapproval and disinterest really to expect much help, let alone have people regard Cath as a citizen with rights. In my resolve to prove to everyone, including myself, that my course of action had been and still was justified, I had always been as independent as possible, minimizing the problems we encountered with Cath. Now, however, I had to change gears and turn sharply in a different direction. I had to swallow my meekness and say that I needed help, I deserved help and I would fight for help, if only because Catherine herself needed and deserved more than I could give her.

This change of outlook wasn't easy, but I was helped by two factors. First, through talking to Alice and learning what was going on in other countries and even in other parts of Canada in the field of handicapped children realizing their full potentials, I knew that Cath could be gaining ground if only the expertise was available. The knowledge hardest to accept about Cath is that if she had had the right therapy, stimulation and training from birth she would be far less handicapped than she is. She might even be walking and talking after a fashion.

Second, I now knew that there were many people who kept their severely handicapped children at home under far more difficult circumstances than myself. Most of them had neither the time nor the energy to do anything more than deal with their lives from one day to the next. I knew many of them were desperate, even if I wasn't, yet.

"You've bought a skirt," commented Ted one day.

"I'm going to start going to meetings and sitting on committees," I said.

And from then on I was in it up to my eyes.

11

In the house, meanwhile, we were all up to our eyes in dust. Cath weighed nearly seventy pounds now and this made the stairs seem interminable and the bath minuscule. We were having a hole knocked through the kitchen wall into the attached garage and transforming it into ground-level quarters for her.

I had spent many happy hours planning the design of this room but now that an irreversible stage had been reached I was nervous. What if the plumber couldn't link the main house system to the pipes necessary for the outsize bath I had devised? He had done a lot of head scratching before saying he could. What if Mr. Victor, our invaluable carpenter, was unable to solve any one of the numerous technical problems that kept presenting themselves? Could he remove a piece of the main joist for the doorway without one side of the house collapsing? What if I dropped dead and Cath had to go to the institution? Ted would be very put out.

I had so many preoccupations these days that it took me a shamefully long time to realize there was something amiss with Dominic. I had noticed vaguely that he was displaying excessive degrees of his normal distress symptoms, such as sleepwalking and Benjy-bashing, but had put it down to his readjusting to Canadian life and his place at school. One morning he came home for lunch and slammed the back door so hard that the window fell out. That finally prompted me to ask some questions.

He was sulky. Nothing was wrong, he said, why did I have to make such a fuss? He was sorry about the dumb door and where was that dumb Benjy because he'd left his dumb boots outside for everyone to trip over.

I was upset. This refusal, or inability perhaps, to tell me his troubles was unusual, and I knew the problem must be serious. During the next few days Dominic came home from school several times with signs of having been in a fight. "It's nothing," he would say. "Just gimme a Kleenex. Quit going on at me."

Then one Sunday I asked him to take Cath around the block in her sleigh. He took off willingly enough but a short while later I heard him screaming obscenities in the back lane. I called him in and as he clumped up the drive pulling Cath I saw two boys running off.

"I'm going to kill those bums," he shouted. Scarlet-faced, he tore off his hat and burst into tears.

"Oh, sweetheart, don't." I had guessed by now. "How long has it been going on?"

He sobbed and sobbed. "Better bring Cath in," he said wetly into my neck when the first storm was over. "It's cold out. Ever since we got back, just about—"

"OK, we'll have a talk in a minute," I said, and between us we hauled Cath up the back steps into the kitchen.

"That crap-headed Spitler kid—what a bummer he is—" As we undressed Cath, Dominic's rage erupted once again but after a while he blew his nose and calmed down.

It seemed that a boy in his class had for weeks been teasing him about Catherine, constantly seeking him out and making his life a misery. You've got a sister that's mental, ya ya ya *ya* ya, and she makes weird noises like this, real spooky, and she waves her arms around like this and boy am I ever glad I don't have such a gross sister. Ya ya ya *ya* ya. Moreover he had persuaded a couple of other boys to join in the fun. Together they were waylaying Dominic on his way home and torment-ing him.

"Do you think it'd do any good if I invited him to meet Cath prop-erly?" I asked Dominic. Spitler entered the school the year we went away, and had seen Cath in her wheelchair outside the house during the fall.

"No. He'd just be super phoney polite. He's smart. He'd agree with everything you said and say he was sorry and then be twice as bad."

"How about if I talked to your teacher?"

"No!"

Nothing like this had ever happened before and I was at a loss how to help Dominic or advise him. I tried to point out that most people have weak spots and sometimes feel they can compensate by attacking those of others. Did Spitler ever get teased about his name, for instance? It was hardly the most fortunate. Sometimes, Dominic admitted. Well then, maybe he should try and bear that in mind. Yeah, said Dominic dutifully, adding a second later that he was really going to cream that Spitler kid one of these days.

We didn't get very far, but I hoped that just by having told me about it he would feel better. That night, however, I awoke to hear him bumping around downstairs and saying something over and over again in a despairing drone. When I reached him I could distinguish the words. "I told her," he was saying. "Oh no, I told her, I told her, oh no—"

"Dominic, wake up." I led him over to the sofa and sat him down.

"—I told her, oh no—"

"Wake, up, darling." At last he did, but could remember only that he had been having a nightmare, not the contents. "You were saying 'I told her'."

"Oh no!" He gave a wail of horror and pulled himself away, staring at me as if I'd grown fangs.

"You told me about Spitler, you mean? But I'm glad you did! Darling, come here. What is frightening you so much?" He inched towards me and suddenly sat up very straight.

"I'm scared," he said looking down with intense concentration at his top pyjama button. "I'm scared you'll put Cath in the institution."

I was mystified. "But why?" I said. "I mean she may have to live somewhere else some day, we all know that, but not now. You know the reason I have to leave you with sitters so often these days is that I'm working to get a *nice* place for her eventually."

"I know all that. But I've heard you and Dad say that if she ever had a bad effect on our family she'd have to go to that place. And—" he paused.

"And?"

"And I know I've been a real pain lately and caused a lot of trouble because of her and so I thought—" He pulled a pyjama button off.

"Oh darling!"

A mass of reassurance and a cup of hot chocolate later Dominic returned to bed, with at least some of his fears allayed. The next day, with his approval, I had a quiet word with his teacher. She was shocked when I told her of the situation. She said she would talk to the class about handicaps, in general rather than specific terms, and see if she could observe the penny dropping with Henry Spitler. To her dismay the plan backfired. She had asked for examples of handicaps within the class and various children had volunteered bad eyesight, crooked teeth, obesity and so on. Then Spitler's arm started waving urgently.

"Dominic's got a sister that's got real bad handicaps," he said. "She's a retardate and she can't walk or talk and," he concluded in tones of deepest disapproval, "I've heard kids teasing Dominic about her and saying he must be mental too!"

"Great heavens," said the teacher, thoroughly nonplussed. "Is that so?"

"Yes," replied Henry nodding vigorously. "But I'd never do such an unkind thing."

"I should hope not indeed!" She and I couldn't help laughing when she told me about it, but didn't know what to do next. Eventually we decided to consult Mr. Johnson, the kind and experienced principal of the school. Dominic, meanwhile, returned for lunch hysterical, and once again banged the storm window out.

"Now the whole class knows about it and they're all talking about Cath and there are only two or three of my friends who aren't making fun of her. Benjy, that's my grapefruit you're eating and I'm never going back to that crummy school again."

"Yes you jolly well are," I said. Ted and I had discussed moving him to a private school but had decided it wouldn't be the answer in the long run. "You've coped very well so far and I think things will change soon. I'm going to talk to Mr. Johnson."

"What can he do?"

Mr. Johnson and I had a long talk, at the end of which he said, "Leave it to me. I think I can sort things out."

He did, and although I thanked him profusely I never asked him how he managed it. But Dominic said that Henry spent a whole morning in the principal's office and emerged perfectly cheerful. He offered Dominic a piece of gum and thenceforth never teased him again nor enticed others to do so.

Although it was a painful experience for Dominic, it was also a useful one. Since that time he has had occasional barbs about Catherine thrown his way by other children but, with his increased maturity and security, he can flick them away before they penetrate. Benjy's attitude towards the whole issue was interesting. Once it was in the open he didn't say much but I noticed he avoided being seen in public with Cath. If I said, "Coming for a walk with Cath and me, Benjy?" he would suddenly remember he had to hammer a poster on his wall. I kept silent and once everything had blown over he began to re-own her, as it were.

References to Catherine's eventual institutionalization seemed to be cropping up constantly of late. Almost since her birth I had had to counter mindless suggestions that I "put her away," but now these recommendations were becoming more acceptable, because they were backed by intelligence and genuine concern. Just before leaving Oxford, the grandmother of a friend of the boys, a woman I liked a great deal, had gently pointed out that the longer I put it off the harder it would be for our whole family to adjust to the separation. I said that before even considering such a step I would have to find a decent place for Cath. But I realized, after thinking about it, that her idea itself was right. And now, shortly after Dominic's experience, my pediatrician's partner, again someone whom I liked and respected, had just presented me with a different argument. After giving Cath a booster shot, the doctor and I started talking about the difficulties Cath presented. As usual I waved them all aside, adding an enthusiastic description of her room, which was nearly completed, and further adding that I was becoming active in setting up community residences for retarded children.

"But the latter are obviously a long way off," said the doctor, "and anyway you still don't seem to think in terms of permanent placement. Have you ever considered that you may be hanging on to Cath for your own benefit?"

I felt my chin dropping and only just managed not to say "Huh?"

"The boys are ten and seven now, aren't they?" continued the doctor. "It won't be too many years before they take off. And your husband presumably could manage alone. But Cath . . . you know that she will always be totally dependent—" She paused.

"On me, you mean."

"On you."

"At least *she* will always need me."

"Precisely."

I looked at my nails but after Dominic's adventures there was nothing to chew. I asked the doctor if she'd been to the big institution. She said no, but she understood that it was improving greatly. For the less handicapped people, perhaps, I said, but if she saw the rooms where children like Cath were she would be shocked.

When I got home I pondered her theory, and have often thought about it since. I think it was a perfectly legitimate one, but I feel, luckily, that I'm secure enough as an individual not to need the reassurance of Cath needing me all my life.

Her new room had worked out even better than I had hoped and enhanced the whole ground floor of the house, opening up and brightening it. The room was well-proportioned, spacious and light. Now that I'd done the painting and furnishing, and made curtains, it was very inviting. So inviting, in fact, that Ted showed signs of moving in before Cath did. As he closed himself in with the folding cedar doors he said enviously that it was by far the nicest room in the house. I suspected that by this he meant clean and tidy and potentially private. I appeased him by promising that from now on the sitting room would be as he had always dreamed it would be, civilized, like other people's. How? he asked not unreasonably. That room had for years been full of the TV, children, broken furniture, food, toys and spills. Simply, I said, by moving the TV and everything else up to Cath's old room, which I would turn into the boys' private sitting room. Ah, said Ted, slum relocation, you mean. But his expression became happier when I pointed out that henceforth the sitting room would be virtually his.

I don't know whether Cath fully appreciated that she had the only wall-to-wall carpeting and picture windows in the house but she certainly liked the room. She had watched its creation with the rest of us, going berserk with delight at the din and confusion. When the moving-in ceremony took place she seemed to realize its significance. She sat up very straight in her chair and achieved an almost regal air as she surveyed her new domain.

That night she was in a state of bubbly excitement when I put her to bed. All her familiar bedroom paraphernalia was around. The mirror was on the wall to her left so she could check that she was still the fairest of them all. Toys and mobiles hung by elastic from ribbons stretched across the ceiling. What really fascinated her now, though, was that if she looked to her right she had a marvellous view through the wide doorway into the kitchen and dining room.

This was intentional. Part of my overall plan had been that even when in bed she would feel in touch with the pulse of the household. But I hadn't expected quite the degree of appreciation she was now exhibiting. There were great whoops of joy every time she saw us and hooting question marks between appearances. When, at one in the morning, Ted grumbled mildly that a lump of bologna had just cost him a five-minute chat with her, I decided the time had come to close her doors. I had planned originally to use them for privacy, rather than shutting Catherine off. She quietened down then, and I thought she'd fallen asleep. But when I quietly reopened them before going up to bed she gave an almighty shout of laughter and was off again. Heaven knows when she finally dropped off; she may well have stayed awake all night. When the boys and I trooped down for breakfast she was wide awake and greeted us eagerly.

The feature in the room of which I was most proud was the bathtub. It was basically a steel tank built to my specifications, 6'6" long, 3' wide and 3'6" high. But once it had been boxed in, painted and tiled, it was like a mini-swimming pool, and cost half what a real custom-built bath would have. The only problem was that I had underestimated the tilt at which it should be set. The first time I put Cath in it, I had to hold her head and shoulders up all the time or she might have drowned. She was plainly longing to have a good unencumbered kick and slosh and I was furious with myself for my miscalculation. I sat and glared at the bottom of the bath afterwards and then I got it. To create the slope necessary to keep her top half higher up, all I needed was a removable wedge. I drew a rough picture of what I wanted and had it made. It worked fine and from then on the bath was the greatest success.

The total cost of Cath's new room, from Mr. Victor's first whack of the sledgehammer down to the pictures on the walls, was nearly $4,000. For what we got this was very reasonable, but we live entirely on Ted's salary, and it was a tidy sum to find.

Since we might easily have saved ourselves this $4,000 by institutionalizing Cath at public expense, I made enquiries at the provincial Tax Department to see if we were eligible for any sort of reimbursement, or at least a tax deduction. The answer to both questions was no. To add insult to injury the next house tax bill we got was much higher than in previous years. The assessor had noted that our property had increased in value!

It made me wonder how people with a child like Catherine managed to meet their needs if they were living on half our salary, or a quarter, or even less.

A couple of miles down the road from our house is a hospital run by the Shriners, a Freemason organization famous in North America for, amongst other things, the good work it does in aiding physically handicapped children. The hospital is a handsome building, set on the river and surrounded by huge trees, but whenever I had gone by in the past I had always felt sad and slightly resentful. I knew that only children with normal or near-normal mentality were treated there.

Soon after we returned to Winnipeg, I took Cath to be reviewed at the Crippled Children's Society. I discovered that a team of doctors, therapists and engineers had recently set up a Special Devices Clinic in this hospital. It was an outpatient clinic where appliances such as braces, walkers, artificial limbs and sophisticated electronic aids were designed and made for children with physical handicaps. This applied to all children, which was the great thing. There was no more discrimination against the mentally handicapped. I couldn't wait to investigate, so one fine spring day I took Cath down.

It was a refreshing experience. Therese came with us as she was concerned about Cath's right hip, which was completely out of joint by now. We met the people on the Special Devices team who were all super and really interested in Cath. They seemed anxious to help and, chalking up a first, able to do so. After long discussions, which Cath joined in with raspberries, they came up with modification plans for the English chair, which she'd outgrown to the point where she drooped forward over the tray like a fuchsia. Her original wheelchair was banned henceforth as it did bad things to her posture, but this didn't bother me because I only used it for travelling anyway. We were promised an all-in-one, custom-built wheelchair by summer. I was really enthusiastic about the whole set-up. It looked like the answer to all Cath's physical complications, and Dr. Letts, the orthopedic surgeon in charge, told me to phone whenever I needed help. I could hardly wait to pass on the news to all the many people I knew who would benefit from the clinic. The Shriners paid for everything, apparently with no help from the government. Ted muttered something about "charity" when I told him about it but, as I pointed out, we couldn't afford to be proud after Cath's room. We'd be in the red for years as it was.

Cath had now grown to the point where I found it almost impossible to take her anywhere by taxi, and after an experimental trip in a handi-cab one day I was hooked on this form of transportation. The driver would fling open the back doors of his van, pull down a ramp, run Cath up and in, secure her chair and off we would go. It was infinitely luxurious not having to heave her out of her chair, shout instructions over my shoulder about packing the latter, aim her into the taxi without catching her feet or letting them dangle in the pools of mud on the floor, and then reverse the process when we reached our destination. Luxurious it may have been, but twice the cost, and I only treated myself in this way when absolutely necessary.

I myself was spending a fair amount on taxis these days getting to and from meetings, and it would have been more had Alice not given me rides whenever she could. I tried going by bus once but it took so long that I ended up spending more on a babysitter than I would have on a taxi.

Another tricky aspect of becoming a meetings person was organizing my life so that I could leave the house. Evening meetings were the easiest because usually Ted could manage to be at home. If a meeting was after four o'clock, I could get a teenager to babysit. During the day it was more difficult. Luckily my friends could usually help and Cath spent many an hour under Ann's piano, on Mary's kitchen floor or rolling around the sitting room in Irene's house. (Irene and her husband Hugh had moved in down the road a couple of years ago and we had shared booze, books, children and catastrophies ever since.) In return these friends landed their kids on me sometimes. Occasionally I had to be out from morning till evening at a conference. Normally Mrs. Bock could come and take over. However, if she had to be at home with her grandchildren, I would take Cath to her house for the day, which was complicated, and make local arrangements for the boys.

I prided myself on the high degree of efficiency I achieved in all these manoeuvres, until the day I arrived at an important meeting armed with a plastic bag full of diapers. I don't know what Mrs. Bock made of the pile of papers she got.

Ever since the end of the summer program Alice, along with one or two other vociferous parents and two progressive school superintendents, had been trying to coerce the Department of Education into providing suitable programs for multiply handicapped children. I was only in on the end of this series of meetings and my impression had been that we were getting nowhere. I hadn't yet learnt that people in powerful, policy-making positions love to keep in the dark those most directly affected by their decisions. I was therefore surprised to get a letter from my school division one day saying that Cath and five other children similar in age and degree of handicap were to join a school for physically handicapped children for the last few weeks of the school year. This was to be a temporary arrangement. In September it was hoped that a brand new program was to start, specifically for children like Catherine.

It was a good thing that the first arrangement wasn't permanent. Most of the teachers had had little or no experience with severe retardation. They did their utmost to incorporate these strange beings into their classes, but I suspect they felt it was unfair to them, their own pupils and the multiply handicapped newcomers. Mr. Tweedie, in whose class Cath was landed, was kind and well-intentioned and made a praiseworthy attempt to understand what Cath was all about. But I realized how impossible he found it to get down to her level when he commented that Catherine didn't seem to *see* too well. It reminded me of my mother's story about a man in London during the war who observed that his friend's doorbell wasn't working, but failed to notice that half the house had been blown away by a bomb.

Cath certainly benefited from going to the school, however. She had two rides in a van each day, which our school division paid for, she was given physiotherapy by Therese, who happened to work at the school part-time, and last but not least she had a break from me.

She had a week-long break from all of us after school ended in July. Thanks to Dr. Letts of the Special Devices Clinic, she was beautifully cared for in the Shriners' hospital while being fitted for her special wheelchair. At the urging of the nurses and also of Hugh and Irene, who offered to act *in loco parentis*, Ted, the boys and I went to the lake.

"Just like an average Canadian family," I commented to Ted.

"Statistically, at least, it'd be hard to be more average than us," he responded. "Not many families have 2.3 children."

It was a pleasant break for all of us. Ted shut himself in the cabin and read fifteen thrillers while the boys and I swam and went on pony trails.

I had thought, when we bought Cath's English chair, that it was very good, but compared to the one built at the Shriners it was antediluvian. The new one was a masterpiece of ingenuity and streamlined design. Into the frame of an ordinary wheelchair, narrowed to Cath's size, had been fitted a removable seat that was padded and contoured to her shape in such a way that, with neat shoulder straps, she now sat up straighter and more steadily than ever before. In fact when I first spotted her in the ward I thought she'd grown about a foot during the week. The seat, armrests and footrests, one of which was thicker than the other for her wonky leg, were all upholstered in a dark green leather-like vinyl and the effect was most elegant, particularly when a large green and orange tray was slotted on.

We met Dr. Letts on our way out and I thanked him for arranging everything, adding that it was gratifying to find a doctor who was prepared to apply his skills to someone as retarded as Cath. His response pleased me; surprised me, even, because it was so unusual. "Catherine may have a severely subnormal mentality," he said, "but she's just as deserving of any help we can give her as a crippled child with an IQ of 150. It would be regarding her as less than a person to think otherwise. Let me know how things go with the chair. We'll have to modify it as she grows."

Shortly after our holiday I had a nasty fright. I was humping Cath up our front steps in her wheelchair when my foot slipped and we both went flying down them again, skidding to a halt on the lawn and nearly overturning. After that I found I was scared of getting her up and down the steps alone. I knew I was strong enough—my arm and shoulder muscles were so well developed that Ted always said I'd be lethal in a dark alley—but now I knew the fear of the unexpected. I could slip again, a sandal strap could break, my back might click out, any number of horrid things could happen.

So we had a ramp built from the top of the steps down to the sidewalk. It cost $150 and, as with Cath's room, produced a derisive reaction when I enquired about possible reimbursement. I felt the same sort of reluctance to get the ramp as I had when getting Cath's first wheelchair years before. It was necessary, but it seemed to make her so obvious.

The day it was built I felt like wolfing a bottle of tranquillizers. Every child in the neighbourhood gathered to watch and then took turns roaring down it on tricycles, trucks, wagons, engines and anything else with wheels; one beaming urchin even went down astride his little sister's doll's carriage. I hated to spoil the fun, earsplitting though it was, but I was terrified of an accident. I told the boys to organize a guard system by the road in case anyone overshot the mark. We parked Cath facing the ramp and she enjoyed herself as much as anyone, looking like a spectator at a wildly funny tennis match as she turned her head rapidly from side to side and hooted with laughter as kids whizzed by.

12

As a result of much hard work and determination on the part of many people, the new school program for multiply handicapped children did, as we had hoped, get going in September. It was set up in two classrooms, with some use of the gym, in an underpopulated primary school. There were eight children, including Alice's daughter Jeanie, Catherine, and the others who had spent a few weeks in the school for the physically handicapped at the end of the previous school year. They were all roughly the same age—young teenagers. The staff consisted of two teachers, two aides and a part-time occupational physiotherapist, who was a bright and energetic young woman and who also, since she worked with Dr. Letts on the Special Devices team, already knew most of the children. The school day was four hours, 10.30 to 2.30, and the children were transported in wheelchair vans. All costs were borne by the individual school divisions.

I had let Cath's wild woolly hair grow during the summer and she looked sweet as I handed her over to her driver the first day in her smart new pants and shirt, clean socks and neat pigtails.

The government of Manitoba has many good qualities but it also has an unfortunate propensity for reinventing the wheel. Although there were already several centres for multiply handicapped children in Ontario, nobody saw fit to investigate them before starting ours. Consequently everything was much harder for the staff and administrators of the program than it need have been. The enthusiasm they felt for the project was dampened at first by their own lack of experience and specialized training and also by the totally unnecessary lack of guidance and support from their superiors.

It was a while before I felt Cath was gaining from the program beyond having a change of scene. When she came home she would be withdrawn and even less responsive than the boys to my eager, "What did you do in school today, darling?" Then one day I heard her hooting as she was pushed up the ramp and she beamed at me when I opened the door. After that she nearly always returned cheerful and I concluded she had not only accepted school but was enjoying it.

Cath being away for a few hours each day made it easier for me to attend meetings with Alice. It also allowed me to pursue more personal goals, such as improving my cello technique and learning to drive.

After returning from England I had resumed cello lessons with my original teacher, Mrs. Vallentyne. She was pleased to hear that I now had more time to practice each day and suggested that I join the amateur university orchestra in which she played. I protested vehemently. For heaven's sake, I said, I'd only been playing for two years and in a dilettantish way at that. It would take far more gall than I possessed to do such a thing and anyway I was still lousy. Nonsense, said Mrs. Vallentyne, I would enjoy it. It would be a great experience for me and wasn't playing with other people what I'd been aiming at all along? Yes, I said, but not yet, in another five, ten years perhaps. She and Ted alternately coaxed and bullied me and eventually I allowed myself to be dragged along. I was so tense the first time that I put my back out just walking to my seat and had to sit at an odd angle all evening. But the exhilaration I felt at being part of an orchestra playing Tchaikovsky's Fifth Symphony was so intense that I barely noticed the discomfort.

"I direct most of my energy," I wrote to my mother, "towards being neither seen nor heard. I hide behind the other cellos and concentrate on bowing in roughly the same direction as them and when necessary, as in the quiet bits, keeping my bow off the strings. The trouble is, most of the music is so difficult that I can barely keep up visually, let alone physically; we sight read Leonora III the other night and I thought I was doing quite nicely till suddenly the rest of the orchestra swept off the final chord—and I had three pages still to go. But I absolutely love it. Not only is it a complete break from normal life but I'm also meeting lots of nice and interesting people. Good old Cath! It was really being so tied to her that made me embark on the cello in the first place."

As a teenager I had been a passenger in a bad car crash and had nursed a neurotic fear of driving ever since. Now, however, being a non-driver was becoming a thorough nuisance. Also, we hardly ever went out in the car as a family nowadays. Getting Cath and her wheelchair in and out of it was such a bore. I could see the time coming when we would have to get a van and it would be ridiculous if I couldn't drive it. Family reaction, when I announced my idea, was mixed. Ted was appalled; it would be far cheaper in the long run if I took taxis and handicabs everywhere, he said. The thought of me driving his car caused him to dive into the fridge before he had even finished his supper. The boys, on the

Nicola using every muscle to push Cath into the van.

other hand, were overjoyed; they would no longer have to suffer the indignity of having the only mother they knew who didn't drive.

I had five lessons and then took what I imagined would be the first of about twenty driving tests. Good, said the tester, very few points lost. I'd passed? The idea of being let loose on the roads with only five hours of driving under my belt, and none of them solo, threw me so badly that for days afterwards I refused to go near the car. Ted was visibly relieved but the boys, like myself, were disgusted.

It was a surprise visit from Chloe that eventually got me going. She, I knew, would appreciate the significance of my achievement. An hour before her plane was due I piled the boys into the car and we crept the four miles out to the airport. She didn't disappoint me. Her amazement and congratulations were all I could have hoped for. Unfortunately, what with the excitement of seeing her and basking in her abundant praise, I got hopelessly lost coming home. Ted, uncharitably imagining the worst, nearly phoned the police.

The following spring we took a deep breath, borrowed from the bank and bought a super Dodge van. Once I had got used to driving such an enormous vehicle and had become less hysterical about the power brakes, steering and lack of gears, it literally changed my life. Ted fixed up an ingenious system of straps to tether Cath's chair firmly, and a friend down the road built a ramp for it. So now I was all set. No more relying on the vagaries of the handicab service, which packed up at four o'clock and had left me stranded more than once. No more wrestling Cath and her chair in and out of the car. No more feeling guilty when I left Ted carless. I was independent, I could take off with all the kids whenever I wanted. It was marvellous.

Ted encouraged me in my outside activities concerning Catherine and always arranged to be at home when I had an evening meeting. He didn't, however, become directly involved, mainly because he just didn't have the time.

Knowing he had worries enough, I tried not to come home from meetings in a temper, but this had been difficult lately. Usually I managed to keep the lid on my feelings by shutting myself in Cath's room to play a few therapeutic scales on my cello, rather than exploding in the sitting room. One evening, however, I came home patently angry. It had been a year since I became a member of CAMR and joined Alice on her community residences committee. Ted asked what was up.

"It's the bigwigs in CAMR," I said. "They're a bigoted bunch of reactionary old fogies and they don't give a bugger about kids like Cath."

"Hm. That's strong stuff. Redundant, however. Reactionary means—"

"Oh, shut up!"

"Sorry, OK." With commendable lack of reluctance Ted put down *Correlation Functions and Spectral Densities*. "Come on," he said. "Let's have it. And let's have a drink, you look terrible."

"Thanks."

When I had met Alice she had told me that as CAMR was supposed to support and represent to the government all mentally retarded people, it was the logical agency within which to work for the needs of our children. Its record in aiding severely handicapped people and their families had to date been abysmal but she was hopeful that this was on the verge of changing.

Once I saw the administrators of CAMR in action, however, I began not only to doubt the validity of this optimism but also to suspect that Alice was being exploited. Here she was, voluntarily masterminding for them the establishment of a community residence for retarded adults, a job for which a professional would be paid a fat salary, yet every time she put up her hand for multiply handicapped children she was slapped down and told she was being difficult. Time and again at meetings I watched her making a calm, intelligent and informed pitch for the multiply handicapped. And time and again the response was a series of vague and pathetic excuses for not acting on her suggestions. The time wasn't yet ripe for providing services for the multiply handicapped; to provide such services would be too difficult, too expensive and show too few results; they must provide improved services for the thousands of mildly retarded people first; the public wasn't yet ready to see multiply handicapped people living in its midst; or, most galling of all,

Alice and Jeanie Rothney.

she must learn to be patient, she must keep working and the time for the multiply handicapped would come.

The introduction of new ideas in any field is often met with resistance rather than acceptance. The perplexing and frustrating thing here, though, was that the basis of all Alice's ideas wasn't new at all. As she said, through the provision of good community services, people like Catherine, rather than being institutionalized, could lead happy, significant and relatively normal lives within the community. The Scandinavian countries had been working along these lines for decades and the trend in the United States and Canada had been similar for several years.

I was constantly amazed at Alice's self-restraint as she faced the CAMR administrators and board members. She herself was a board member, but became unpopular when she showed an irritating tendency to want to *do* things. She was forceful, but she was always polite and dignified, even if people were extraordinarily unpleasant to her at times. But what impressed me most was that she very rarely, if ever, mentioned her own fraught life with Jeanie. She spoke instead in general terms and, when wanting an example, used another family. I was normally quite quiet at meetings but once, when a high-up member of the executive told her it was "unrealistic" to expect funding for a home-help program for people with multiply handicapped children, I found myself asking him if he had any idea what it cost Alice and her family to come to these endless and fruitless meetings. Did he realize that today, for instance, she was functioning on three hours of sleep because she had spent half the night down at the hospital having a gash on Jeanie's head sewn up? And that she had had to call her husband home from the university to look after Jeanie so that she could be here now? Yes, yes, said the bigwig uneasily, we all had those days, didn't we? I learnt later that I had been labelled "emotional."

"So," said Ted when I paused for breath. "What in particular set you off tonight?" He filled our glasses without so much as a glance at his book.

"We had a committee meeting about the second house CAMR is buying to provide 'normal living accommodation for retarded people' and—"

"Hang on. What is the process exactly? Who pays?"

"The committee finds a suitable house," I said, "an ordinary family house in an ordinary neighbourhood, close to buses and stores and churches. It then writes a proposal to CAMR about what alterations are needed, how much they would cost, etc. CAMR then buys the house and the committee organizes the changes, furnishes it, finds staff and suggests inhabitants. The upkeep and *per diem* costs are paid by the government. It pays for everything, really, but through CAMR."

"I see. Carry on with today."

"Well, the CAMR bigwigs promised Alice ages ago that they would ask the government if some of the inhabitants of this next house could be under eighteen. I told you that, remember? It's the assumption we've been working on, what's kept us going. But today they informed us that they're not prepared to do it. This one will be just for adults too. And the next and the next, as far as we can see."

"Why?"

"Because, they say, it's not government policy to fund community residences for people under eighteen. Period."

"Good God! You mean we have to wait for six years before Cath even stands a chance?"

"Apparently. Not that Alice was expecting children as bad as Cath to be let in. She realized everyone would balk at that because of the expense, but she wanted to establish a precedent. To get some kids in, uncomplicated kids who could go to school and be treated pretty normally. But they blocked even that!"

For a while the only sound was my stertorous breathing. "It seems to me," said Ted finally, "that not only does CAMR not represent children like Cath but it doesn't intend to, either. I think that in fairness to the administrators you should realize that they have their work cut out trying to cater to the majority, the mildly and moderately retarded adults. Hang on, don't interrupt. What I mean is, that's what they tell themselves. Probably you and Alice and other people who have children who constitute misfits by not conforming to the criteria laid down by these agencies should break away and start your own organization. Be your own representatives to the government. A government that was, incidentally—" here Ted's own prejudices came into force "—founded on humanitarian socialist principles and hands out money with abandon to criminals and—"

"Yes. You can be honorary advisor then, you lazy bastard."

"Busy bastard."

Alice and I and several other involved parents had in fact been considering this possibility for some time. Alice, foreseeing more clearly than the rest of us how much work it would involve and the amount of resentment we would incur, was reluctant, but the recent community residences blow decided her. Our first action was to make an appointment to see the Minister of Health. We wanted to inform him of our predicament and to discover what plans his department had for children like ours and their families.

It was an astonishing meeting. The Minister apparently had no idea that there were people as badly handicapped as Jeanie and Cath living at home. He thought they were all in institutions. So much for CAMR's ability to represent us! At one point he turned to a senior civil servant and asked him what assistance the department gave families like ours. That gentleman went very red and after a lengthy silence muttered something about foster homes. Alice and I stared at him. He made some uncomfortable noises in his throat and the Minister tactfully changed the subject.

The Minister was sympathetic but bewildered. The upshot of the interview was that he asked us, which meant Alice, to write a brief describing the total situation in Manitoba regarding the lack of adequate community services for multiply handicapped people and the reasons for this lack. It seemed odd that he didn't consider it the responsibility of his department to do this but, as Alice commented afterwards, at least this way a true and complete picture would be presented.

As I have already indicated, Alice and I were by no means the only parents in Winnipeg fed up with the paucity of services for their children and themselves. There were at least sixty families in and around the city who had a severely handicapped—and handicapping—child. Many more had already had to institutionalize their children and were desperate to get them back into the community. The nucleus of our new organization, however, comprised just four of us at first: Alice and myself and two other mothers who had been very active on the community residences committee—Gwen, a widow whose youngest child Stevie had Down's syndrome and cerebral palsy, and Helen, whose daughter Diana was a severe epileptic like Jeanie, though not as retarded. They were both at their wits' ends for a place where their children could be cared for when necessary. "I'm longing to have a nervous breakdown," as Gwen put it, "but I keep having to postpone it because what would happen to Stevie?"

In the area of daytime programs for our children, Alice and I were one step better off than Gwen and Helen. Cath and Jeanie had their four hours a day in the new program for multiply handicapped children. Diana had a mere two hours each day in a school for the retarded, and Stevie was still at home twenty-four hours a day because Gwen lived four miles outside the boundary of metropolitan Winnipeg. Her school district refused to pay for him to go to the program, though there was a place for him there and it was where he should have been.

Alice dug herself into writing the brief and we decided that if we were to represent a large number of people we should dignify ourselves with a name. Action for the Dependent Handicapped (ADH) was really only a tentative title but before we had a chance to improve on it we received some unexpected publicity and it became permanent. At the end of October I noticed that the Manitoba Theatre Centre was soon to present *A Day in the Death of Joe Egg,* by Peter Nichols. I knew it was a tragicomedy, drawn partly from personal experience, about a young couple with a retarded spastic child. I borrowed a copy of it from my friend Irene and sat down at once to read it.

Never have I reacted so empathetically to a piece of writing as I did to that play. Chunks of it were so familiar that I felt Peter Nichols must have sneaked into our lives on occasion and taken notes. I sat engrossed, one minute close to tears and the next howling with laughter at his black-streaked humour. My immediate reaction on finishing it was to place a phone call to him in England to thank him for having written it. Realizing the impracticality of this I called Edward Gilbert, the director of the Winnipeg production, instead. My original idea was that my experiences with a child not too dissimilar to Joe might somehow be useful, but within days this had snowballed into almost unmanageable proportions.

As soon as Eddie and I had replaced our receivers he came round to see me. We had a lively discussion about the play, Catherine and related topics, and together we concocted a plan that we hoped would benefit both of us. I was beginning to see that the play could be an excellent vehicle for telling theatregoers that helpless Joe Eggs and their unhelped families were not just a figment of a playwright's imagination, they existed right here in Winnipeg. Perhaps a note to this effect could be put at the end of the program? Or would that be taking too much of a liberty? I almost wished I hadn't spoken but Eddie pounced on the idea. He loved the play but was apprehensive about its reception in Winnipeg, fearing that the subject matter and some of the "controversial" scenes might raise criticism. If the play was somehow extended into real life, putting it on would be validated. Nobody could then accuse him of presenting it for shock value. He suggested that I write an information sheet describing the local situation and explaining why Action for the Dependent Handicapped had come into existence. He then offered to have it printed at the theatre so that I could hand it out to people after the play. This would be at once less intrusive and more personal than having it in the program notes. He also suggested that I meet the actress who was playing the role of Joe Egg's mother, Pat Galloway.

He started to tell me about Miss Galloway's reputation as one of Canada's most distinguished actresses but I needed little telling. I had admired her in both serious and comic roles at the Manitoba Theatre Centre and had often heard her on the radio. For years, too, I had been reading reviews of her fine performances at the Stratford Festival in Ontario.

I was nervous about meeting her. I tidied up the house and Catherine and wondered whether to make tea or coffee. I filled the kettle and blew the dust off the company teacups and jumped every time I heard a car.

"Miss Galloway?"

"Mrs. Schaefer. I'm so pleased to meet you."

It was odd to hear that husky voice, so familiar, on my doorstep. I was even more nervous.

"I'm so pleased to meet *you*, do come in. Let me take your coat. Isn't it a vile day? It's so good of you to come; you must be awfully busy. Would you like some coffee?" Jabber, jabber.

"That would be very nice—"

"Or tea? I can make tea if you'd rather—"

"I really don't mind, either would be lovely—"

"Well, perhaps you'd like to get warm by the fire while I pop a kettle on?"

Halfway to the kitchen I stopped. "Miss Galloway," I said slowly, "would you by any chance like something a little stronger?"

She hesitated just long enough to be polite and a short while later we were curled up in front of the fire with drinks and chattering away as if we'd been buddies for years. Cath lay on the floor between us and looked at Pat cautiously through the fingers of her left hand. After a while she started to pull a vivid silk scarf from Pat's pocket.

"She likes you," I said. "She only pinches things from people she likes."

"I like her too. She's got a nice, funny character—haven't you Catherine? I say, she's got it all out now. Clever girl!" She bent over and hugged Catherine, who cooed happily. "You know," she said turning to me, "I was petrified of meeting her—a real live Joe Egg—God! And you—what would you think of me acting your role, so to speak. But now I'm so glad Eddie suggested it. Gosh, she really likes that scarf, doesn't she? Bit naughty of you to train her to be a pickpocket, isn't it?"

"Got to find some use for her."

"Nicola! You're as bad as me and Bri in the play."

"It's essential," I said. "Part of the survival kit."

During the few remaining days before the play opened I phoned everyone I could think of—friends, students who had worked in Alice's program, volunteer organizations—and made up a list of people willing to hand out information sheets after each performance. There were four exits to be covered so I needed three people plus myself every night and four for matinees when I couldn't make it. The play was to run for three weeks, so it was a long list.

Together with a number of friends, a gang of us from Action for the Dependent Handicapped (ADH) went to the dress rehearsal. I had become curiously protective about the play and felt sudden panic before the curtain went up. I felt sure that Pat's performance would be right, but what about the others? How would the girl acting Joe be? I knew that Eddie and the cast had been out to St. Amant and seen children like Joe but it was bound to be tricky all the same. How would such-and-such a scene be handled? Would this be like seeing a favourite book done all wrong in the film?

I needn't have worried. Everything about the production was superb, with riveting performances from everyone. Watching the play come to life was an unexpectedly moving experience. I found it magnified and intensified all the emotions I had felt when reading it. Gwen nudged me at one point and said she kept thinking it was me up there, and I realized it was because Pat was incorporating into her performance many of my automatic gestures—the way I played with Cath's hands, touched her, looked at her. Even *I* thought she was me at moments.

It was a hectic but stimulating three weeks. I must have driven at least three hundred miles, picking up volunteers and going back and forth from the theatre. At first I found it embarrassing to wave a sheet in front of people as they approached the exit, especially as they were often in a state of shock after the play. But when I realized the interest that was being aroused I found it easier and became more assertive. Every night a number of the audience stayed behind to talk about the play and its significance. The other four adults in the cast, whom I got to know over post-performance drinks with Pat, were very enthusiastic about what was going on, as were the theatre staff. They churned out thousands of information sheets and helped in every way possible. Eddie was delighted to see that the theatre was not merely putting on a good play but was, as one critic put it, "using its power to move out into the community to support a worthy cause."

A day or two after the opening the news media latched on to the stir the play was causing and the CBC called me down to do an early morning interview on the radio. Ted and the boys, praying that I would be wider awake and more coherent than I usually am at that time of day, listened over their breakfast.

It was a phone-in program and as soon as the switchboard was opened all the lines lit up. Most of the calls were sympathetic and friendly but the voice of one woman caller rings in my ears to this day. She accused me of being smug because I hadn't institutionalized Cath. I shook my head and looked at the interviewer in alarm. I didn't think I'd been anything of the sort, and I most certainly didn't feel smug. She gestured that she agreed with me and cut into the caller's angry tirade. I had, she pointed out, specifically stated that I was thankful to have been able to keep Cath at home so far; maybe I had been misinterpreted. It transpired that the caller had a child in the big institution, about which I had admittedly been less than enthusiastic, and that the child was happy and contented there. I said, sincerely, that I was very glad, and she rang off.

The incident was a lesson to me. All parents, including myself of course, are defensive regarding the awful decision about whether to keep or institutionalize a handicapped child. I didn't realize at the time that many people who do take the latter course are faced with the accusation, sometimes veiled but often viciously explicit, that they don't love their child. Since then I have made a particular point of saying how fortunate we've been in having been able to avoid institutionalizing Cath. If we ever did have to, I hope we might be regarded with understanding and sympathy.

The day after the interview a producer from the CBC asked if the TV people could make a documentary about our life with Catherine. Since my original idea in this whole enterprise had been to inform the public about, and create an interest in, the sorry state of all multiply handicapped people in Manitoba, I wasn't particularly pleased that everything was now focussing on me. However, I was told that this was the most effective way to get the point across. Alice and Gwen and everyone else interested in ADH encouraged me to go ahead, so for the next three days the house was an obstacle course of wires, tripods, blinding lights and cheerfully cursing technicians. The resulting twenty-minute film was shown soon afterwards on a local public affairs program. Once I had overcome the discomfort of seeing myself, I watched it as objectively as possible and thought it was extremely well done. Most of it was me talking, or Dominic and Benjy and myself doing things with Cath; I was determined that the boys should be included. Interspersed at relevant points were short clips from the play, shots of Cath and the other children in their new school program and me dishing out my propaganda at the theatre.

One person noticeably absent from the film was Ted. He supported my involvement, as he did my Joe Egg activities, but refused to appear himself.

"You go ahead and make a public spectacle of yourself if you think it'll do any good," he said lightly, "but count me out." I stuck my tongue out at him but understood his reaction. He is an intensely shy and private person and had never really coped with Cath's conspicuousness on our street, let alone further afield. The idea of appearing in people's sitting rooms with her made him feel quite ill. I had doubts myself about subjecting us to the public, and vice versa, but felt it was worth it.

The immediate result of the program was that the phone didn't stop ringing for three days. Several women called to say that they either had, or knew of, a child like Cath who was getting no help from anyone. I was appalled at some of the stories I heard of the run-arounds people had been given by doctors and other professionals, although I was able to direct one or two of them to suitable agencies they didn't know about. Some people called to offer money to ADH but since we were still so new, and were not a registered charitable organization, all I could do was take names for future reference. And many people simply wanted to get more information and to offer general support.

Later in the year the CBC made the film longer and more significant by juxtaposing the happy scenes of Cath at home with horror shots of children like her living in the big institution. This version was shown right across Canada at least twice. To this day strangers approach me to say how deeply affected they were when they saw it and to ask whether the government has done anything about the situation.

I hadn't planned to take Dominic and Benjy to the play because I thought it might be too strong for them. Pat and other cast members were often over at our house, however, usually for lunch followed by merry, if chaotic, carol-singing sessions initiated by Pat. The boys became increasingly curious to see what everyone did in the play, particularly since we were constantly talking about it. So I took them and was glad I had; they took most of it in their stride and said they enjoyed it far more than children's plays they had seen.

I was exhausted by the end of the run but in a pleasant way. I felt I had been able, with many people's help and encouragement, to make a contribution towards opening the public's eye to the plight of multiply handicapped people and their families. En route I had made many new friends, both for myself and for ADH, and I had enjoyed myself immensely.

13

The greatest joy in Cath's life these days was eating, and one of my great joys was observing and encouraging it. Gone was the time when she only became excited at mealtimes; now she started grinning and reaching out eagerly with that left arm whenever she saw anyone eating or drinking, or even chewing, and we all delighted in giving her bits of whatever we were having. As a result she was becoming, in her

Cath enjoying an apple. MICHAELIN MCDERMOTT PHOTO

own way, as bad a nibbler as the rest of us. The very suggestion of food turned her on. I found it impossible, for instance, to peel an apple, crack a nut or just open the fridge door without hearing a hopeful chirrup behind me and, when I was within reach, being tugged at. Probably one of the oddest thrills of my life was the day one of the teachers at school phoned to say that Cath had stolen a candy from Jeanie. Apparently Cath had been lying on her stomach on a wedge and Jeanie had dropped a chocolate on the floor as she walked past. Before she could retrieve it, Cath had shot her arm out, picked it up and popped it into her mouth.

If I put food on her tray she could get it into her mouth quite successfully with her left hand but I had to be careful. She tended literally to bite off more than she could chew. Several times recently I had had to stick my finger down her throat and hook up a large lump of food. It seemed impossible to restrain her from cramming in too much so I tried, by moving her lower jaw up and down and saying "Chew!" to instill the idea of adequate mastication. She was slowly getting the hang of it, although she plainly thought I was daft.

All this eating was, of course, causing a great increase in her size. I was lying on the floor beside her one evening and when Ted unravelled her he said there were only inches between us in height. I'm 5'5". She was at last beginning to look well-covered, too, and in addition was blossoming into womanhood. "She's better endowed than you already," pronounced Ted, "but there is usually an inverse correlation between the size of brains and the size of boobs. Usually," he repeated glancing dubiously in my direction. I happened at that moment to be standing on one leg like a bird, staring at the wall in a yoga position I had just learnt.

I could no longer lift her over my shoulder but managed to move her around quite well by holding her under her arms and knees, cradle fashion. Then one day I bent down to pick her up and got stuck there. I knew there must be a trick to lifting Cath's eighty pounds without crippling myself so I phoned around and a girl from the Arthritic Society came to show me the correct method. It was very simple and I should have thought of it myself. Rather than bending over and heaving, with barely bent knees, this method involved squatting down, back straight, knees bent out, as close to Cath as possible, grabbing her and then slowly rising, keeping my back almost straight and using my legs to produce the power. Once my legs had accommodated themselves I was delighted with this new lift. As well as no longer having back trouble I was able confidently, as opposed to hopefully, to assure people that I could still lift Catherine. She could increase her size by another twenty pounds or so before it would bother me.

At Christmas I was very glad of my new lifting technique because I suddenly had to move her around much more than usual—from her bed to the floor and back about ten times a day. She was very ill indeed with pneumonia and the doctor said it was essential to get the mucus out of her lungs or she would have to be hospitalized. Clearing her lungs meant tipping her, head down, and then turning her from side to side and thumping her back so that the mucus drained into her throat. I knew there were tilting beds and tables for doing this at the hospital but I was anxious to keep her at home. I improvised by lying her on the short ramp leading from the kitchen down to her room.

It worked, but it was a miserable and exhausting experience for both of us. When she eventually got better I enquired about getting a hospital bed for her. After trying all the obvious agencies, a neighbour told me about a government-run pool of home-care equipment. I soon acquired, on permanent loan, not only an excellent and attractive bed that could be wound up and down in all directions but also an electric suction machine in case Cath ever choked on the stuff I pounded out of her. Luckily I've never had to use the machine but the bed has been indispensable. It's a great help when Cath's chest gets congested or when I have to feed her in bed. It also serves to entertain her when she's bored. "Cath's whining," one of the boys will say. "Shall I wind her up and down?" And at once she's shaking with laughter as she feels herself mysteriously undulating.

One of the most rewarding aspects of having met so many people with multiply handicapped children was that I now had others with whom I could share my worries and frustrations and, conversely, my laughs and joys. We could also exchange useful information; whenever I received help the first thing I did was to contact anyone else who might benefit from the same source. So as soon as the men had staggered in with Cath's bed I called Tom, whose daughter, I knew, could do with a bed like ours.

I had met Tom a short while before and I still shudder with embarrassment when I recall our meeting.

Normally I'm as aware as most that only a small number of severely physically disabled people like Cath are also very retarded, and I act accordingly. But one day while pushing Catherine in her wheelchair in the park I saw coming towards me a man also pushing a wheelchair. Sitting in it was a girl who looked so similar to Cath that I thought I must be imagining it—same size, same fair hair in pigtails, same spastic movements, even the same shoeless feet. The man, presumably the girl's father, and I smiled tentatively as we approached each other and stopped when we met, exchanging some weather pleasantries. Then the man turned to Catherine.

"Hi," he said.

"She can't talk," I said. "She's very retarded. She likes the attention though, so you needn't stop talking to her." Then I looked at his daughter. "Hello," I greeted her. "It's nice to be out for a walk, isn't it?" and then, turning to her father again I said, "Does she enjoy being out like this?"

"Sure she does, don't you Vicky?"

The girl's face contorted, her arms jerked and she said with almost perfect clarity, "Thanks for asking. Yes." She threw back her head and jerked her arms as she took another breath. "It's much better than sitting around watching the idiot box." She giggled and took another breath. "What's your daughter's name?"

I was quick to catch the ball but my humiliation was awful. Luckily no irreversible damage was done and Vicky and her family have been good friends of ours ever since that day.

Tom became an active member of ADH shortly after we met. Unlike the rest of us, he and his wife had had more dealings with the Society for Crippled Children than with CAMR. Vicky's mentality was normal but she was academically backward because of visual and other physical impediments. For years they had gone through the same sort of embittering experiences as we had. This included working hard on committees and never getting what they needed for their own child, and being unable to find anywhere for Vicky to live when the family needed a break. They had been told that a place could be found for her in the big institution if they declared Vicky to be mentally retarded. "We were overwhelmed with the generosity of the offer," said Tom.

Tom was a great asset to our group; he produced good ideas, was forceful and eloquent and had a wry humour which saw us through many grim moments in the months ahead. One of his first suggestions for making ADH more widely known was to have T-shirts made for all the kids, with the initials of Free Us Crippled Kids stamped on the front. We rejected the idea only with great reluctance. Above all, Tom was a man, and his joining us made it harder for bigwig civil servants to imply that we were a group of hysterical women, to be kept at bay with compliments, pats on the head and promises.

In January, 1974, the CBC national network started a fortnightly TV program called *Ombudsman*. The Ombudsman, a Montreal lawyer, presented and tried to remedy cases in which the bureaucracy was preventing Canadians from obtaining their legal or moral rights. One night at *Joe Egg* I had handed an information sheet to a girl who was working in the research department for this program. She later asked me if ADH's problems could be aired on one of the first programs. Alice felt it would be unfair to attack the government on general issues before it had had a chance to respond to the brief she was writing, so we decided instead to give prominence to an individual case—that of Gwen's fourteen-year-old son Stevie, whose school division was refusing to pay for him to attend the special class.

The case was presented to the viewers and then the Ombudsman questioned the provincial Minister of Education who had been flown to Montreal to be in the hot seat. The Minister was, to put it charitably, vague. It seemed the government had discovered a loophole in the Schools Act. Because the multiply handicapped program was a pilot project it wasn't covered. He did, however, say he would look into the situation. From then on pressure was put on him to do so. Gwen herself knocked on doors; her social worker prodded CAMR to prod the government; her MLA asked questions in the House; Alice raised the subject at school board meetings; and finally, the superintendent of Gwen's school division was questioned and prodded. But he stoutly refused to have anything to do with asking the division to pay for Stevie's education. I wouldn't have believed this had I not been at the meeting where he made his announcement.

He won the day. Stevie never did get into the program. Indirectly, however, the publicity created by the *Ombudsman* program did help. In August, a year after Stevie had been offered a place in the multiply handicapped program, he was admitted to a day program run at St. Amant where he made good progress. He was over the age limit but was admitted because he was small for his age and easy to handle.

Catherine was by now clearly profiting from her program. Going out each day and being exposed to new people and new ideas was encouraging her to become far more sociable and aware of life. Her whining-from-boredom rate at home had dropped. She was getting more physiotherapy than I gave her and was taken swimming once a week, which of course she loved. The principal of the school in which the program was based had never had anything to do with wonky kids and admitted that when they first moved in he had been anxious. Now he was adapting himself to the situation well and was encouraging his own young pupils to mix with our children. When I dropped in one day I was pleased to see a girl of about Dominic's age throwing a ball to Cath in her wheelchair and trying to show her how to throw it back.

This is how it ought to be, I thought. Our kids should be in a program suited to their level of mentality and physical ability but at the same time surrounded by normality. Society should adapt itself to them rather than exclude them because they couldn't adapt to normality. I thought again of all those miserable Cath-like people stuck out in the institution and wondered how long it would be before programs and residences would be set up so that they could escape their incarceration and have a chance at living more normal lives in their own communities. A group of parents in Winnipeg were working on this but were impeded at every turn by the government.

Alice spent the winter writing the brief. It was sixty pages long, but considering the ground it covered it was short. As I typed it out, piece by piece, my admiration for her doubled. It was well-constructed, clear, log-

Cath and Diana (Helen's daughter).

ical, well-documented and packed with constructive criticism and ideas aimed at bettering the lot of all retarded people, particularly the multiply handicapped. Had a government-hired consultant written it, s/he would have been paid a minimum of five thousand dollars. This is not my opinion but that of people who have been commissioned to write similar reports.

While Alice was working on the brief, the rest of us in ADH prepared as an adjunct to it a folder of profiles of a variety of dependent handicapped people. When the brief was read by the uninitiated, it could then be understood at once what sorts of people we were talking about. The format was simple and striking: a photographic portrait, beautifully done by Tom, set beside a three- or four-paragraph description of the child, the family, the services they were receiving and those they needed. The final paragraph was a summary, and even a casual reader of the profiles could hardly fail to notice that the same three needs cropped up in each summary: practical support for the family, year-round stimulating developmental programs for the children and, last but not least, short-term care for them, and ultimately permanent care, in a community residence.

The government had been playing musical ministries lately and there was now a new Minister of Health. This man had a reputation both for humanity and intelligence, and he was also known for getting things done. We were hopeful that he would support us. On March 14th, 1974, a delegation of ten ADH members and involved friends presented him with copies of the brief and the profiles. He was civil and sympathetic when Alice explained who and what we were and he promised to read the brief carefully and to be in touch with us. An interesting point emerged during the meeting. As an example of the discrimination practiced against multiply handicapped dependent people, Gwen told him about the trouble she was having getting Stevie into school. He was amazed. He had, he said, written the legislation for the new Schools Act himself when, a short while ago, he had been Minister of Education. He thought it had been written so that no school division could possibly wriggle out of its responsibility for paying for any child's education.

We all felt positive towards the Minister and emerged from the Legislative Building cheerful and optimistic. We had left copies of the brief in the offices of several other ministers and senior civil servants. The government would now no longer be able to profess ignorance of ADH's concerns.

As we crossed the grounds Helen pointed to one of Winnipeg's newest and most renowned buildings, the public convenience in Memorial Park. The controversy surrounding the planning and erection of this edifice had been of gargantuan proportions. The last straw for the anti-convenience faction had been at Christmas when the facility had been mysteriously locked up during the Santa Claus parade when thousands of shivering children and their parents had hoped to use it.

"If $100,000 of taxpayers' money can be spent on that," said Helen, "just think what our super socialist government might spend on multiply handicapped children!"

"Hang on there, Helen," said Tom. "You must remember that politicians are full of more than just compassion."

In the fall my nephew, Richard, dropped in on a hitchhiking trip across North America. Not only was he delightful to have around, he was also very useful, especially with Catherine. When he saw the rutted, squidgy mess between the sidewalk and the road he flexed his muscles and said he'd lay a flagstone path. He did a very professional job, which included a good deal of loud construction-site language, to the glee of the boys and their friends. I was glad to dispense with my precarious arrangement of stones and strips of plywood.

Catherine loved Richard, partly because he treated her with friendly roughness and partly because he was very noisy—a perfect combination, in her view. So vigorous were his gestures and so loud his sound effects that she often got the giggles just by watching him telling me a story. "Oh, belt up Cath," he would say. "It's not that bleedin' funny," and he would whizz her around in her chair or on the floor until she was helpless with laughter. Not one to make light of physical exertion, he pleased her enormously by producing histrionic moans and exclamations when he lifted her from her chair or carried her more than three feet. Once he nearly dropped her and she laughed so hard that she choked. "You're a bleedin' nuisance, you are," he said fiercely when, thereafter, he had to pretend to do it again. "OK, here we go—Gor!" She followed him with adoring eyes whenever he was in sight and looked puzzled if he neglected to shout "Hello pest!" and give her a few fake punches in passing.

He added a permanent new dimension to her life by giving her a pair of headphones. She had always loved and responded to music but hated having anything on her head, so we wondered which feeling would win. We wired her up and she started to tug crossly at the headphones but the moment the record started her hand dropped and a look of amazement filled her face. She froze for a few seconds, then looked at us with big eyes, smiled absently, and the next moment retired into a world of private joy which made her grin, chuckle, drool and nod her head while flapping and jerking her limbs. Her whole demeanour, plus the apparatus on her head, suggested that she was undergoing some form of pleasant and prolonged electric shock treatment. Since then, listening to music through the headphones has been a source of endless amusement for her. We've weeded out the records she likes best and as she listens she bangs an arm or a leg in rough time and makes humming-cum-droning noises as if trying to sing along. I'm sure there must be a way of teaching her something through this form of entertainment. Maybe someone will come up with an idea some day.

In my perennial desire to lead as normal a life as possible despite Catherine I had rarely been thwarted. Camping, however, which the boys had almost given up plaguing us about, had so far defeated me. Actually this was due more to Ted than to Cath; he thought camping was most abnormal and the word had only to be mentioned for him to launch into his "mosquitos, black flies, bears, smelly cans, fishing, transistors, not even the privacy of a cabin, oh God, the tedium of it all" speech. Now that I had the van, however, I figured I could take all the children by myself if I had to. The first time this wasn't necessary. I had persuaded Richard that a long weekend in the wilds of Ontario would be the perfect way to round off his sojourn with us.

Our first night was so disastrous that had my stubborn pride not been at stake we would have returned home the next morning. No serious problems arose until bedtime. We had survived the hot, hundred-mile drive on the highway. We had found our way, despite the absence of a vital signpost, down apparently interminable dirt tracks to the small secluded campsite. There, by prearrangement, we had met Harold and Ann Lugsdin and their children and set up camp together. We had had a terrific supper and were now on our fourth bottle of wine around the campfire and thinking deliciously in terms of sleep. The pyjama'd figures of the five children flitted screaming, shushing and giggling between the trees. "Bed, kids," we said unconvincingly whenever they appeared in twos and threes to do one more marshmallow. "Bedtime now." But they vanished into the black again before we could nab them. Eventually, when we heard bears rooting around in the garbage cans at the other end of the site, they allowed themselves to be posted into their tents. Richard tucked down in his sleeping bag by the remains of the fire and the boys crawled into their tent. Harold and Ann called goodnight from their camper and Cath and I prepared to settle in the back of the van.

It was pitch dark so I switched on the flashlight, cleverly hooked up inside by Richard. I heaved Cath from her chair and threw her into the disorganized heap of blankets and clothes. Panting, I then hoisted in a bucket of hot water and shut the door quickly behind me. But not quickly enough; a million mosquitos and black flies had spotted the light and rushed in. I knew they would drive us mad so, before I attempted to undress and wash Cath, I swatted for half an hour. Then, dizzy with tiredness, I crawled around trying to bring some semblance of order to our sleeping arrangements. As I tugged a blanket from beneath Cath I felt a tiny stab in my finger.

"Harold?" I hissed a minute later at the Lugsdins' camper, "Harold!" He unzipped just far enough to poke his head out.

"What is it, dear?"

"Harold, I'm frightfully sorry—goodness you do look funny—but have you got a pair of wire cutters?" He blinked, and I held up my right hand.

"Oh, my *God* Nix—"

"I know, I'm sorry. It got worse as I tried to untangle myself."

Soon everyone had seeped out of their tents to see what was up. Once it was established that I wasn't in agony, peals of muffled laughter rang out on all sides. The thumb and middle finger of my right hand were caught together with two parts of a three-pronged fish hook and from the hook dangled a six-inch painted tin fish. Between us we had every possible piece of camping equipment, including axes and saws, but wire cutters we didn't have, so I couldn't even undo myself enough to drive.

Harold and Ann both offered to drive me, but Harold won the argument and took me forty miles to the hospital in Kenora. It was all very, very humiliating.

Cath was still awake when, at 1:30, we returned. Once I had changed her and given her a drink she seemed to think a new day had started. After slaughtering another batch of insects and checking my net and masking-tape arrangement over the windows I collapsed beside her, and despite being kicked and bashed and hooted at enthusiastically I fell into a deep sleep.

The next thing I knew I was sitting bolt upright and staring at an awful face six inches from mine. For a moment I thought it was my reflection in the window, but it was Richard, urgently demanding entry. Bears, he said trembling as he clambered in, bleedin' great bears crawling all over the Lugsdins' car, into which he had sneaked because he awoke chilly at 3 a.m. I told him crossly that it was his imagination, that bears only go for food, not people, and that I knew we had cleared up all the food. Bears, he insisted loudly, bleedin' great black things with little red eyes, and he wasn't going out there again. He had just draped himself across the seat when there was a tap at the door. It was Dominic and Benjy. They had been awoken by bears, they said, and they weren't staying in the tent. It wasn't bears, I said, it was Richard. But they wouldn't budge. So now we were five in the van.

"And then they all had to get out to pee," I reported to the Lugsdins the next morning, "and made such a fuss they woke Cath up again."

"It was bears though," said Ann. "Look!" She could hardly speak for laughing. "You took it all the way to Kenora and back! It must have driven the bears mad trying to get it—" I looked at the top of the car. Wedged into the luggage rack was a plastic dish containing the remains of Cath's supper.

I spent half that day asleep, but after that the holiday was a great success, though I must admit I don't think Cath thought much of it. She inevitably spent much of the time on the floor in the van or being shaken up in her wheelchair as we hauled her from place to place over the rough ground. She did enjoy it when I took her into the lake. It was shallow and warm and she lay elegantly on Dominic's blow-up canoe and laughed as we bounced her around and splashed her. But it was such an effort hauling her in and out that once a day was my limit.

I couldn't stand the thought of Ted hearing about the fish hook incident so everyone was sworn to silence. And nobody, not even the smallest Lugsdin, normally an irrepressible chatterbox, ever told.

Some weeks later Ted was sitting at the dining-room table dealing with the monthly bills. Cath lay at his feet and was trying to pull the sandal off one of them.

"You think that's funny Cath," he said. "I think this is."

"What?" I asked casually.

"I've just written out a cheque to the Ontario government."

"What on earth for?"

"For the removal of two fish hooks from Mrs. Nicola Schaefer." He turned to me with a broad grin. "Out-of-province patients are billed directly," he said, "and they addressed it to me. You didn't think of that, did you?"

14

The Minister of Health was impressed with Alice's brief and disturbed by its contents. In May he demonstrated his faith in her abilities by appointing her to the board of the Health Sciences Centre. He then asked ADH to write a proposal for "the development of a community-based training and residence program for dependent handicapped youth."

Alice had stressed in the brief that community programs for the dependent handicapped should be the responsibility not just of the Department of Health but also of Education and to a lesser extent Recreation. We had wondered how the Minister would respond to this and were pleased when he told us that the brief was shortly to be discussed by a sub-committee of Cabinet known as HESP. These letters stood for Health, Education and Social Planning; the committee comprised the relevant ministers and other civil servants. He put us in touch with the man who prepared the agenda for HESP weekly meetings, Daniel Goodman.

Daniel had been a civil servant for many years but unlike most of that breed he was bright, progressive and open. He delighted us by the interest he showed towards both us as an action group and the new ideas contained in the brief. He, in conjunction with his assistants, soon became one of our chief champions.

While awaiting the Minister's response to the brief, we had acquired official status by incorporating ourselves and had also had over a hundred copies of the brief printed. They were in hot demand and we were distributing them to doctors, therapists, teachers, social workers, friendly politicians and other interested people. Now, however, the real work was to begin and one of our problems was money. Since our formation six months ago we had dug from our own pockets well over a thousand dollars to cover expenses such as stationery, printing, travelling and, costliest of all, sitters for our children while we were at meetings and, in Alice's case, writing. These expenses were unlikely to diminish and when we explained the situation to Daniel he advised us to apply to HESP for a grant. This we did, and thanks largely to his prodding HESP members, we heard at the end of May that the grant had been approved.

Immediately upon receiving the Minister's request for a proposal, Alice and the rest of us started discussing and planning. Then we pooled our ideas with those from a number of professional people who were anxious to help us. These included a man who had helped organize and run a developmental centre for multiply handicapped children in British Columbia, a church minister with knowledge of how community residences for the multiply handicapped were run in the States, and a professor of architecture who had designed facilities for handicapped children in Australia and England. The outcome was a plan for what we soon started to think of and refer to as the Centre.

We saw the Centre as a uniquely designed one-story structure that would supply year-round developmental daytime programs for about forty people like Cath and Jeanie. It would also provide temporary residential care and recreational facilities for hundreds of other disabled people. Everything would be geared towards supplying the students with stimulating surroundings and stimulating activities, the twin aims of which would be to increase their knowledge of themselves and the world, and to help them step by step towards their full capabilities.

Parents and family would be welcome at any time at the Centre and would be encouraged to regard themselves as fully qualified members of the team that was planning and implementing developmental objectives for their child. They would never, as happens in even the best institutions, feel they had lost control over the child's destiny.

The hub of the Centre would be an indoor swimming pool and garden, roofed with glass to utilize the light and the heat of the sun, and surrounded on three sides by classrooms, medical treatment and therapy rooms, kitchens, a multi-purpose gym, a cafeteria, offices and so on. The fourth side, which would get most of the day's sun, would open onto a playground and garden area.

Branching out behind this hub, either attached or close by, would be three self-contained home-like units, each containing six beds, where children could live and be cared for on a short-term basis. Twelve beds would be for scheduled use, such as planned holidays, and six for emergency use. Accommodation would be available for parents who wanted to spend a night there settling in their child. Although one of the most important functions of the Centre would be to enable people to keep their handicapped child at home, we knew that even if it sprang up overnight there were some families who would want their child cared for permanently elsewhere. Knowing we might be accused of planning a "mini-institution" if we provided beds for such people within the Centre, we would convert one or two ordinary houses close by into community residences concurrently with the building of the Centre.

Our Centre would be designed to be highly functional both for the people it served and for the staff. Equally important, it would be visually attractive, inside and out, and situated in pleasant, easily accessible surroundings. The reason for this was that we wanted to get away from the idea that the severely handicapped couldn't appreciate and didn't deserve nice surroundings. We would hardly achieve that if we set up shop in a warehouse down by the railroad tracks, as one bright civil servant had suggested. Our underlying reason, however, was even more revolutionary.

As I've already indicated, the trend in North America and Europe during the last few years has been towards helping physically and mentally handicapped people to lead as normal a life as possible. But there are many people like Cath who, even if they do well by their own standards, will always be totally dependent on others for all their needs and will never be able to adapt to normal living. The terms "normalization" and "integration," so popular with sociologists, cannot be applied to them in the same way as to other handicapped people. They are not realistic objectives, however desirable they might be.

So rather than make futile and expensive attempts to fit multiply handicapped dependent people into the community, which is what is usually done now, we should try to do the reverse. We would create an ideal environment for them in the Centre so that we could then say to the community, "Look everyone, we've got something terrific going on here! Come and join in!" We wanted to make it such an attractive and exciting place that people would want to work there, want to help there, want to be part of it. The more aesthetically appealing it was, the more likely it was that people would respond.

This then was our basic idea; to build for our society's most handicapped and least privileged members an innovative Centre where we could show that giving them the highest quality teaching, training and care was not just the most humane but also the most successful and, in the long run, the most profitable way of providing for them.

"You ought to buy Cath a bra, Mum. I can't wait to see Pat's farm. Hey, look at my blood blister! Want to play a duet?"

It was very hot. I happened at that moment to be thinking that if we had our Centre Cath might be enjoying a swim instead of lying listlessly on the lawn. She lay there without even the energy to play with the balloons I had strung over her between the lilac bush and her wheelchair. My mind slowly focussed on Dominic's flow of non sequiturs.

"You're right," I said. "I'll get her a bra. Now listen, don't get too excited about the farm because I'm not sure about driving all that way. Yes, that's a super blister. No, don't pop it. OK, let's do 'Greensleeves.' Phew!" He had been taking piano lessons with Ann Lugsdin since our return from England.

This holiday idea had started when Pat Galloway was in Winnipeg playing in *A Day in the Death of Joe Egg*. We had become fast friends and she had invited us all to stay with her economist husband, herself and their menagerie of friends and animals on their farm near Stratford, Ontario, where she had been based for years. I said I didn't know about Ted because he was planning to remain in his lab for the whole summer to catch up on his research. The children and I, however, would certainly come. There had been a number of empty bottles around when this invitation was issued and accepted. It was only when Pat had phoned to see when we were coming and I had said gaily "in a month or so" that I started seriously to think about the trip.

I decided that since Toronto was so close to Stratford we would first go there and stay with Mia while looking up other friends and relatives nearby. Then we would drop in on Ted's sister Irma and her family in St. Catharines. It was ages since we had seen them all. And Alice had told me about a developmental centre for multiply handicapped children close by so I thought I would see that too. Then we would go to stay with Pat. I thought it all sounded great fun and very sensible.

Ted thought it sounded insane.

"What are you trying to prove?" he said.

"Nothing, for heaven's sake." I was indignant. "I admit I was trying to prove something that time we went camping but now I simply want to go on a holiday and there's no reason why I shouldn't. I also admit it would be easier without Catherine but as you very well know there's nowhere I can leave her. But with the van it'll be easy, particularly since the boys are really useful now. And I've got a mattress for Cath to lie on in the back when she gets tired of sitting."

When he realized I was adamant he sighed. "Do you honestly think you can cope?"

"Yes."

"What makes you so sure?"

"Sixth sense," I said blithely. I was getting crosser.

"Sixth sense!" He strode into the kitchen. "I wish to God you'd use your other five occasionally! I'll bet you haven't even got any maps. Where's the cheese?" He sighed histrionically. "You can't even organize a bloody fridge and yet you're planning to travel three thousand miles with—"

"I have got maps. And your senses of smell and vision are on the blink." I handed him the cheese. "Right in front of you. Listen, I promise you this trip'll work."

"Hm."

In the end he came along, a happy decision for all of us. He justified the frivolity of a holiday by planning to rent a car and tour eastern university chemistry departments while the children and I were staying with Pat.

One of the most pleasing aspects of our holiday was that Cath, rather then just tolerating it, as we had expected, actively enjoyed it, particularly the travelling. Invariably the most wide-awake member of the family in the mornings, she seized up and whooped when the time came each day for Ted to push her into the van. Once ensconced she sat there contentedly looking around and murmuring sweet dribbly nothings into our ears as we bowled along the highway. She quickly caught on to the signs indicating that something interesting was about to happen. When one of us fiddled with the side window beside her, for instance, she grinned widely because she knew it meant that she would soon get blown about; eyes shut, mouth open and pigtails streaming behind her, she was the picture of ecstasy. And when we stopped the van and got out her expression became serious and liplicking because she knew that food was coming.

One definite if curious contribution she made towards our travels was that she saw to it that we received instant service in restaurants. She adored eating out and viewed each new place with interest. As soon as we were settled at our table she would start pulling at the tablecloth, reaching out desperately for cutlery, thumping on her tray and blowing impatient raspberries. Not wanting to embarrass people, but unable to quell the racket, I soon learnt always to have an apple handy. This helped, but even so she hardly represented the average restaurant-goer. I found I had only to raise my eyebrows and smile anxiously to have waiters flocking to our table.

Ted gained something unexpected from our holiday. He overcame, to a significant extent, his embarrassment at being seen in public with Cath.

Having carried, pushed and pulled Cath around everywhere for thirteen years I had long since become inured to the stares and nudges she attracted. Ted, though, is easily embarrassed and lives in perpetual terror of being noticed. Cath, much as he loved her, could hardly have been more of an attention-getter, so he had always contrived to be seen in public with her as little as possible. At home it was fine, but as soon as he was outside with her he became a stranger, talking in a loud ho-ho-ing Santa Claus voice or whistling with awful, tuneless nonchalance and banging into things.

During our travels we both noticed he was much more relaxed than usual about her, even to the extent of willingly coming into restaurants

Cath and Ted enjoying each other's company.

with us. I had thought that day would never come, as he usually found the boys and me embarrassing enough. I don't really know what caused his new attitude; perhaps it was being all together on such a concentrated basis for the first time. But it was lovely, and it lasted. Every evening during the following fall he took Cath out for "a cigar:" a walk around the neighbourhood lasting as long as a Brazilian Black.

As the children and I bumped down the poppy-banked lane to Pat's farm, I looked ahead and saw the English country garden that she and Bernhard had created around the house itself. Lawns were interspersed with trees and shrubs and gorgeous, splotchy flower beds. There was a pond with a rough rock garden around it and a tree-covered island in the middle.

A gardening fork waved from within a mass of delphiniums when we drew up and Pat emerged, muddy and welcoming. A black dog the size of a Shetland pony followed her and then ambled over to greet an astonished Benjy.

"This place," I said to Pat, "is stunning. Is there an entrance fee?"

"Well darling, visitors aren't forbidden to weed."

Our week there proved to be one of the most idyllic in all our lives, full of beauty, fun, laughter and endless good company. There never seemed to be fewer than fifteen people floating around, either staying like us or dropping in. Once, on the occasion of an afternoon garden party that lasted till the next morning, there were nearly a hundred. The numerous animals, all of which considered themselves domestic rather than farm, earned their keep mainly by being charming rather than useful. I remember Cath's awed delight one day when she was lying in the hammock, a dog curled up on her feet, and a horse with a rose hanging from his mouth clomped up and nuzzled her.

One particularly good day for Dominic and Benjy included falling off the donkey, swimming in the pond with ducks, milking goats with Pat, then having a huge lunch party on the lawn with theatre people telling funny stories and using naughty language. The afternoon was full of swinging on ropes in the barn and then helping Bernhard with a bonfire that got excitingly out of control. Finally, the boys went to the Festival Theatre in Stratford and saw Pat and other friends in *The Imaginary Invalid*. Afterwards, they were taken backstage to see how everything worked.

As I tucked Benjy down that night, with Jessica, the huge black Newfie occupying three-quarters of the bed, he made an observation.

"I'm glad we've got Cath," he said.

"Same here, sweetheart," I said. I had brushed the worst of the barn from his hair before going to the theatre but was still extracting the odd strand of hay. "What makes you say that particularly though?"

"Well, I don't mean I'm glad she's like she is because—ouch—I'm not. But if she was ordinary we'd never have met Pat, and all these other guys, would we? Or even got the van, or the new room. Or a whole lot of things really."

One of the reasons I had wanted to go on holiday that August was that I felt I had to escape, if only for a while, the frustrations of being a member of a citizens' group attempting to work with civil servants. June and July, the months following the Minister of Health's positive reaction to ADH, had been horrible in this respect.

Everything would have been fine, I think, had we been allowed to prepare our proposal for a Centre with the help of the professionals we had found, and then presented it to the Minister. As it was, one of the conditions of our getting a grant was that we work with, and be approved of by, something called PIC. This was a group of civil servants, mainly from Health, many of the most influential members of which we knew, from bitter experience, hadn't allowed a new idea on the subject of mental retardation to enter their heads since joining the service.

We slogged on, hoping that one fine day PIC might wake up and listen, or listen and wake up. But as I looked at all those closed, obdurate faces around the table one unproductive meeting after another, such hopes seemed whimsical. Tom often cheered up these meetings for Alice, Gwen, Helen and me by passing around wicked cartoons of the PIC people. He always did it with a very serious face, as if it was an important message he was sending. I often had to dive under the table with a fake coughing fit when I opened the paper. I once met Gwen under there and we wondered whether we would ever stop giggling enough to surface.

Thrown together by chance, Alice, Tom, Gwen, Helen and myself had got to know, respect and best of all like each other very quickly, spending almost as much time in one another's company for enjoyment as we did for work. We have drunk many a toast to our children for having caused our meeting. There existed between us not only friendship but a binding spirit of optimism and determination—determination not to allow people and circumstances to get us down. Sometimes one of us would wobble or collapse, but we knew the others were there to steady, pick up, console and cheer on.

When I returned home in August, I found that two good things had happened during our holiday. First, after a good deal of prodding on the part of Daniel—our civil servant supporter—our grant had arrived, together with an official letter from the Minister of Health wishing us luck and saying he expected our proposal in by December 23rd, four months from the date of his letter. Second, Alice had had a talk with a bigwig in the Department and he had asked her to hurry up with the proposal so that the government could act on it quickly. This seemed encouraging.

PIC stood for Policy Implementation Committee, an astonishing misnomer since its chief function appeared to be to sweep new ideas under the bureaucratic carpet with all possible dispatch. It *was* now government policy to provide community programs for all retarded people but PIC apparently hadn't heard the news. Its members seemed to do an excellent job of obstructing us by using tricks, such as making sure that at each meeting there was either a new colleague present to whom ADH had to be explained, or an important colleague missing so that no decisions could be made. Although one or two people understood what we were aiming for, as a group they were either deaf and poker-faced or overtly resentful. When it became known that HESP—Health, Education, Social Planning—had approved a grant for us to be taken from PIC's budget, there was an absolute outcry. Daniel, at least, spoke up for us at this point. HESP had read our brief, he said, had viewed it favourably and had approved the grant and that was that.

I suppose we were resented, particularly by the more senior civil servants, because we were an embarrassment. We had exposed a problem nobody wanted to know existed and we would not, despite every discouragement, shut up about it. Worse, we were being taken seriously at ministerial level.

And as if all this wasn't enough, those whom we represented couldn't be neatly categorized. Had they been only severely retarded, only spastic, only epileptic, only over or under eighteen, the civil service mind might have been able to cope. Our idea of providing a centre that would be mutually beneficial to people of all ages and with different combinations of handicaps was apparently incomprehensible.

Because we had insisted that the Department of Education be involved in plans for the dependent handicapped, one of the stipulations of our grant was that we work on our proposal with specialists in the education of handicapped children from that department. They were far more friendly than the people from Health but we soon realized that most of them knew rather less about the subject than we did.

While on holiday in Ontario during the summer, I had visited the developmental centre near St. Catharines that Alice had told me about. It had made my mouth water. It was a beautifully designed and well-equipped building surrounded by an imaginatively planned playground. Most significant of all, a large number of badly handicapped children and adolescents were being encouraged to acquire new skills and having a thoroughly good time into the bargain. When I commented to the director that there was a comparatively small number of children with as severe a degree of handicap as Catherine, she drew my attention to a boy sitting at the water table. This was a huge, waist-high tray of water on legs, with a deeply indented circumference so that children could stand, or sit in wheelchairs, and be surrounded by water as far as their arms could reach. The boy was absorbed in a game of pushing a boat back and forth to a friend. His movements were jerky but he was managing well.

"When he came here three years ago he couldn't even hold his head up," said the director, "and his arms were useless appendages curled up to his chest. His legs too. I think he'd been labelled hopeless and left in a foetal position in an institution all his life, cared for like a baby, nothing ever expected of him. Now he can play. He's learning to feed himself, too. And we have him riding that built-up tricycle over there, with help of course."

She then showed me written and photographic progress records of many other children who had entered the centre labelled, for one reason or another, hopeless. All had progressed, some even to the point where they could now attend special classes in regular schools.

When, as an example of what could be done for multiply handicapped children, I related this story to people from the Education Department, it was clear that many of them preferred to continue believing that babysitting services were what children like Cath really needed. However, as with the Health people, we carried on and kept hoping that the one or two people who understood and supported us would help us fight through the muddle of ignorant and discriminatory attitudes of their colleagues.

It's usually the people who actually work in specialized programs who know and learn more than the theoreticians and planners above them. It was certainly the case with the staff of the multiply handicapped class that Cath and Jeanie attended. Those five young men and women were doing a terrific job with our kids and yet their superiors took only the most cursory interest in what was going on. Some of these people hadn't even been to see the program, although it was in its second year.

The same sort of situation, only worse, existed in a program for multiply handicapped people over twenty-one which had creaked into existence soon after ours and was run by the Department of Health. With one or two exceptions, the apathy shown by the department and the government in general was staggering. Nobody was concerned, it seemed, that the program had already twice been shifted from one completely unsuitable location to another, that the staff/student ratio was ridiculously low, and that the staff and parents were constantly aware that the program was lurching from one grant to the next without any assurance that it wouldn't simply be dropped. The staff members themselves were excellent. I had known several of them, and most of the students, since the time of Alice's recreation program, where they had been volunteers. They were keen and committed people but how long could they be expected to carry on under such hopelessly inadequate conditions?

Catherine was glad to return to school that fall. When I took her out to await the van the first morning she looked disturbed, because she was well aware that this wasn't the usual time of day for a walk. I had told her what was happening but it hadn't sunk in. "You'll see Tony again," I said, "Tony your teacher and second-favourite man rolled into one who swings you around in his arms till you beg for mercy and who is hoping to have you feeding yourself with a spoon before the year is out. And you'll see Mrs. McKenzie, who stretches your arms and legs every day for you and is getting to know you almost as well as I do. And you'll see all the children again, too. Jeanie will be there loping around. Maybe she'll drop a candy or a piece of fruit for you again. And you'll be bounced on the air mattress and, I hope, taken swimming once a week, though when we have the Centre you'll be able to go swimming every single day, which is what you need and would like." When the van arrived my pep talk seemed suddenly to penetrate her foggy mind. She scrunched up her arms and legs and hooted cheerfully and off she went.

While sticking a backlog of photos into the album I found one I had taken of her exactly a year before, when she was twelve, and a *bona fide* schoolgirl for the first time in her life. What a change! She had grown so much during the year, both up and out, that an entirely new back and seat had had to be made for her wheelchair. Also, I had been forced to take Dominic's advice and buy her a bra. When I found she needed one two sizes bigger than me I decided that such cheekiness should not go unremarked and bought her a T-shirt with "Out to Lunch" written on the front; some people thought it naughty of me but it attracted a lot of notice, which she loved. When I commented to friends that she was getting fat they protested. And it was true, she didn't look fat, just beautifully healthy. But I could see that her voracious eating was resulting in a layer of padding quite unnecessary to her and a nuisance to me. So the day she hit ninety-five pounds I put her on a diet; not a mean one, just less sugar and starchy stuff and masses more fruit and vegetables. She didn't mind at all; in fact she liked it because this way she could eat more.

Cath's growth spurt had produced a far more serious side effect than the necessity to buy her a bra. (The start of her periods, incidentally, was far from being the terrible problem so many people had assumed it would be; it was simply a matter of popping a plastic-backed diaper inside her normal wad at each change.) A few months previously I had taken her to the Special Devices Clinic and Dr. Letts had ordered an X-ray of her backbone. I had noticed that since getting so tall and heavy she had developed a hump on one side which was particularly noticeable when she was sitting in her chair before I strapped her up. When we looked at the X-ray I was horrified. Her spine looked like one of those sectional bamboo snakes one buys in novelty stores and it had a distinct S-shape to it, more pronounced at the top.

"That looks awful. What on earth does it mean? And what can we do?"

Dr. Letts sat me down and explained. The bend was called a scoliosis and was caused mainly by Cath's dislocated hip and by her lack of adequate trunk control. There were two courses of action: one, improve her holding-up straps and see what happened, and two, put a steel brace down her backbone, inside her.

Before I had a chance to go into hysterics Dr. Letts whipped out before and after X-rays of a patient on whom he had performed this operation. There on the screen was a spine with a curve twice as bad as Cath's and next to it an almost straight spine with a foot-long rod beside it, hooked into a vertebra at either end.

"She's a different girl now," said Dr. Letts, "self-confident and happy instead of feeling, in her own words, like a creepy freak."

"Yes, but she was mentally and physically OK other than the scoliosis," I said, "right? I mean Cath doesn't think she's a—"

"Yes. I'm not saying we should do this on Cath. It's just a possibility." In answer to my tremulous question about what such an operation would mean for Cath he said, "She would wake up in a heavy body cast, spend six months on her back in it and another six, but not on her back, in a lighter one. Then she would have a nice straight back." While I was still trying to organize my face he repeated quickly that this operation was only a suggestion and that even if I said go ahead he would think seriously about the pros and cons in Cath's case before operating.

"Certainly no decision has to be made right now," he had concluded. "She's what, nearly thirteen? Plenty of time yet."

I don't often kid myself that all is well when I know it's not, but during the summer I had almost managed to blot from my mind the knowledge that the scoliosis wasn't going to disappear miraculously, and that sooner or later a decision would have to be made about whether to have it operated on. The photo I was looking at showed that a year ago she was sitting considerably straighter than she was now, and if I was honest I could see a change in her shape when she was lying on her stomach, too. The S in her spine had become more pronounced and her right leg was higher up her hip.

A second X-ray and another talk with Dr. Letts confirmed my fears and banished the hope I had clung to—that the deterioration could be stalled or even reversed by comparatively ordinary means like crafty padding in her chair and better supporting straps. I began to think of the pros and cons of having her spine straightened with a rod.

I found it hard to be objective. It was terrible to know that leaving it alone would almost certainly lead to worse deformities, arthritis and squashed innards. But so was the thought of the bewildering pain and misery she would have to endure if we had it fixed. Ted kept saying he knew I would make the right decision and then asking technical questions I couldn't answer. I became so worried and depressed that eventually he braced himself and came with me to discuss the matter in detail with Dr. Letts. At the end of the discussion the blackboard was covered with diagrams and we were both feeling unwell and even further from a decision than before. Dr. Letts was unwilling to decide for us and the three of us sat in glum silence for a while. Anxious not to induce a finger-drumming spell on anyone's part I suggested getting a second opinion and the relief was general.

"Who will you take her to?" Ted had to turn his head to ask this. He was striding down the corridor to get out of the hospital as quickly as possible.

"Chap I sit next to in orchestra," I said, jogging along behind him. "He's Hungarian and very bright and a good cellist. Do slow down. He's straightforward, says what he thinks. Gets impatient when I'm cowardly about high notes and soft bits. Do slow down, I'm getting a stitch. If he made a decision for me I'd accept it, he's been in it for years!"

"What are you jabbering about?" Ted stopped abruptly and I cannoned into him.

"Don't get so cross. I was just going to tell you, he knows all about this operation. He's an orthopedic surgeon." We were both on edge.

My friend was against the operation and I felt far happier after I had seen him. He examined Cath and her X-rays and we had a long talk about her and then went over the arguments for and against the operation. Cath probably used only a quarter of her lung and heart capacity, he said, so what if she lost part of it through being squashed? Sure, the possibility of respiratory complications would increase as the years rolled by but did I really want her to live to a ripe old age? She would look better with a straight back, but who would benefit more from that, she or I? He wasn't quite as blunt as this but left little doubt about what he thought. I was grateful to him for being honest and glad that he had strengthened my instinctive feelings against the operation. So was Ted and so too, I suspect, was Dr. Letts; not to mention Cath.

Something had to be done, however, so the Special Devices people once again improved her holding-up straps and we talked about the possibility of a body-jacket for next year sometime.

Cath has always had a knack of compensating us for the various worries she puts us through. Not long after her back problems, Tony phoned me from her school and asked me to come down. He and Lindy, the other teacher, thought I might be interested in something Cath had to show me. I knew they had been trying to teach her to feed herself with a spoon but they had wanted her to achieve a measure of success before I was given a demonstration. I suspected the moment of truth was at hand. I grinned and said I was on my way.

To see my daughter enthusiastically feed herself a meal from a plate, with a spoon, almost unaided, had a strange effect on me. I neither exclaimed nor wept nor laughed; I just stood and gaped. It didn't matter that her spoon had been bent inwards and had had its handle built up, nor that her plate was specially shaped and secured to her tray, nor even that her elbow was tactfully guided by Lindy as she lifted up each mouthful. What mattered was that she had learnt, step by step, to grasp her spoon, scoop food on to it, lift it up, put the food into her mouth, chew and then recommence the process, and all without releasing the spoon. This last point was significant because it meant she had achieved a controlled and sustained grip, a very difficult task for her.

I think the most significant aspect of this self-feeding demonstration was that Cath had performed it with her right hand. Had it been with her left I would have been delighted but not amazed, but her right arm and hand had always tended to be tight and spastic. When I tried to persuade her to hold an object in her right hand she either transferred it to her left or held it in a vice-like grip until she was able to relax and fling it away. It was the occupational physiotherapist who had helped organize the program who had suggested that she be taught to eat with her right hand. On my way home I dropped in at the Shriners' hospital to ask if the Special Devices people could provide me with a built-up spoon and plate for Cath so that I could continue her self-feeding program at home. They were, as always, most obliging.

Elated though I was by Cath's accomplishment I had a moment of acute anguish that night as I thought of the progress she could have made had she been taught earlier. She was now well past the prime developmental period of her life and her body was stiff and creaky, yet she had managed to learn the complicated process I had just witnessed. What could she not have learnt before! The moment passed and I thought instead about the director of a large service club whom I had talked to earlier in the day. He had read copies of both our brief and our recently completed proposal and had assured me that as soon as the government had clarified its policy towards dependent handicapped children and adults his club would be anxious to contribute a major donation to the Centre. A swimming pool, perhaps? I said. Could well be, he responded. He realized how important water therapy was for our people and liked the idea that the pool would be used not just by those attending the Centre regularly but also by hundreds of other handicapped people who were unable to use public pools.

We were getting this sort of response from other service clubs and foundations to whom we had given copies of the brief and the proposal. Once we had opened their eyes to the lack of community facilities for multiply handicapped people they assured us of their willingness to assist in making the Centre the success we knew it could be. But before they could help us they had to know that the government would take the major responsibility and guarantee the day-to-day operational costs. When did we think the government would respond to our proposal?

We wished we knew. Alice, the others, and I had spent the weeks before Christmas completing and co-ordinating into draft form the many sections of our proposal. Working out the Centre's architectural plans, capital and operational costs, programming, governing policies, and so on, was incredibly complicated and required weeks of investigation before being even tentatively written up. Due to her greater experience, it fell to Alice to do most of the organizing and writing. We wished we could do more to assist her. She and her family were having a frightening time with Jeanie, whose epilepsy had taken a drastic turn for the worse. The thought that kept her going was that once this mammoth task was completed we would be on our way to getting our Centre. One good thing was that we no longer had to get the proposal approved by PIC, because this so-called Policy Implementation Committee had ceased to exist. We never found out why but assumed it had self-destructed. Its members were, however, still very much present in the government to be grappled with in the future.

Daniel and his staff were always willing to give us advice on how to write the proposal in a form that would be acceptable to the government. They had a rare understanding of the strain under which families with children like ours lived and were as anxious as we were to see something materialize from all our work. As our deadline drew closer they began exhorting us to get the proposal in as quickly as possible. We didn't understand this urgency until we heard to our dismay that the government was playing musical ministries again and that on December 23rd, the very day the proposal was due to be handed in, we were to get a new Minister of Health. Daniel had been hoping we could deliver it earlier so that the present Minister could act on it before he left.

But we couldn't. We were going flat out already, writing and typing into the early hours of every morning. On the designated day we presented a copy of the proposal to the departing Minister, who was apologetic about the timing of his exit and promised to keep in touch. We left one for his successor. Then we went home and dealt with our turkeys.

This had been six weeks ago. While writing the proposal we had been led to expect an invitation to discuss and if necessary defend it almost at once, the change of Minister notwithstanding. We had distributed copies to people in all levels of the departments of Health and Education so we knew everyone had had a chance to study it. But despite numerous follow-up letters and phone calls we had heard nothing. We were frustrated and alarmed at this silence and Daniel, indignant on our behalf, advised us to arrange a meeting with the relevant senior civil servants from Health and Education.

This we wearily did, and finally, one morning in March, Alice, Gwen, Tom, our architect and I found ourselves outside a government meeting room awaiting our summons to enter. We were eager to get going but also nervous. This morning, after all, was in effect the moment we had been working towards not just since starting on the proposal but since the formation of ADH over a year ago; this morning we would discover how and when the government had decided to act on our plan for surmounting a major social problem it had hitherto disregarded.

We were beckoned in and found ourselves faced by about twelve top policy makers, mainly from Health and many of whom had been in PIC. Only two did we regard as friendly. We braced ourselves. It was obviously to be a long and trying morning, with lengthy discussions and a barrage of questions to answer.

But the first question completely threw us. Why, asked one of the Health people, were he and his colleagues here? Alice, after a moment of bewildered silence, responded. To discuss ADH's proposal, she said. Ah, said the Health person, well he was sorry, but nobody present was at liberty to do that. One or two of his colleagues grunted in agreement while the rest stared at their briefcases. Alice glanced at them and then at us; but we were speechless. Very well, she said, the government was apparently critical of the proposal. But why? How could we improve it to make it acceptable? What help had the people in the room to offer? She was dignified and polite—but determined—as she asked each person these questions. Nobody would answer her.

The silence in the room became so thick that her voice was beginning to sound muffled. At last the chairman of the meeting, a man in the financial end of Health, muttered that our proposed Centre would be too costly. Alice was ready for that one, of course. The construction and *per diem* costs quoted in the proposal were, she said, drawn directly from developmental centres and community residences already in operation in other parts of Canada. Our proposed Centre was not a pie-in-the-sky ideal, it was perfectly realistic. ADH was, however, aware that the government did not have unlimited funds so we were obviously open to reasonable compromise. Perhaps the discussion could be taken from there?

There was no response, just a lot of looking at watches and muttering. The meeting was apparently at an end. Stunned, we trailed out. Afterwards one of the people whom we had expected to support us told Alice he had come to the meeting prepared to discuss the proposal, about which he felt very positively, but had been ordered not to show us his written response to it. The implications of this apologetic statement were ominous. It looked as though the government was directing more time and energy towards silencing us than it was towards responding to the proposal. There were no jokes between us as we left, not even from Tom. "They're out to shaft us," he said, and none of us could disagree.

I had to hurry away to pick Cath up from school. She had an appointment for another back X-ray. I was filled with rage and despair about what had just happened but as I climbed into the van I was suddenly overtaken by fear. I felt dizzy and breathless and then I started sweating profusely and my heartbeat doubled its rate. I sat bent over the steering wheel and told myself not to be stupid. After a while I felt better and took off.

I had experienced these spells often lately and once my doctor had ruled out the deadly possibilities I had suggested, I had accepted that they were nervous in origin and tried to pinpoint their cause. Reluctantly I realized they occurred whenever I had to take Cath out in the van by myself. At first I tried to kid myself I was still nervous about driving the van but eventually I faced the truth. I had become terrified of getting her up and down the ramp, particularly when there was ice around and I couldn't get a firm grip with my feet. She and the wheelchair combined weighed about a hundred and forty pounds, ten pounds more than me, and the ramp was steep, so I suppose it wasn't surprising I found it tough. Nevertheless I knew I could do it if I told myself I could. It needed perfect co-ordination and all my strength but I could do it. The trouble was, I was sounding increasingly unconvincing to myself and there had been a couple of times lately when I had skidded badly. After that I carried a pail of sand in the van and scattered a handful at the end of the ramp; but it didn't work because I was still scared of slipping on the ramp itself.

When I got to the school Tony offered to push Cath up into the van. "Thanks, I can manage," I said. I had meant to say it airily but instead it came out with a ferocity that surprised us both. I got her up through sheer bravado. At the hospital the ground was very icy so I cheated and asked the help of a man who happened to be parking next to me. But would anyone be there when we came out? Why worry, I said to myself, I could do it. I was clammy with sweat and my ears were humming.

While I was holding Cath up for her X-ray, which was a difficult process, especially since I was weighted down with a lead apron, I got so dizzy I thought I would crumple to the floor with her. What was the matter with me? So it was a bit icy out there, so what? It had been icy all winter and I had managed. What was so special about today? I could do it.

But I couldn't. As soon as I clenched my teeth and aimed Cath at the ramp I knew that this time I couldn't get her up it. I got her halfway up and had to let her roll back down. I tried again and the same thing happened. It happened because I knew I was no longer able to convince myself I could do it.

"Let me give you a hand." I jumped. It was one of the Special Devices engineers.

"Thanks. It's slippery."

"No problem." He pushed and I pulled and we got her in.

"Thanks," I said. He nodded and hurried off. He was embarrassed because I was crying.

I tethered Cath down and then sat down myself and cried and shook helplessly.

Ted would have been mystified had he known I was crying because I couldn't push Cath up the ramp. He would have told me we could get an Ironside hoist or whatever was necessary. But to me it wasn't as simple as that. In the last two years we had spent $10,000 because of Catherine. It was true that we all benefited from her room and the van but we could easily have done without them and spent the money on a decent car for Ted, on trips to England, on a good piano, on all sorts of things not related to Cath. And now I found we still weren't equipped to cope with her physically. I knew the hoists cost about $2,000 and there was no way I could justify spending that amount on something that would be no use to the rest of us. Anyway, we still had two years to pay on the van.

Oh, hell. I must stop this crying and get home to change Cath and get myself into a better state of mind for the boys. I dug around in the unspeakable depths of my bag and extracted my key. I found, though, that I couldn't aim it into the ignition. I was shaking too much. This precipitated a fresh bout of tears and suddenly all the worries I usually kept under control broke loose in an unruly demand for attention. Had I, for a start, made the wrong decision thirteen years ago when I refused to consider putting Catherine away? Had I been wrong to hang onto her ever since? Would the lives of the rest of us have been better without her? Usually my answers to these questions were unequivocal but now I couldn't be sure. If I had institutionalized her I certainly wouldn't be sitting here now in the most wretched despair I had ever known. On the other hand I might be in a loony bin as a result of the unhappiness and guilt I would have felt at rejecting my child.

Then there were the present anxieties. I thought the right decision had been made about Cath's back but Dr. Letts had just told me she would soon have to wear a stiff body jacket, starting at her armpits and ending below her waist, and it would be for keeps. Should we reverse the decision about the operation? Which course would be the least awful for her? And what was I going to do about the pressure sore on the inside of her right ankle? It had been caused by her rubbing her foot on the floor as she kicked and I had been applying heat and rubbing alcohol every day for weeks. I suspected, however, that unless I immobilized her leg entirely the skin would break and I would have a major problem on my hands. And how on earth would I immobilize her leg, anyway? String it up from the ceiling or something? Dear God, would these physical problems with Cath never stop?

It wasn't just worry that was causing my apparently endless flow of tears. It was fury and frustration. Together with Alice and the others in ADH I had put a great deal of time and effort into doing something constructive about our difficulties, and those of many other people who were even more burdened and less able to cope and speak out than we were. But where had it got us? Nowhere apparently. What in God's name did those Health people want? Did they and their superiors intend to ignore us until we paraded our kids in front of the Legislative Building or made a stink in the papers or dropped dead or what?

But why should we be driven to such ignominious lengths? We had done everything, and more, that had been asked of us by the government and it was now refusing even to discuss our proposal. If it was their wives who dealt with feeding, wiping, lifting, giving enemas, washing stinky diapers, guarding, worrying about and living with a child like Cath, then something would happen all right.

I sat up sharply and held my breath. A pain had zoomed down the back of my leg. What was it? Neuritis? Something growing in my spine?

Nerves, for heaven's sake. It was my nerves.

"AAAAAAAAAAH!" I saw that crew-cropped boy in the big institution again, even saw down his throat and felt his slippery grip on my arm.

The big institution. When we had returned from our sabbatical in England I had faced the possibility of Cath landing in there and had roused myself sufficiently to try and do something about it. Now, two and a half years of raised and lowered hopes later, I knew that if I died it was still the place where she would have to go.

I cry when I'm angry or frustrated. When I'm frightened—really frightened—I smile and carry on.

"The boys must be home, Cath," I said. "Better be getting back."

I hadn't been out to St. Amant since Cath had stayed there in 1971 but I had heard that the entire institution was being taken over for the care of up to two hundred and seventy-five young handicapped children and that exciting things were happening. Gwen's son, Stevie, was now doing well in a day program there and she urged me to go out with her one day to have a look. As we went in we happened to meet the nun on whose ward Cath had stayed last time. She greeted me with characteristic warmth, asked all about Cath and then eagerly offered to give Gwen and myself a guided tour.

It was easy to see why this offer was made so enthusiastically. The St. Amant Centre, as it was now called, was surely on its way to becoming one of the best and most attractive institutions for retarded children in North America. Whoever had been in charge of the renovations had succeeded in making the whole place both beautiful and practical. It comprised many of the physical features we wanted for our own Centre, including an indoor pool and garden. The old wards were still depressingly crowded but this situation would be remedied as soon as the alterations on the wards in the new wings had been completed. One of these was already finished and occupied. It was a dramatic improvement on the old.

The small school program for the brighter kids living in the institution had been moved to new and better quarters, as had the program for twenty-five or so severely handicapped children like Stevie who were still living at home. We had a good look at both and also at the cottages, which were small home-like units where the least handicapped resident children could learn how to live as normally as possible.

The great thing about St. Amant had always been the loving and devoted care given by the nuns and other staff to every one of the children. On the three occasions that Cath had stayed there, I had known that while she might be bewildered and bored, she would at least never be neglected or ill-treated in any way. What had not been so good was the attitude towards children as badly handicapped as her and less so; that they were not capable of progressing and that giving them love and care was all that could be done for them. But I was encouraged to see that along with the physical improvements of the institution there was a marked increase in developmental activities for the more mildly handicapped children and much more talk about what could be done with those like Cath. The latter were still up on the wards most of the time but now one could at least hope that programs would be created for them eventually. "We're going as fast as we can," said a physiotherapist when I talked to her about this. "Give us a chance."

As we were leaving, our accompanying nun did something odd. I had just finished telling her how impressed I was with the new St. Amant Centre and she put her hand on my shoulder and said, "Maybe we'll see Catherine here this summer. You look as though you could do with a break."

I laughed. "Certainly I could, Sister, but she's nearly as big as me now—I told you, remember? And she was way past the age limit last time she was here so—"

"Yes," she said, "that's right I guess." She looked as though she wished she hadn't spoken and bade us farewell rather awkwardly. "You never can tell," she said as she waved goodbye. Gwen and I looked at each other and wondered.

Elucidation, and a change in my entire outlook on life, followed days later when I heard that one of the new policies of the St. Amant Centre was to admit and care for multiply handicapped non-ambulatory children of any age; and not just for holidays, but indefinitely if necessary.

Relief of the magnitude that I experienced on hearing this news, which was still semi-secret but which I had made certain was true, sinks in only slowly. For a long time I literally could not believe it; the sudden evaporation of the nightmare of the big institution was too much to accept.

When at last I did allow my taut mind to relax enough to be grateful I discovered that this gratitude had produced another feeling—courage. A few weeks ago I had felt defeated. Now, with the edge of personal desperation removed from my life, I found I had new determination to continue working for the community needs of myself and others.

15

We in ADH were naive, I suppose. We believed that once our socialist government knew of the monumental apathy and discrimination with which multiply handicapped dependent people and their families had hitherto been regarded, it would clap a hand to its forehead and leap into action. Instead, with the exception of one minister and a handful of senior civil servants, it seemed to do everything in its power to obstruct and silence us. The result is that now, nearly two years later, absolutely nothing has happened in the way of community residences and developmental programs for the dependent handicapped. We can never even be sure that funding will continue for the programs that do exist. We can only conclude that those most in need and least able to help themselves have the lowest priority in the government's eyes.

Shortly after our meeting in March, 1975, with the PIC people, we discovered that the Minister of Health had delegated the responsibility of dealing with us to one of his top civil servants, the same one who a year earlier had encouraged Alice to hurry up with the proposal so the government could act on it. This man, now that he was actually expected to do something, became instantly unavailable, refusing to answer phone calls and letters and being uncivil to the point of rudeness when physically confronted by us. We soon realized that rather than acquaint himself with our brief, our proposal, or us, he had chosen to rely on the advice of the PIC people and that of a government-hired specialist in community residences for the retarded—a person who, it transpired, had extremely biased views about our sort of handicapped people because he had had no experience with them.

Despite numerous attempts on our part, and prodding from within by Daniel and his people, there followed a period of several more months when we were refused any sort of constructive meeting with our critics and detractors. By the beginning of 1976, it was pretty obvious that our proposal had suffered a wholesale rejection. It wasn't until June that we managed to persuade a friendly senior civil servant to write us an official letter to this effect so we would have something definite to react to. In July, eighteen months after our proposal had been handed in, we finally arranged a meeting with the Minister of Health and some of his advisors, a meeting that the Minister had been promising Alice since January. She, Tom and I went, and afterwards treated ourselves to an extremely good lunch. We felt it was the least we deserved.

Any hopes we might have had at that meeting of correcting the department's misconceptions about our proposal were immediately dispelled by the Minister when he announced that the proposal was dead and he wasn't prepared to discuss any aspect of it. Alice, the rose in her lapel quivering only slightly, asked why this was so. We realized how grim our situation was when he gave us precisely the same negative, prejudiced and misinformed objections to the proposal that we had been hearing from his advisors for so long. He appeared to have no idea of either the philosophy behind the proposal or its actual contents. He then told us that the only way we might expect improved services for the dependent handicapped was if we dropped our campaign completely and toed the government line. The latter, unfortunately, was, as far as we could ascertain, virtually nonexistent; such services as did exist would be "improved" in some unspecified way at some unspecified date. When Alice, Tom and I all asked for a little more detail, the Minister became most indignant, implying that great strides had been taken recently and that we should be grateful that the multiply handicapped are no longer kept in cages!

At the end of a completely unproductive hour and a half we were told that it was recognized we were "sincere" and that we would be welcome to discuss our concerns with a ministerial advisor henceforth. We couldn't help feeling that the meeting had been a mere formality.

Why has ADH not created a public outcry all this time? For one thing we have kept hoping the government would accept its responsibility towards the hundreds of people we represent. For another, creating a public outcry demands far more time and energy than we have been able to muster recently. Three of our key members have been reduced to institutionalizing their children, a traumatic and enervating experience. Gwen, worn down after years of caring for Stevie and her other children without a husband, was persuaded to place him in the St. Amant Centre. Vicky, whose parents had to declare her mentally retarded, is there too. And Alice and her husband, exhausted and ill from the strain of caring for Jeanie, whose epilepsy became far worse, finally capitulated and took her to St. Amant also.

The St. Amant Centre is, as I have said, improving constantly. Jeanie, Stevie and Vicky are all well looked after and relatively happy. But it is nevertheless an institution and therefore cannot avoid having at least a few of the drawbacks of any institution. Also, a point of the utmost importance, there are many dependent handicapped children who would not be accepted there because they are ambulatory; Jeanie is there and not in the big institution only because she is tied into a wheelchair most of the time. Finally, there is a long waiting list for the St. Amant Centre. It is already full.

There are glimmers of hope. The conservatives in the executive of CAMR are gradually being replaced by more enlightened people and while there are still some staunch reactionaries at the top of the Department of Health, there are others who now share ADH's philosophy. The

Entering the van via remote control.

attitude within the Department of Education, too, is becoming far more positive towards our children. Also, many people in the community now recognize the needs of dependent handicapped children, including the director of a local YMCA, who last year organized a splendid summer recreation program for them.

With the support and encouragement of these people, and others, we in ADH will continue, individually and collectively, to work towards our ideals.

It's a gorgeous day, warm, windy and swirling with golden leaves. The whole neighbourhood is out enjoying this prelude to winter, the adults bedding down their perennials and doing last-minute, rather leafy painting jobs, and the children playing.

Catherine—she's sixteen now—and I are out too; she, beautiful and rosy with her unruly hair drying in the wind after her Sunday bath and me, dusty and disheveled after removing the matting from the ramp, scribbling on the step beside her. Two feet away Dominic and Benjy and about ten friends are taking turns whizzing perilously down the ramp on skateboards. I find it not a little distracting, but Cath thinks it's marvellous, scrunching herself up and hooting and laughing.

Cath and Nicola, 1977. TOM PRESCOTT PHOTO

Discarding my notebook and chewed pencil for a moment, I unscrunch one of her feet, rubbing it and bending back the toes as far as their deformities will allow. She coos, and I look up to respond to the grin I know is there. A fleecy pad is tied around her right foot under her sock; we acquired it courtesy of the Department of Health and it protects the pressure point on her ankle. While on the subject of the physical problems I've encountered with her, I might mention that the reason she's sitting in her wheelchair so straight and stately, like something on a prow of a ship, is that she's in a body jacket. It was made by the Special Devices people last summer. It bothered her at first, suddenly to feel trapped, but now she's grown accustomed to it and likes the support. She kicks and laughs whenever she sees me approaching with the two white shells. She knows it means a ride in her wheelchair, and that usually means either food, a walk, or a drive in the van. Taking her out in the van is no problem these days, thanks to an economical and efficient winch fixed in it last year. It pulls her up the ramp, or lets her down, and all I have to do is guide her. Even Dominic and Benjy can get her in and out of the van alone now. And she's learned to duck her head rather than hang onto the roof to prevent her head being bumped.

I think Cath has stopped growing now, for which I thank God. Her body has stopped growing, that is, but her brain continues to develop. Comments about her increased alertness and responsiveness have been coming thick and fast lately.

She must have known I was writing that, because she's just touched me delicately on my head. It's one of her most charming gestures, a quiet demonstration of love. I look up and we exchange a smile. The first time she touched me like that was last summer soon after I took her home from St. Amant, where she had stayed while the boys and I were in England. I was busy telling her what a lovely time she'd had, with her father visiting her and lots of other people dropping in to see her, and she reached out and simply touched me, and smiled. It seemed to be a sort of reassurance.

It's quieter now. The boys and their friends have temporarily abandoned their skateboards and are raking up huge piles of leaves in which to bury themselves and each other.

Ted has just joined Catherine and myself; he has been poring over a student's thesis all afternoon. When Cath sees him she reaches out and pulls him down for a hug. She notices he has a cigar in his hand and knows it's walk time.

"OK, Cath, let's give your mother a chance to get on with that interminable book."

I glare at him. "I'm just writing the last sentence now. Hang on, I'll come with you—"

"Ah, I see. We all walk off together into the sunset, you mean."

I rise stiffly to my feet. "Something like that," I say, and off we trundle.

Autumn 1977

16

It seems hard to believe that nearly five years have passed since Ted, Catherine and I trundled off into the sunset. We trundled back, of course, and our lives have continued; usually merrily, occasionally miserably, but never monotonously.

It's a mid-summer Sunday and my daughter, who recently turned twenty-one, is sitting in her wheelchair beside me on the porch. She grins at me bemusedly and I ask her what she thinks her admirers would like to hear about in this update to her official biography. Perhaps overcome with the enormity of the question, she reaches out for a hug. She perfected her hugging technique about two years ago; she pulls one down by the neck with her left arm, clinches the deal by slowly hooking her right arm over and then grunts endearments as one hugs her back. It's lovely.

Out for a walk with Coda.

Ted, who has been patching the stucco, comes up behind us.

"I'm getting too old to go up ladders," he says. "Where are the boys?" His tone changes suddenly. "Oh God, not another book." He has spotted the loose leaf folder he thought had been thunked permanently shut five years ago. "I'm off to the lab."

"A mere update," I shout as he retreats. "Sorry Cath, I didn't mean to deafen you." She grabs me tighter.

"Are you sure you've got time to write an update?" says Ted reappearing somewhat mollified through his cloud of Gitane smoke. "I've never seen anyone as frenetically busy as you since your book came out. You're constantly flying to some conference, yakking to groups, off to a vital meeting, being interviewed or poring over some bloody manuscript." His cigarette ash showers down onto his shirt creating a new crop of little holes. "What will you give up to do this writing?"

"How about a martini and some cheese straws in your comfy garden chair when you get back, sweetheart?"

"Hm. The conciliatory approach. OK, that sounds good. Bye then, 'bye Cath."

Just as I hunch over my folder again a new distraction appears. Huge and hirsute—they're both 6'3"—Dominic and Benjy lope towards the house from opposite ends of the street, Dominic with tennis equipment hanging from one hand and Benjy sounding like a motorbike trying to start as he sucks up the remnants of a Slurpee.

Dominic sees my folder. "Oh God," he says in unconscious imitation of his father. "Not another book. Give me strength!"

"How long will we be orphaned for this time?" Benjy enquires. "Hello Coda! Gimme that. Good girl." He removes one of Cath's flimsy Indian shirts from the dog's mouth. Coda, the gorgeous golden retriever I bought as a puppy with my first book money, a present for Cath, has been shuffle-clicking around the house all morning looking for a cool spot and finally spread herself out on the basement floor like a polar bear carpet. The sound of the boys' voices, however, has galvanized her into a panting, tail-swiping greeting.

"Could you take her for a quick walk, Benjy?"

He groans. "But I was going to play the piano a bit! I've got some great new sheet music. Anyway," he continues more brightly when he sees my look, "it's Sunday, so aren't you taking her and Cath for the usual walk?"

It's tempting. Every Sunday during the summer, the City bans motor vehicles from a beautiful broad river road near us. We can walk for miles unimpeded by sidewalk edges. Coda, with her lead hooked over a wheel-chair handle, helps pull Cath. We're constantly overtaken by Winnipeg on wheels: black-bottomed, helmeted, serious cyclists whistling through whole families on bikes and trikes, kids on roller skates, tube-topped girls with their bare-topped fellows on lookalike bikes and the occasional person humming along in a powered wheelchair.

Yes, it's tempting. We could go as far as the bend in the river, rest a while and then stop on our way back for refreshment at one of the friendly watering holes we've developed along our route. Then I think of last Sunday, when I slaked my thirst at one such oasis with two glasses of white wine and barely made it home with my curious caravan. I refocus on Benjy.

"No," I say, "I must do this." He and Dominic agree to take Catherine and Coda round the block. As I watch them go I recall Dominic and his girlfriend taking Cath for a walk recently and realize that we've passed a hurdle I saw approaching a few years ago, the day when my sons acquired girlfriends and might suddenly become embarrassed at having Cath for a sister. Judging by the amount of time they spend with their faces two inches from the mirror, though, and by the number of girls they usher into the house, they're far more self-conscious about their own looks than their sister's.

Catherine looks marvellous today, bright and happy and healthy and much like any other young woman in the neighbourhood. Her hair is loose and she's wearing a T-shirt and sweat pants; around her neck is a gold chain, a gift from her friend Zana; on one finger, like me, she has a

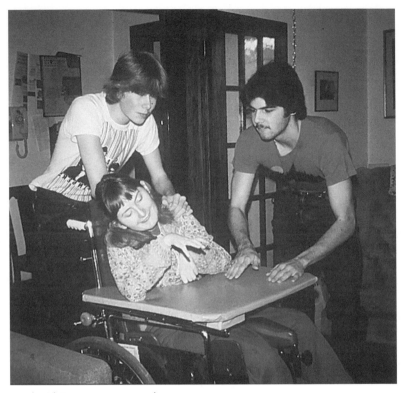

Benjy and Dominic entertaining their sister.

gold signet ring with my family crest on it; and on her feet are runners, carefully chosen to accommodate her curled over feet. The only obvious difference is that she's in a wheelchair.

Her life, too, is similar to that of many of her contemporaries. During the school year she goes to school and in the summer she attends a recreation program. Most people her age spend the summer working, it's true, but in a sense she's contributing to society as much as Dominic—he's cleaning buses for the City between university years—because she's training assistants to recognize the strengths and needs of people with severe handicaps.

The developmental program we helped establish in a regular elementary school in 1973 ran into trouble about three years after it started. The non-handicapped population dwindled and moved elsewhere and the empty quarters were taken over by a day nursery. It seemed terrible to me that our kids had nobody their own age around, and that the little ones in the day nursery were learning that big people with severe handicaps belong together in a clump. A friend and I started pushing for a change and finally, two years ago, our program underwent both a move and a metamorphosis. There are now fifteen students between the ages of fifteen and twenty-one and they have three teachers, three aides and a part-time physiotherapist. The program occupies four rooms in the hub of a large junior/senior high school near the centre of town—which means there is the opportunity for extramural activities like exploring the museum or having lunch at the local hamburger joint. Since one of the aims of the program is to teach the students basic life skills, the main room is like an apartment, with carpeting on the floor, sofas, comfortable chairs, a stereo and TV, a dining area and kitchen apparatus. Round the corner are bathrooms and chang-

School photo.

ing rooms, and down the corridor are a physio room and two small, distraction-free rooms for individual learning sessions. Exciting things happened within weeks of the program opening: one girl, who can walk but has uncontrolled epilepsy and is severely mentally handicapped, learned with delight how to stack the dishwasher; a young man learned to choose what he wanted to eat in the school cafeteria rather than hurl food he disliked across the room; another grasped the idea of vacuuming the floor from his wheelchair; and Catherine embarked on a new life in a powered wheelchair.

The hair on the back of my neck stood up the first time I saw her move across the room independently. She was taught by means of her favourite thing, food. A university psychology professor heard about this and, since he'd never seen anyone as handicapped as Cath do anything so dramatic, he came to see. It was funny to see a tweed-jacketed, tied professor backing down the corridor holding out a spoonful of yogurt and saying, "Come on Cath, let's go!" and then scribbling down her reaction for the paper that is doubtless in the making. She's not too good at corners yet but she can go the whole lengh of the corridor. She might eventually achieve what I suspect is her ambition—to mow me down in retaliation for all the ghastly things I've put her through during her life.

When the teachers told me they were planning to teach Cath to control her environment, I had visions of her slashing through a jungle with a scythe. What they meant, though, was that she should learn to make choices, rather than have them made for her. To this end she now spends part of each day bashing various long-handled switches and sorting out which will give her, for instance, music in her headphones or a slide flashed on the wall. She has been quick to pick this up and I'm hoping to get a similar setup at home. How lovely if she could choose a TV channel or radio program, and operate the machines, rather than be subjected to what I think she wants! That reminds me: she chose the shirt she's wearing today. When a friend suggested that Cath might choose what to wear I thought he was batty but nevertheless started offering her a choice of shirts. At first she took no notice but I waited till she inadvertently touched one and then put it on her. She soon caught on and now very often decides what to wear.

She's also, by pointing at large photos of herself in action, beginning to communicate what she wants to do. Her teacher last term says she now actively searches for the one that shows her eating. I hope that in time she will absorb my lectures on the benefits of physical activity and point instead to the one of her in the gym.

One of the best aspects of having the program located in a high school is that the handicapped students are highly visible, moving from room to room like everyone else. Oddly enough they in fact become invisible, because they are surrounded by kids who aren't handicapped. They seem to have been accepted in the school very well, and a number of the non-handicapped students enjoy working with them on a regular basis, even forming friendships that extend beyond school hours.

Catherine is enjoying her summer program at the Y, as she has since it was inaugurated six years ago. She loves the daily swimming (and looks splendid in a bikini), the outings and the camping trips, the latter complete with a bonfire, marshmallows, singalongs and leaky tents.

It's my custom, on Cath's birthday, to appear at lunchtime with a cake. This year, as everyone plunged into eating it, I was struck by the number of young people who were spending their second, third and even fourth summer working in the program. The work is far from easy. The program tries to serve individuals with a variety of disabilities so it involves chasing after people ("Where's John? I've just found his clothes"), feeding, changing, washing and lifting them, wiping up every imaginable kind of mess and occasionally being bitten or kicked. And the pay is lousy. I asked one assistant the reason for his recidivism. "I guess it's because I can't think of anything I'd rather do," he said. "I really like Cath and the others. Besides," he added with a grin, "there's always Cath's birthday to look forward to. Hey Dale! Get out of Sharon's lunch, please."

I asked a new assistant how she became involved. "I'm a volunteer," she answered. "I wanted to do something worthwhile after grade 12 so I went to the Volunteer Bureau and picked this program. I love it, in fact I'm hoping to be an assistant here next summer. Oh dear, Jacques and Hugh are having problems, I'd better go."

I find it extremely upsetting, when I look at Catherine's life, to think that some people still argue in favour of segregated education for students with severe handicaps. Today's children are, after all, tomorrow's parents, teachers, bus drivers, politicians, street cleaners, lawyers and so on. Surely they deserve the opportunity to meet and learn to appreciate *all* their fellow citizens from nursery school on. Equally upsetting is the knowledge that there are hundreds of individuals who are unable to attend a school program like Cath's or a community recreation program because they are forced, by our slowness to arrange community alternatives, to live in institutions.

The phone rings. This is unusual these days when the boys are at home. They're usually on it already.

"It's for you Mum. Quick!"

"Tell them I'm out."

"But it's Cordelia!"

"My mother? For heaven's sake why didn't you say so?"

"I just did."

All I can hear when I canter to the phone is a transatlantic hiss. Then, "Darling? Oh good, I was just getting my drink. How are you all sweetheart? Good. Poor Benjy, I thought he was Dominic. Damn, forgot the lemon. Ed?" she shouts to my brother, "Ed, get me a piece of lemon would you darling? In the fridge probably. No? Well try the windowsill. No? Well just hunt around, I'm talking to Nix. It's what? Well cut the moldy bit off. So sorry darling," she says to me, "just getting organized. You're doing an update? Well don't you dare put me in, I nearly sued you over the original. Yes, we're all fine, Harry's chopping up wood and going a marvellous colour in the sun. Richard and Eleanor were both down with their friends last weekend—Richard's working with wonky kids, did he tell you? He loves it. Oh dear, I must have a cigarette. Ed? Get me my tin, would you? It's in my bedroom cupboard under my paintings. I hide them from myself," she says to me, "now where was I? Quick Ed! Oh yes, Greatham's teeming as usual, all the Fishers are down and flourishing. So are my beans, I might add. I do wish you and the boys were coming over—but last summer was heavenly, wasn't it? Now listen darling, I've made a decision—oh thanks Ed—"

It transpires that she's coming to spend Christmas with us, news that delights us all. She came for Christmas in 1980 and the visit was a terrific success. She arrived wearing a hairy skirt with a fringe, a smart black raincoat with a line of large white stitches on the shoulder ("Caught it on a tree, darling, and didn't have any black thread,") and striped knitted socks kept up with elastic. On her head was what I took to be a tea-cosy but on inspection proved to be a fur hat I'd sent her twenty-two years ago.

"Nix! All ready for your famous winter," she cried, and lifted the hairy skirt to reveal long pink underwear.

"Very nice," I said trying not to notice the gathering crowd, "but your knees—" We eventually got her woollen legwarmers, and in these, a pair of Benjy's outgrown boots, and a mildewed sheepskin coat of mine tied round the middle with a suitcase strap, she took off daily for a walk, dropping in on my friends along the way.

I threw a fundraising dinner for the Manitoba Chamber Orchestra while she was here. She made the punch, and the speed with which the party got off the ground was such that people swarmed around her asking for the recipe.

"A bottle of gin, two of white wine, four big ones of cider and tons of fruit. Unbeatable. More darling?" My friend already had his glass over the bowl.

"Mm. Fantastic punch, Cordelia. Let's see. Bottle of gin—" He weaved away.

"Nice boy," said my mother.

"He's a judge."

"Goodness. Heads will be rolling at *his* next party."

Before we hang up today she asks me to give Cath a hug and is glad to hear she's feeling chipper.

This time four years ago Cath was far from chipper. She was having a rotten time with her right leg which, as Dr. McInnes in Edinburgh had predicted when she was a baby, had dislocated at the hip. The inside thigh muscles and groin tendons had shortened and tightened, so that the whole leg was being pulled up and rotated inward. This meant it was permanently bent up and twisted in. It made washing and dressing and keeping her sore-free extremely difficult. Far worse than that, though, I knew from her expression that she was always uncomfortable and very often in great pain, especially when we lifted her or went over a bump in the van. Eventually Dr. Letts agreed that cutting the muscle and tendon was necessary. She looked extraordinary afterwards, with her legs stretched wide apart and encased in heavy plaster. She seemed to have grown dramatically, but it was simply because I'd never seen her legs in that position. She looked surprised and cross but otherwise all right. The next day, however, she was as grey and sweaty as a mushroom under cellophane and I knew instantly that she had pneumonia. Dr. Letts' stand-in, an officious twit who heaved deep sighs and twiddled his stethoscope while I talked to him, said she just had mucus in her throat. At this point I got angry and said I wouldn't budge till he ordered an X-ray of Cath's chest. When I called him later he said the X-ray was normal. I shot to the hospital and found Cath looking much worse and with a raging fever. I found another doctor and explained her problems. He took one look at the X-ray and said, "Definitely pneumonia. I'll order antibiotic in her IV at once. Lucky you were around." Lucky, yes; it made me wonder what happens to people who are similarly handicapped but who don't have parents or advocates to speak on their behalf.

Catherine's whole skeletal structure seems to have settled now. Her leg is still fine and the scoliosis in her backbone has been kept in check with the plastic body jacket she wears when she's sitting. There have been other health problems, though. About three years ago she, Benjy and I were about to have supper one day when her face and whole body suddenly started to contort and shake wildly. Her eyes strained wide open and rolled upward, her teeth clenched, her face went white and her lips blue, and she began frothing at the mouth and making terrible death-rattle noises. Benjy rushed from the kitchen and then peered round the door fearfully, just as he did when he was little and watching a horror movie on TV. Had he not been there I'm sure I'd have panicked. As it was I had to keep calm, so I dragged him in and explained that Cath was having a grand mal epileptic seizure. Although she looked appalling, I said, she was unconscious, couldn't feel anything, and we should get her onto her bed, keep her warm, and stay with her till she recovered. This we did, and we were immensely relieved when, after a minute or so, she loosened up and fell into a deep sleep. Afterwards Benjy shiveringly observed that he wasn't surprised that in the olden days they thought people with epilepsy were possessed by the devil.

I had always been grateful that, unlike most people I knew who had extensive brain damage, Cath didn't have a major seizure problem, and my reaction to the incident was to ignore it. I ignored the next few grand mals, which were spaced several months apart. Then one morning she had three in a row, during one of which she bit through her tongue and then upchucked blood. I finally took her to a neurologist and he put her on a regular dose of anticonvulsant medication. She's been on it ever since; it's a low dose and does the trick.

Like her mother, Catherine had impacted wisdom teeth. Before she had them out she often avoided chewing properly and as a result sometimes food became lodged in her esophagus so firmly that it had to be removed under a general anaesthetic. On one such occasion recently we encountered a doctor with values dramatically different from those of Dr. Letts' stand-in. When the ambulance delivered us to the hospital—the general one rather than the Children's Centre now that Cath is an adult—she was in a wretched state. She was shaking with exhaustion from my attempts to unclog her with my electric suction machine, her hair and clothes were awry and littered with vomit and drool, and she kept retching and moaning. When the young doctor came in he looked at her in astonishment.

"Catherine! Nicola! Whatever happened?"

I was in such a tizzy that it took me a moment to realize that he was the son of a friend from way back, one of Ted's colleagues. He examined Cath, talking sympathetically and reassuringly to her all the while. Emergency wasn't busy for once, so after he'd arranged an X-ray and woken up a surgeon he came back to chat. Another doctor and a couple of nurses dropped by.

"Do you know these people, Hardy?" one of them asked. Hardy took my daughter's hand.

"I certainly do," he said. "Catherine and I used to play together on our lawn while our fathers painted the picket fence. Oh, and this is her mother, Mrs. Schaefer." I could have hugged him.

Did you ever get the Centre you wanted? How are you getting on with the Canadian Association for the Mentally Retarded these days? What does Catherine's future look like? I'm constantly asked these questions by kind people who have read my book.

No, we never got the Centre. And, incredible though it may sound, I'm in many ways glad we didn't.

When we were planning and pushing for the Centre there were two distinct groups of people who were against the idea: those who held people like Cath and Jeanie in such low esteem that they thought it would be a waste of time and money, and those who thought it would be ideologically wrong.

In the first group were wishy-washy politicians, the old guard of CAMR and, most unsavoury of all, civil servants who, because they had spent years working in the big institutions or sitting behind a desk issuing Orders of Supervision, were now self-proclaimed experts on the subject of mental retardation. Not, you will note, experts on persons with mental retardation, but the condition itself, as if the two were separable. In the face of irrefutable evidence to the contrary, these "experts" had—and have—the gall to state that most profoundly retarded, multiply handicapped people can't progress and are perfectly happy in institutions.

In the second group, which was much smaller, were people like the Executive Director of CAMR's Winnipeg branch, my friend David Wetherow, who valued individuals with multiple handicaps as highly as they valued anyone else. They maintained that building a special centre for such people would tend to set them apart as basically different from other people, further delaying the already horribly slow process of persuading generic services like schools, recreation centres and housing agencies to adapt to their needs. It was essential, they said, not only that people like Catherine lead as normal lives as possible but also that they be seen as an integral part of their communities.

I was impatient with both groups, the first for its total lack of vision and the second for its apparently unrealistic vision. I agreed with that vision in principle, of course, but I recall saying snarkily to David that presumably he figured Cath should get a job or go to university when she left school and move out into an apartment. Yes, he said, perhaps just that. Ha bloody ha, I said.

In the past five years, however, I have gradually dropped my dream for a Centre. I have now read, heard, and best of all, seen that even individuals whom our "experts" label "impossible to manage in the community" can, with a good support system, lead dignified and fulfilling lives in ordinary settings. Shaun K. is a good example. Shaun is labelled autistic, and his parents, no longer able to cope with his unpredictable and often violent behaviour, were forced to institutionalize him when he was about thirteen. Ten years later they finally managed to have him transferred to a community residence near them but he was so disruptive that he was kicked out after a year. At this point David and his gang wangled funds to rent a small house for Shaun and to pay for two live-in assistants. In the succeeding months he changed dramatically: his anti-social actions decreased; his attention span increased; he became more willing and able to communicate his needs (rather than tear his clothes off and screech around in a fury of frustration); and he learned to work, with assistance, in a local sheltered industry. He became, in short, a much happier young man. It cost money, to be sure, but only marginally more than to keep him zonked out neatly on a chipped iron bedstead in the big institution from which he came.

At this point I'd like to draw attention to something very frightening that's happening in several regions of Canada. While most people at least pay lip service to the concept of deinstitutionalization, some seem to think this means emptying monstrosities like the big one here and relocating the inhabitants to obsolete hospitals or other grotty old buildings no longer used by ordinary people. There are even those who would build new institutions.

Institutions by their very nature gobble up millions of dollars, with singularly little benefit to their residents, so if anything like this is happening in your area I would ask you, on behalf of my daughter and all citizens with a mental handicap, whether they live in the community or in an institution, *please* to question it.

My relationship with CAMR has improved enormously. Its attitude towards individuals with multiple handicaps has become so civilized that meeting their needs in the community is now its top priority. It's a reflection of a refreshing new direction in the organization across the country. I now have many friends in CAMR locally, provincially and nationally—people whose values I share, people with whom I really enjoy working and people upon whom I can always count for support. An example of our cooperation will, with luck, occur at the end of the summer. I've been invited to give my views on "Parent Partnership with Professionals" (an almost unheard-of topic until recently!) at a global conference in Toronto. I told the staff at headquarters in that city that I wouldn't have anyone to care for Cath at the time so they invited her too, and are laying on assistance so that I can work and she, rather than being bored out of her mysterious mind with me, will be entertained in town. What's more, David is also attending the conference and has arranged his schedule so that he can fly there and back with us. Normally when I leave home for a few days our friend Zana moves in to care for Cath. Zana appeared in our lives during the second summer recreation program, in which she was working, and since then she's virtually become part of our family. As long as Ted or the boys are around to lift Cath, she can pretty well replace me. She's resourceful, bright and she makes me laugh. "According to some of my colleagues," she said recently (she works in the community with people who are mentally handicapped), "Cath requires servicing—as if with a realignment and new spark plugs she'd run just fine." Cath enjoys my absences because Zana often loads her into the van and takes her to parties with her friends. "Why not?" she says, "it's time she had a few nights out."

It's good that Cath is getting used to being cared for by different people and in different places (last summer she stayed, very successfully, with a neighbourhood family while the boys and I were in England) and it's also good for me to know that she survives perfectly well without me. The thought of her living somewhere else permanently used to make my stomach lurch and my ears hum in horror. Now, though, with the help of Zana and David and other friends, I'm beginning to look at it from Cath's point of view, rather than my own. I realize she has as much right as the boys to leave home eventually.

Things are looking up for people with multiple disabilities in Manitoba. Babies with significant developmental delays are being diagnosed and helped earlier; there are some good, though segregated, programs for young children, plus integrated programs in two departments at the University of Manitoba; elementary-aged children are now being integrated not just into schools but into regular classrooms; there are the programs Catherine is in; there are two good but overcrowded residences for adults; and more of the people like Cath in the St. Amant Centre now have individual programs.

Alas, all these improvements, and some exciting plans CAMR and other groups have for the immediate future, are too late for my dear friend Alice. Her daughter Jeanie died last September. Alice says the staff at the St. Amant Centre were very kind during the six years Jeanie had to spend there, but although the Centre provided most of the medical attention Jeanie needed it was, of course, unable to give her the stimulating life and personal care her family always gave her. I'm bound to say she would have received this treatment in our proposed Centre. It's typical of Alice that she is now anxious to help other families who want to keep their sons and daughters at home.

Catherine's future has always been misty and has sometimes had big black institutional clouds hanging ready to envelop her. Now, though, as I have suggested, some positive plans are beginning to take shape.

Until recently the idea of her living in her own apartment was, as I said to David, ludicrous. However, I've now met many people across Canada, some with even greater needs than Cath, who are living happily and successfully in small houses or apartments, usually with one or two friends who are handicapped, and with the necessary assistants either living in or being there on a shift basis. Judging by set-ups I've already seen, I think one of the most attractive and practical ideas for Cath would be an apartment. There are several blocks near us that are wheelchair-accessible, have a swimming pool and nice surrounding neighbourhoods in which to go for walks, and are as close as we are now to such amenities as hospitals and stores: in fact the only basic necessity not already in place would be her bathtub, which could easily be transferred.

I see Catherine's apartment being one of a network of such individualized living arrangements in Winnipeg for people with severe disabilities. The network would be run by a small staff who would find and train assistants and negotiate financial arrangements on behalf of Cath et al. This staff would be responsible to, and supported by, a strong community board of parents (including me, I hope!) and friends and allies willing to provide voluntary professional input. Funding for the plan would be acquired through existing social allowance schemes.

Friends are encouraging me to start arranging this move now, and I must admit that I'd like to see Cath well settled soon rather than wait for a crisis, which would be unfair to all of us. While I still hate the idea of not having her at home with us, I tell myself we'd remain very much part of each other's lives; in fact I'll probably drive her nuts by phoning and visiting her daily at first.

So now, in our mind's eye, we have Catherine in a well-supported, comfortable living arrangement. But what will she do during the day? In the summer she can continue going to the recreation program but what about the rest of the year?

Once again, that brief interchange with David years ago may have been prophetic. Aware that there is an abyss for Cath and many others after the official school-leaving age of twenty-one, our school division has kindly told me she can stay in her current program for an extra year. After that, astonishingly, she may indeed go to university.

The University of Winnipeg, in the centre of town, is comparatively small and cozy and has a more philanthropic approach to education than some such institutions. When it recently announced that it was now almost entirely accessible to students with physical handicaps my mind started whirring.

David and I arranged a meeting with the new Dean and, taking a deep breath, suggested that the university establish a developmental/educational program for a limited number of adults with severe or multiple handicaps.

I have on countless occasions been part of a group making a proposal to Government and I can usually predict how the recipients of the proposal will react. They start out nodding and smiling, then they get fidgety, and then they say no. In this meeting almost the reverse happened. The Dean and his two colleagues present began by being friendly but cautious, then they sat up, became really interested and said what a fantastic idea, let's see if we can do it! They even anticipated us by noting the benefits of such a program to the university—that it would be a practicum setting for students in subjects like education, psychology and communications, and that the university would be one of the first in North America to open its doors to students with mental as well as physical handicaps.

We've had several meetings since then, all positive, and though I say this with the utmost caution, it looks as though there could be a program ready to start in the fall of 1983.

It occurs to me that I should ask my daughter what she thinks of all these plans I'm making for her. It's been a long day and she's looking a bit droopy.

"Hey Cath, I've got an important question for you, darling. How would you like the idea of moving into your own apartment and going to university?"

She looks dazed for a moment. Then she reaches out for my hand, looks directly at me and grins broadly.

Fortuitous? Perhaps. But who knows?

Summer 1982

PART TWO

1983—99

It's a handsome house. Old, wood-framed and painted white with a black roof and trim, it has three stories. It faces a pleasant park where one can enjoy concerts, picnics, celebrations and evening saunters in the summer, as well as crunchy walks along its paths in winter. The house is in a friendly, elm-shaded neighbourhood close to downtown Winnipeg. It's five minutes from where Catherine grew up and it's been her home since July 18th, 1986.

"Is it the one on the corner with the curved path sloping up to the back door," someone asked recently, "the one with the lovely flowers everywhere?"

"That's it, yes. And the path is actually a disguised ramp. I'm glad you were fooled!"

This conversation took me back nearly a decade, when planning began in earnest for Cath's move to her own place. The idea of her living in an apartment with the necessary supports had lurked at the back of my mind for some time, but then an even better plan had presented itself.

Five years previously I was at a conference in Winnipeg, telling the story of Catherine's life, and had met a charming psychiatrist, Hugh Lafave, who would later become the Executive Director of the Canadian Association for Community Living (CACL)[1] in Toronto. Hugh told me that my apartment idea reminded him of when he was a medical student: he'd thought how great it would be if a house could be set up to meet a variety of people's needs. Hugh imagined a friendly, middle-aged couple—maybe retired but still active—living in a third floor, self-contained apartment; they would be responsible for running the house. Four younger people would have bedrooms on the second floor. The ground floor would be their communal space—the sitting room, dining room

---

[1] Encouraged by the leadership of People First of Canada (an association of people who had lived and struggled with the label of mental retardation), the Canadian, Manitoba and Winnipeg Associations "for the Mentally Retarded" were renamed "Associations for Community Living (ACL)." In March, 1986, our local branch became the Association for Community Living—Winnipeg. CAMR Manitoba Division followed suit in May, and the national body became the Canadian Association for Community Living (CACL) in October.

and kitchen. Three of these young people would be students, in subjects like medicine (that's where Hugh would fit in), psychology and teaching, and the fourth person would be someone with a disability who needed friendship and support to lead a good life. The result: a congenial abode and a learning experience for all concerned.

I thought the idea a marvellously innovative one—one that would work well for a person with less complex inconveniences with which to contend than Cath—but felt it wouldn't be the answer for Cath herself. Then, because there was no funding for such an undertaking in sight for anyone with Catherine's sorts of needs anyway, I forgot about it.

•

I'd always been grateful for the existence of St. Amant as a place where Cath could go when I took off for England with the boys, but I was never exactly thrilled to leave her there. When the automatic front doors opened and I wheeled her in, Cath's expression seemed to undergo a subtle change—nothing as specific as unhappy, anxious or displeased, but the slightly lowered eyelids and suspension of her customary arm-flapping suggested quiet resignation, an emotional shutting down. I'd also become increasingly uncomfortable running around talking about community alternatives to institutions, then sheepishly admitting that I still occasionally made use of just such a place.

A small but significant occurrence the last time I'd picked Cath up from St. Amant after going to England finally spurred me to action.

As I walked down the main hall of her ward, I passed an alcove wherein a group of about fifteen residents were propped up in, or hanging over the edges of their wheelchairs. They were grouped in a semicircle around a huge colour TV showing a steamy scene from a soap opera that looked as though it was called *The Doomed and the Dreary*. A couple of attendants standing behind the group were watching the show but, as I cast my eye over the residents in wheelchairs, I noticed not one of them had their eyes anywhere near the TV. It was utterly irrelevant to them. I walked to Cath's room but she wasn't in it.

"So you've lost my daughter?" I said to the nurse at the desk. She looked up and smiled.

"Hi, Mrs. Schaefer, good to see you. Now you know we wouldn't do that. She's watching TV. She's been no trouble at all, as usual."

Puzzled, I walked back to the group. I scanned it slowly and, sure

St. Amant. KEN GIGLIOTTI PHOTO

enough, there was Cath in the middle, head drooped on her chest, fast asleep. I was horrified to realize that I hadn't seen her the first time, hadn't been able to distinguish her from all the other bored young people in the wheelchair circle.

Cath had, in a sense, disappeared.

Well, I thought, I don't know how I'm going to do this but that's the last time Catherine is going to St. Amant. I have to cut the umbilical cord. Maybe I'll just have to give up going to England.

Later I took a deep breath and told my thoughts to our friend David Wetherow, ACL Winnipeg's Executive Director. He put his arm around me and gave me a big squeeze.

"Good for you," he said, "good for you! We've been wondering when you'd have the courage to do this."

I was taken aback. "You have? And who is *we?* Who have you been discussing me with?"

"All of us who care about you and Cath. We decided we shouldn't say anything to you, though. It had to be your decision. But now you've made it we'll be there for you. Rest assured, we'll sort out something for Cath next time you go to England."

I had an almost identical reaction from Zana—"God! What a relief you've finally come to that conclusion!"—and from several other friends.

Early in the summer of 1983 I put everyone to the test by announcing that while Dominic was planning to clean buses for the City for most of the summer, Benjy and I wanted to go to England for the month of August. It would be too difficult to take Catherine.

In 1980 a community residence had opened in Steinbach, a small town near Winnipeg. It was created largely due to the efforts of Martha, a friend of mine who, despite the fact that her daughter had died some years before in the big institution, continued to be active in procuring good alternatives in the community for people with multiple disabilities. Apart from having been forced by the government to accommodate too many people—six plus two "respite" beds—the home ranked high in many people's estimation, including mine. Debbie, the house manager, heard that I was looking for a place for Catherine and kindly invited her to stay for the last two weeks of August.

Zana came up with an imaginative if scary plan for the first two. She worked for ACL Manitoba at the time and was in charge of its summer holiday program for people with complex disabilities. Cath had, incidentally, been the catalyst for creating the program a year or two before. Zana had funding from various sources but no building so, with encouragement from Dale Kendel, ACL Manitoba's Executive Director, she set about planning for Cath and two other young people in the program to take a trip to the Rockies.

Although at first I was intrigued by the idea, I soon developed a daunting list of possible disasters. Cath had camped overnight before but this was different. What if, for instance, despite the carefully planned menus which included loads of fresh fruit, veggies and bran, Catherine's innards clogged up? What if she developed a chest infection that didn't respond to the antibiotic I was sending along? What if a bear took a fancy to her? I decided that the concept of allowing people who have disabilities "the dignity of risk," i.e. not over-protecting them, is all very well but only when applied to *other people*. However, my qualms subsided, somewhat, as I heard the details of the expedition develop.

There were five assistants accompanying Cath and her two friends— three women, including Zana, and two men. All were at university, studying a variety of subjects that included education, chemistry, psychology and theology. Three of them had experience working with persons who had severe disabilities, four had camping experience and two were certified in First Aid. In addition to this expertise, they all had tremendous enthusiasm about the proposed trip. They spent individual

Enjoying Lake Louise (Cath on left, Zana in hat).

time with the three protagonists and their excited but dubious families, and became knowledgeable about their regular routines, habits, medications, diets and preferences. Then they set up rough meal plans, precise medication charts, and began to work out routes.

Next they rounded up camping gear, mostly borrowed: two tents, air mattresses, sleeping bags, lanterns, cooking equipment, coolers, umbrellas, a daunting box of disposable undergarments, a bike pump for the wheelchairs and a Trivial Pursuit game. When all the equipment was massed from wall to wall and ceiling to floor in our dining room, everyone wondered how it, plus eight people, would fit into our van and the small car they were taking. But it did, and hours after Benjy and I boarded the plane for England, off they set across the prairies.

There were the minor problems common to any such trip, such as burnt food and lost roads, but nothing went seriously wrong. The eight friends thoroughly enjoyed a memorable camping holiday together. Cath brought back a photo album of the jaunt and a diary kept by the assistants. We still enjoy looking at these books. To give a taste of the trip, here's an extract from an article written later by Zana:

Three days later we (the women) joined the guys in Banff. We camped at Tunnel Mountain, a beautiful spot. We decided to cut Jasper out of the trip, spend more time in

Banff and return home via Calgary. This allowed us to adopt a slower pace and see more of Banff, which is a lovely town. We strolled around, watching the other tourists and admiring the Rocky Mountains. We spent a full day at Lake Louise and managed to walk halfway around the lake before the path got too steep to manage the wheelchairs. A picnic at Coral Creek with a red-and-white-checked tablecloth; a spaghetti dinner with home-made sauce and two bottles of wine; the gondola ride at Sulphur Mountain; shopping for souvenirs for ourselves and our families—these are the memories from the Rockies.

We drove to Calgary, down from the clean, crisp mountain air to the muggy prairies. Mounds of laundry and eight baths later, we all spruced up and went out to a highly recommended Chinese restaurant. We had a great time, with cocktails followed by lots of fine food. As had been the case throughout our trip, we received excellent and respectful service, with the waiters going out of their way to get to know us all and what would please us. After dinner we took a stroll through a beautiful island park in the heart of Calgary and listened to performers at the Folk Festival. The city and park were all lit up and so were we.

All through the holiday we drew double takes and long looks. We welcomed them, especially from children. We would always smile (or smile back) and try to start a con-versation. Children wanted to know why some people couldn't walk or talk, and then wanted to know what they could do. Adults were amazed that we were on holiday, all the way from Winnipeg. Fortunately they were so struck by this fact that they forgot to tell us all how wonderful we were for doing this. What we could probably never have explained to them was how much fun we had had on the trip ourselves.

Everyone seemed powerfully affected by the trip to the Rockies but none more so than Jay, one of the assistants. He was a chemistry student at the beginning of the holiday, but by the end of it had decided to switch to medicine. He wanted to become a neurologist so that he could help peo-ple like Cath and her friends. The last I heard he was well on his way.

•

Several significant events occurred in the late '70s and early '80s that were to change the lives of many people with disabilities in Manitoba, including, for the first time, those with complex problems such as Catherine's. In the summer of 1979 Dale Kendel, ACL Manitoba's Execu-tive Director, and John Robertson, an enthusiastic and community-spirited journalist, headed up a group of people who organized a twenty-six-mile marathon to raise funds for community projects aimed at support-ing people with mental handicaps. Some four and a half thousand runners took part and it was immensely exciting. Zana, Cath and I camped overnight in the van where the race started so that we could be up at 5.00 a.m. to help stick numbers on competitors' shirts. Then we had a protracted breakfast at a nearby pancake house while the runners ran, after which we waited at the finish line (the race was circular) to cheer everyone as they returned. The professionals merely shook off their sweat and checked their time. Others, arriving much later, wobbled and weaved their way down the final stretch and collapsed into the welcomers' arms.

The Manitoba Marathon has continued annually. As of 1998 it has raised three and a half million dollars and has been a terrific instrument for public awareness.

Says Dale:

The significant impact of the Manitoba Marathon has been the strategic use of these three and a half million dollars to initiate new concepts (apartment living, smaller community residences, shared accommodation, employment options, etc.) that have now become commonplace. These concepts, once successfully implemented, have received ongoing provincial government funding and the designs have been replicated. Apartment living, for instance, started with twenty-nine people and now supports four hundred and fifty individuals throughout Manitoba. Overall, in excess of forty million dollars have been attracted to projects over the last decade and a half, and in total, two hundred and forty-three projects have been supported, so clearly the Marathon has played an extraordinary role in influencing the services and supports that have been developed in Manitoba.

One year, I went down to the river road which Cath, Coda (our dog) and I regularly walked, to yell encouragement to the runners at the midway point. A middle-aged man plodded grimly past, his mouth open, a bandage holding one knee together. "Doing it for Cath," he managed to croak, "my way of helping." Further on he veered off to the side of the road to pass under a shower someone had thoughtfully rigged up with a garden hose. It was only then that I recognized him as a friend from the Chemistry Department at the University of Manitoba. I felt a twist of guilt but realized he wouldn't be doing it if he didn't want to, and that the Marathon was a way for people to do their bit for the cause even if they couldn't become directly involved in people's lives.

A New Democratic Party (NDP) government was returned late in 1981 and some two years later, Muriel Smith, a human rights activist and an old friend of Alice's and mine, became the Minister of Community Services. Muriel understood the necessity of making it possible for people with disabilities to lead decent lives. One of the first things she did as Minister was to launch what became known as Project Welcome Home. Under the auspices of this plan some two hundred and twenty people would be sprung from the big institution, St. Amant, and another small but isolated institution. Funding would be provided to help an equal number of adults with disabilities move from their parental homes into the wider community. The process was to take about three years and rural areas were to be addressed first.

Initially, there was chaos, rather similar to the scenes one sees on TV when a planeload of food lands amidst thousands of starving people. Many of us had almost given up hope that we would ever see money going towards creating alternative living situations in the community, rather than being used only for improving, or adding to, existing institutions.

A confusion of committees was set up to sort out how the whole process would work. This alone took almost a year. There had to be equal representation from community agencies and relevant civil servants— some of whom had been regurgitated from the bad old days and were neither relevant nor civil. I was reminded of the excruciating time when Alice and I and other members of Action for the Dependent Handicapped (ADH) had to wrestle with these people when they had no intention of listening to us, let alone doing anything constructive. Muriel's policy, and her determination to make it work, made a difference this time.

I forget how many committees I was on—at least four—but much of my life seemed to be spent shut up in one of several artificially-lit, stuffy board rooms arguing vociferously and trying to make sense of what someone was diligently writing on the flip chart. Alternately, I was travelling to or from one of the institutions. Teams of pertinent people—the individual concerned, family members if any (very often, sadly, people had no known relatives), social workers, institutional staff, community agencies which could potentially serve the person—were created to plan the resettlement in the community of those chosen to be sprung.

Like many of my friends, I worked on several of these teams as a sort of bi-partisan community advocate. The sense of ear-humming, sweaty horror I'd felt ten years previously, when I went to investigate the big institution, never failed to stun me every time I entered the place. And even though we were doing something positive, it was sad and frustrating to know that only a few of the hundreds of men and women in the place would escape to a real life.

Staff members were almost universally pleasant and eager to cooperate but a curious attitude was prevalent. They divided inmates into two groups: those who were "ready for the community" and those who, due to the complexity of their disabilities, were not. "Mary shouldn't be in here, she doesn't belong. But Lucy, in that bed over there, she'll always be with us." We heard such comments often. We knew that each individual in the place could live in the community. It was more a question of whether the community was ready to provide the necessary support to welcome each individual.

Reviewing the lists of people for whom we were to plan, I found it depressing to see that they were described mainly in negative terms: "#3593, M., 47, wheelchair, seizures, profoundly retarded," or, "#4487, F. severe retardation, non-verbal, self-abusive, violent." Several people had "wanders" listed among their non-attributes. A typographical error on one turned this into "wonders." I'll bet he wonders, said someone.

I remember on one trip we met a dignified, middle-aged fellow called Max who shyly told us he dreamed of living in his own place back in Altona, where he came from, and that he got angry when people tried to make him do things like spend the day unscrewing widgets and then being told to screw them up again. His notation read, "Wheelchair, non-compliant." Who wouldn't be infuriated under these circumstances? We began automatically to admire the spirit of anyone who had "non-compliant" by their name. Conversely, we suspected that "compliant," which was used as a positive adjective, meant squashed spirit.

My desk, a table in Cath's room, became a repository solely for piles of proposals and documents associated with Welcome Home. The paperwork spread inexorably down to the floor and thence, after a spell, onto the fridge, into the dining room. My normal desk stuff—mainly heaps of unanswered mail and an alarming file labelled "to be dealt with now" dated two years previously—was moved to a space between the piano and the wall, where at least I couldn't see it.

My typewriter, a comfortable old manual full of dog hair, stayed put, usually buried amidst the papers. This was because Dominic seemed to be turning into an academic, a breed that has always puzzled me. He was working towards an Honours English degree and periodically, after holing up in his room or at the university for days at a time, he would appear white and bleary-eyed with, for instance, an armful of erudite essay on Eliot which had to be typed (by me) and handed in tomorrow. He habitually did this while Cath was watching the late night news and I was ready to drop. My screams of outrage caused her much merriment. My sleep pattern had been the same for years: some six hours a night during the week and terrific lie-ins on the weekend. Now, though, there were even meetings at 9.00 on Saturday mornings.

Having hauled myself out of bed on one such occasion, I fed and dressed Cath, felt like passing out at the meeting and returned home more than a little fragile. Ted tried to help. "You look awful," he said. I mustered a glare. "You've been at it for months now, but how many people have come out of the institutions? And when is anything going to happen for Cath?"

I'd already tried to explain to him that Welcome Home, after the initial and seemingly endless planning, was concentrating on people from rural areas. Only later would those from Winnipeg be helped. Wanting to be alone, I traipsed down to the basement to do the laundry.

Even when and if Cath's turn did come, I thought, how would her new living situation be arranged and the necessary continuing support co-ordinated? None of the existing community agencies catered to people with her kinds of needs. God, we'd have to start one. How? Who? Tears of tiredness joined the wash as it churned around. When I went upstairs Ted had left for the lab but there was a vase of roses on the kitchen table. "I worry about you," he said later. As one does, I rallied and carried on. The work was relentless but we truly were helping people have a life rather than an existence. That thought kept me going.

•

One ray of hope for Catherine was another initiative of the early '80s designed to benefit people with disabilities. This was the founding, in 1982, of a housing co-op in Winnipeg which incorporated a small percentage of people with physical or mental disabilities. Called Prairie Housing Co-operative, it was dreamed up by David Wetherow. In his role as ACL Winnipeg's Executive Director, David made himself responsible for inventing new ways for people with disabilities to lead good, well-supported lives. Although Cath didn't become a member of the co-op until four years later, he says that she was one of the two people who inspired the idea. "If it won't work for Cath I'm not interested in pursuing it," he said.

Co-operative (working together) housing has existed for decades in many countries but it is a relatively new concept in Canada and only just beginning in the United States. The basis of any co-op is the members, who buy a membership for a nominal sum, refundable if they leave, collectively rent or buy the house, the apartment block, or whatever it may be, and are collectively responsible for running it. Co-op control and responsibility are democratic—one member, one vote— but the usual practice is for the members to elect a board of directors from amongst themselves, to look after the financial and general management of the co-op (the rents cover the costs and anything extra goes towards an "improvement fund"). Fundamental issues are voted on by the general membership.

Sometimes, when a co-op becomes too big or time-consuming for the board to run, a manager is hired. The policy and direction of the co-op, however, always remain in the hands of the board, and the board, in turn, is always responsible to the general membership. As David says in an article about co-op housing in his book, *The Whole Community Catalogue*:

One of the continuing lessons for members in all kinds of co-ops is that there is no 'them.' Ultimately, all action, or inaction, and all responsibility is 'ours.'

Co-op housing is attractive for many people, particularly those with low incomes, because there's no middle person wanting to make a profit. Co-ops can provide decent, affordable places to live, and there's more likelihood of having friendly neighbours.

One of Prairie Housing Co-op's first buys was two pairs of side-by-side houses a few streets from us. Three of the houses were occupied by typical groups of people: a family of three in one, a family of four in another and a young couple without children in another. All these people agreed, when they joined the co-op and moved in, that they would be friendly and supportive of one another but particularly of the people in the fourth house, two women who were friends and both of whom had a disability. These women received paid support from a social agency in necessary areas, such as job-training, but were able to rely on their co-op neighbours for help with shopping and similar chores with which they had not yet become familiar. (Not much chance to go shopping in an institution.)

All members of this four-house cluster spent time in each other's homes because they enjoyed one another's company, and because they shared the chores and pleasures of a communal fenced back garden. Although most of the households in this cluster have changed today, the pattern remains the same.

David and I often found ourselves attending the same Project Welcome Home meetings. After one of them, about a year after my attack of the miseries, I unburdened myself to him concerning Cath's future and where she'd eventually live. He suggested I begin practising what I'd been encouraging other parents to do for their children when I'd spent time with them in the course of Welcome Home—dream, he said, dream about the best possible living arrangement for her.

There were many factors in Cath's favour at the moment, he noted. Prairie Housing Co-op was running smoothly and now had several clusters of housing similar to the one near us, so Cath could link into the co-op as he, David, had always envisioned. Welcome Home had for some time been providing funding for those Winnipeg residents who needed to move away from their parental homes, or who were in danger of being institutionalized because of family problems. The provincial government was making renovation grants available to groups of five people or more who wanted to set up house together, as long as one of them had a disability and would not otherwise be able to live interdependently within the community.

I was a board member of ACL Winnipeg and had been in on Prairie Housing Co-op since its inception, so many of these facts were not new to me. What David said made sense. I should start dreaming for Catherine. I must admit, though, I was reluctant at first, because I felt we might be taking unfair advantage of the system. But when David added that the money wouldn't last much longer, so it might be now or never, I went home and embarked on some serious dreaming.

Finding out about the renovation grants for groups of five people or more reminded me of Hugh Lafave's idea as a medical student—living in a house with a diverse group of people, one of whom required support. Why not a house? I thought.

Two of the most negative aspects of having significant disabilities, particularly if one has trouble communicating, are the propensity for loneliness and the likelihood of having only people in one's life who are paid to be there. Catherine, it seemed to me, might well be prone to these problems if she lived in an apartment with shift staff, however hard we tried to build in supports.

Catherine had grown up in an ordinary house in a friendly neighbourhood. From babyhood, she had always been as widely recognized, accepted and liked for who she was as any other child. Wouldn't she be more comfortable in a setting similar to that in which she'd always been?

Maybe with, instead of her family, a group of friends more or less her age?

But what friends?

Cath and I had been connected with Winnipeg's l'Arche community since 1979. L'Arche, the French word for "the ark," is an international federation of intentional communities, of various sizes, in which men and women who have a disability, and their assistants, live, work and share their lives together. The assistants are never known as staff; they receive board and room and what amounts to pocket money.

Winnipeg's l'Arche community consists of twenty-five people with disabilities. They live with assistants in houses, duplexes or apartments all within a few miles of each other. Jean Vanier, a visionary Canadian philosopher and theologian, founded the first community in a village in France in 1964. There are now about one hundred l'Arche communities in thirty countries all over the world, including several in England. Many of the assistants in Winnipeg's community have been and are from Manitoba but over the years others have come from outside Canada. I'm pleased to have been instrumental in importing, to date, three from England. Assistants live within a community for weeks, months, and sometimes for years. Whichever the case, the experience seems to have a profound effect on them; one writer friend of mine here spent a summer in our community when she was a teenager. She is still, years later, quite connected, writing articles for and about l'Arche, and retreating to the original community in France when life overwhelms her.

I was invited onto the board a couple of years after Cath and I became l'Arche friends. Soon after, at a retreat (a weekend in a Benedictine nunnery) for board members and assistants, I was asked what I thought I brought to l'Arche. I could think of not one single thing. I felt I received more from l'Arche people, both with and without a disability, than I could ever give. Eventually, I looked at my daughter and said, "Catherine," and was gratified to find that others agreed with me. Cath ranks high in a community where vulnerability is virtually a plus, because of what one can learn from those who are vulnerable (including discovering one's own fragility). L'Arche communities across Canada are beginning to welcome people with more severe disabilities, and when it happens in Winnipeg, I'll know Cath has played a part in the move.

In 1985, I travelled across Canada and through the United States, speaking at conferences about Catherine, and about growing up with her. I enjoyed all these trips but the one that gave me the most joy and satisfaction was when Cath herself accompanied me. We travelled on behalf of l'Arche Winnipeg to spend a weekend in Edmonton with the l'Arche communities from Edmonton, Calgary and Illinois. There were about forty-five of us on the trip, including those with a disability, the assistants who lived with them, board members and friends. We travelled by train, nineteen hours each way, and a journey I'd rather dreaded (trains are not designed with users of wheelchairs in mind) proved to be a positive and enjoyable experience. Everybody along the way pitched in to help Cath; people helped people, in fact, and the same was true of the entire weekend, which underlined (for me) the absolute necessity of assisting those with disabilities to create around themselves a network of steadfast friends.

As I considered friends who might like to share Cath's house, the first people who came to mind were Lauchie and Evelyn, former l'Arche assistants who had recently moved out of the community with their small daughter, Marie. They'd be perfect, I thought, a settled, cheerful family. Evelyn was a Montessori teacher, although at the moment she was mostly at home with Marie, and Lauchie was training to be a nurse. They liked Catherine, and they would bring an air of stability and warmth to the household.

I explained the plan for the house and then asked tentatively if they might be interested in taking part. My lengthy speech about how I understood why they couldn't take me up on such a wild idea was overridden and I was literally speechless when they immediately said yes, how soon? It transpired that they had been dissatisfied with their living situation and missed being part of the give and take of a larger household.

I went to David Wetherow once again with my thoughts about a house. "Go for it," he said. "Look for a house and report back when you've found one you think would be suitable." Prairie Housing would then give the place the once-over, as would the Canada Mortgage and Housing Corporation, which was helping Prairie Housing obtain low-interest mortgages. A small group of architects and city planners (friends of Winnipeg's Association for Community Living) would also want to see the house because they would be designing the renovations as well as handling the licensing and other bureaucratic necessities.

As I searched for the right house, I had several considerations in mind: it had to be within easy cycling distance of Lauchie's hospital, close to a nursery school for Marie, not too far from us, and in a friendly

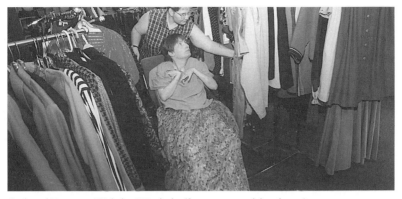

Cath and Darcy in Wolesley Wardrobe (favourite second-hand store). KEN GIGLIOTTI PHOTO

neighbourhood. After several false starts I found a house that fulfilled these requirements and Lauchie and Evelyn and I went to nose around in it, as did the fellows from the planning group.

There was a ground-floor apartment, two smaller ones on the second floor and a fourth on the top floor. With a bit of imagination, we could visualize the ground floor becoming a comfortable living space for Cath and two roommates. There was a huge kitchen with plenty of space for a table and six chairs, a good-sized sitting room, a bedroom and bathroom, which would be for Cath's roommates, and a dining room, which could be transformed into Cath's bedroom and washing facilities. In addition, there was a small room by the laundry room in the basement, plus a bathroom.

Because Lauchie and Evelyn needed a larger space than any one of the three upstairs apartments provided, we figured we could rearrange the latter into one large apartment for them and still have room for a small bachelor apartment for another person.

The house was very attractive on the outside. It had a front porch and a balcony above that on the second floor. There was a nice front garden and lawn surrounded by lilacs and other bushes. In short, it looked like what it had originally been—a large middle-class family home. In the park immediately opposite the house was a playground (perfect for Marie) that included a water slide down which children were happily shrieking.

Reflecting the multi-generational nature of the neighbourhood, next to the playground was a green on which some elderly people in hats were bowling away the afternoon. At the other end of the block was a street with some of my favourite stores: Prairie Sky Books, Tall Grass Prairie

Bakery, The Green Earth Environment Store, Harvest Collective and Wolseley Wardrobe. Close by, too, was Impressions Café (where Benjy often worked). Portage Avenue, one of Winnipeg's main streets, was only a block away from the house, so it would be easy for people who didn't have cars to get to the house by bus.

That summer, 1985, while I was involved in Prairie Housing's acquisition of the house, Dominic finally carried out a long-standing threat, and he and a university friend moved into their own apartment in an old block in an unfashionably grotty part of the city.

"Why you guys wanna move in here anyway?" asked the caretaker suspiciously, as a cop car burned rubber round the corner, racing to deal with a fight in the back lane. "Because we're poor," was the answer. Dominic was finishing off his degree, cleaning buses for the City just often enough to pay the rent. Most of his time, though, was spent working for a small advertising firm which produced, amongst other things, a sort of "What's on in Winnipeg?" magazine. Dominic wore a tie and his father's 1950s suit to work (considered very smart by his contemporaries) and had a pocket full of company cards with his name and "advertising consultant" on them. Part of the job, as might be inferred from this information, was flogging ad space in the magazine, but he was also writing the odd—very odd, he said—article and learning the art of putting a periodical together.

Dominic was also learning, of course, the art of living independently but, in the tradition of all sons leaving home, he would appear every few days for a shower, a meal, and use of the washing machine. We loved seeing him, even though the house became increasingly denuded as he would stagger out to his fifteenth-hand car after each visit with anything he could persuade us we no longer wanted. I drew the line at the sofa.

The idea of leaving the nest seemed to be catching. Benjy was talking about moving out when he finished high school at the University of Winnipeg Collegiate. Benjy had always been clever at inventing jobs for himself during school breaks, and outdid himself this year. Winnipeg had been plagued by cankerworms for the last four springs. These pests appeared just after the leaves budded, and gobbled them up, leaving naked trees and a revolting mess on sidewalks and roads. Benjy offered to trap the moths, which hatched in the ground and crawled up the trees in the fall to lay their eggs. He travelled round the neighbourhood ringing trees with a band of a gluey substance called Tanglefoot—stuff that became ubiquitous around our place and could also have been called Tanglefinger, Tanglehair, TangleTed (which irritated him) and Tangledog. However, Benjy did good business. When he returned to school I had to deal with many a cryptic phone call, e.g., "Is the worm man still ringing?" or "Can I speak to the worm-glue guy?" These days, when young people come round in the spring asking if we want our trees banded, I think of my entrepreneur son, and remember those days.

•

Like other Canadian adults with a disability, when Catherine turned eighteen she began receiving social allowance cheques which, in theory, covered her living expenses. Until then, she'd never had anything more than the family allowance that parents receive for all children, so the $350 a month social allowance seemed like a bonus and I spent the first cheque getting my teeth fixed. If she was eventually to move into her own place, however, this income would barely cover her rent and food, let alone her care.

Welcome Home funding was to be provided on an ongoing basis to assist Catherine and others with severe disabilities in new living arrangements. It had to go through a government-approved agency and, as I've already indicated, nothing of the sort existed. David, having observed that part of ACL Winnipeg's mandate was to provide alternatives for people with Catherine's kinds of needs, created the necessary agency.

We called it l'Avenir Community Co-operative (l'avenir being the French word for "the future, that which is to come"). The co-op began in 1983 around Catherine and a young man named Arnold who had spent years in the big institution and whose family desperately wanted him out. Anyone who has started a new organization knows it takes a huge amount of planning before anything much happens. And so it was with l'Avenir. Nevertheless, when the time came for Arnold and Catherine, and several other people, to move to new abodes, everything was in place. We even had a General Manager, Cindy. Cindy and her husband had recently spent two years with CUSO (Canadian University Service Overseas) in Africa and she had experience working with people who had complex disabilities. Cindy was calm and capable, and she was clever at making good use of limited resources, a skill she'd picked up from her CUSO experience. We could not have found a better person to help l'Avenir grow once David had brought it into being.

Many times, a person with a disability has his or her housing and other needs met by a single agency. This is dangerous; in fact I've known several people who have been booted out of an agency because of "difficult" (probably angry and frustrated) behaviour—losing both their housing and service provider simultaneously. David recognized this potential problem, and intentionally created Prairie Housing Co-op and l'Avenir as separate entities. Should Catherine, for example, for some reason leave Prairie Housing to live in other accommodations, she'll still be a member of l'Avenir and have help with other aspects of her life. Conversely, should she find a better support agency than l'Avenir, she can still live in her house with Prairie Housing.

L'Avenir Community Co-operative's stated purpose is: "to provide the supports which will enable people with mental and/or physical disabilities to live with dignity, fulfillment and security."

Our goals are:
- to help members create for themselves meaningful life styles that are focused on relationships,
- to respond creatively to the evolving needs and wishes of members,
- to enable our members to explore the risks and rewards of life's full spectrum,
- to support families by addressing their concerns for the lifelong needs of their sons and daughters.

We are:
- a small community of members, their families and networks (friends and support staff) living throughout Winnipeg,
- an agency that supports those members in their homes and places of work and leisure,
- a co-op in which the direction of the agency is determined by the people served,
- an agency committed to supporting people with significant and challenging disabilities,
- not buildings or property, but PEOPLE.

Most of the points are self-explanatory; at least I hope they are, because we spent a long weekend concocting the brochure from which they have been quoted.

I would like to elaborate on a couple of them, however, because I think they are the aspects of our agency that make it an unusual one.

"To help members create meaningful life styles that are focused on relationships." Good governments, good agencies, good staff, all these entities tend by their nature to come and go, so one must rely ultimately not on these official bodies, but on family members and friends. I can confidently say that should I disappear right now, Catherine has a network of relatives and loyal friends who would look out for her. In l'Avenir we work to make this a reality for all our members.

"A co-op in which the direction of the agency is determined by the people served." Most agencies similar to l'Avenir have a couple of parents on their board, but the direction often stems from people who are interested and concerned but not involved directly. Our board, on the other hand, consists almost entirely of l'Avenir members plus family members or close friends.

Soon after l'Avenir's inception, incidentally, our friend Vicky, whose father Tom was part of Action for the Dependent Handicapped back in the '70s, left St. Amant to live in her own apartment within Prairie Housing Co-op. She became a member of l'Avenir at the same time and either she or Tom have been l'Avenir board members ever since.

To continue being technical for a moment (I'm constantly being asked how l'Avenir works, so I may as well provide at least the framework), the number of people served by our agency has fluctuated over the years, but we've found that if we try to assist more than twenty people, we're in danger of burning out our Manager. Salaries for our Manager and Assistant Manager are drawn from a percentage of the members' social allowance. That is, Cath uses part of her income to pay l'Avenir to manage the supports and services she needs. L'Avenir usually has about sixty people on the payroll, some of whom live with and are responsible to our members while others work for our members on a part-time or respite basis.

•

When I wrote in 1982 that an educational program for a small number of people with severe disabilities might be established in a year's time at the University of Winnipeg, it's a good thing I preceded it with the words "though I say this with the utmost caution." The program did not actually get started until a year later, in the fall of '84, and it was not at the university. I was never quite sure what happened but it seems that politics, both internal, i.e. the university, and external, i.e. the provincial government, were involved and that funding was a major stumbling block. I'll always regret it, partly because I knew from Dominic and Benjy that probably the most important activity at the university was not, as one might think, attending lectures on philosophy, science and so on, but *hanging out*. And it was while people were hanging out, in cafeterias, in the gym, in the bookstore, at special-interest meetings and in the hallways, that Cath and company, with help, would have had the best chance of interacting with the regular students and making friends.

If the University of Winnipeg missed the opportunity of having an interesting group of students in its midst, Red River Community College did not. Red River is a huge educational institution that grew out of the community college movement of the sixties. A couple of the senior instructors there, including the dean of Continuing Education, heard of our proposed project and became excited about it, with the result that, after months of intense planning on the part of David and his staff, the government Department of Education and Red River, Cath and three other young women (as it happens) went to college. We called the program Project Inclusion.

The co-ordinator, whom we found but whose salary was paid by the Department of Education via Red River, was a sparkly young woman called Sandee, who had become involved as a teenage volunteer with people with disabilities. She had worked in the summer program at the Y where Cath had been years before and was also one of the assistants who had been on the Rockies camping trip. Catherine and the other students each had a program designed around their individual strengths and needs. Four eager young women, whose salaries were paid partly by a government grant, were hired as "facilitators."

Our gang didn't go round in a clump but, like the other students, did their own thing and met up for lunch or an outing. Cath, for example, amongst other activities, went swimming three times a week—a long ride into town in the hired van for which the project had a grant—and had her daily physio alongside other students exercising in the gym. And Vicky started to learn the rudiments of word processing. She planned eventually to write her life story.

Catherine's facilitator evolved a neat trick in the gym: she could lift Cath out of her wheelchair and onto the mat by herself but, knowing her friend's penchant for dark hairy men, suggested quietly to her that she point to someone she fancied lifting her out that day. Cath would point, or seem to point, at some young man pumping iron and looking strong and masculine and Cath's friend would then ask him if he could help Cath. The young man, even though he might initially find this somewhat alarming, would invariably comply. Two gains were made; Catherine would emit a shout of pleasure at having her day made in this way and the fellow learned that she wouldn't snap in half when he lifted her and stretched her out on the floor. He also learned that if a streak of drool landed on him in the process it could be kleenexed off with no permanent damage to him.

Realizing that the regular students at Red River might be puzzled to see four admittedly unusual people at the college, a few of us, including a representative from the student council and Cindy, who found herself deeply involved on l'Avenir's behalf, wrote an explanatory pamphlet in a question and answer format. Who are these people? Why are they here? What can they learn? How can we be supportive? etc. It was pleasing to meet people outside the college and have them tell me, when they discovered I was Catherine's mother, that they thought it was a great idea to have people with disabilities incorporated into the place. Some of the teachers were far from enthusiastic at first ("they should be in a special class somewhere") but most of them eventually realized that having our gang wheelchairing or loping around was, if nothing else, consciousness-raising.

I was grateful that the college program was running smoothly when negotiations about Cath's house began. One way or another, the house required my attention on an almost daily basis, and I would not have been able to cope had Cath been at home full-time.

Once the house had been officially bought by Prairie Housing Co-op, I began lobbying to have a neighbourhood organization of home renovators make the necessary repairs and adaptations to the building. They were a friendly group of men and women, all of whom were part of a Christian association of folks living in the area. Collectively, these families and individuals were known as the Grain of Wheat community, and I was already friends with some of them. Many came from a Mennonite background, and wanted to give something more tangible to the wider community than their mere presence. Their leader was Jake, and he and his wife and their two sons lived immediately behind Cath's house. I took Cath over to meet him and explained the concept of her new home. Jake became increasingly intrigued and was keen to take on the job.

The Grain of Wheat carpenters began work on Cath's house late in

Catherine's house. KEN GIGLIOTTI PHOTO

the fall. Stan, one of the architects from the planning group working with Winnipeg's ACL, had done a brilliant job of rearranging the inside of the house on paper, but Jake and his mates encountered myriad difficulties in practice. I suppose this happens often, but it made me feel guilty when, enthusiasm personified, I'd drop by to see how things were going only to be met with tales of woe coupled with some fairly unchristian comments and language.

The worse the problems, the more exotic the cookies I baked for the team—but my discomfort was never quite expunged. Nevertheless, overall, the building went according to plan, and Jake told me how pleased he and his friends were to be working on a house designed for someone who would bring an unusual "gift" to the neighbourhood. Later, Jake would found Winnipeg's branch of Habitat for Humanity, and he said that Catherine was one of his inspirations.

I was particularly pleased to see the dining room being transformed into Cath's bedroom, in the design of which she and I had participated. I was also delighted with Stan's imaginative plan for the ramp up to the back door, which was the one Cath would use. Rather than going straight up, it curved round from the back lane and had a corresponding terraced garden area on either side.

Finally, the ramp was finished and I was able to push Cath up it and into the house. She'd been inside before but we'd been forced to haul her bumpily up the original steps and manoeuvre her wheelchair in backwards. Now, what had been a minimal back porch was a sturdy wooden deck, and inside the new main entrance was a room that would house a Jacuzzi. Then came the kitchen, and the rest of the ground floor.

Lack of space prevented us from transferring Cath's big bathtub from our house, and I had resigned myself to settling for a shower area which she'd use in a chair designed for the purpose. David suggested the Jacuzzi. Not only would Catherine love relaxing in its warm and bubbly water, it might even work to de-stiffen her somewhat. And other people in the house, along with their friends, would like it too. Not everyone can say, "Come over to our place for a Jacuzzi party!"

When my attempts to get a grant for the Jacuzzi, on the grounds that it was necessary for Cath's well-being, failed, Ted and I bought it as a present for the household. It has proved to be worth every penny of the cost.

Several photos in Cath's album picture her in her prospective living quarters at different stages of its development. Cath looks baffled in most of them, as well she might, or she's studying her left hand closely. We explained the renovations and their purpose, but I'm fairly certain that, as far as Cath was concerned, being in the house held the delicious possibility of someone falling off a ladder, an exciting incident which happened on her first visit. I don't, though, believe she ever thought that this strange, sawdusty, furnitureless place might become her home.

The house and its intended use created intense interest on the part of many people. Dominic and Benjy were fascinated and often helped with the work, and Cath's friends from Red River would also stop by as part of an outing. Colleen, who had taken over as manager of the community residence in Steinbach where Cath had stayed after the Rockies trip, was another interested party. Cath had stayed at the residence several times when I was out of town and she and Colleen had became good friends. Colleen was returning to Winnipeg to take a master's degree in Business Administration and asked to look at the house. By the end of her tour, and having met Lauchie and Evelyn, she decided she'd like to move into the bachelor apartment.

"That's fine," said Ted, "all very nice. But who's actually going to live with Cath?"

This was not the first time Ted had asked this reasonable, but annoying, question. I knew, absolutely, based on nothing but instinct and faith, that the right people would turn up at the right time. I tried to justify my certainty, misty though I knew it seemed to Ted, by saying that many people I knew lived with men and women who had disabilities, in l'Arche for instance.

"The l'Arche people can walk—"

"And run away," I countered. "Cath's never done that."

Ted sighed. "I just can't imagine anyone willing to do the messy stuff and all that lifting."

"We'll find someone, don't worry."

"Hmm."

"Cynic."

"Realist."

Ted's apprehension was understandable. He could not believe our love for Catherine, which transcended the difficulties she engendered, could be felt by anyone else. I agreed with him in the sense that no one else would ever love our daughter in the same way that we, her parents, did, but I believed Catherine had intangible qualities which attracted people. Ted had not been with her as much as I had, and he hadn't had the opportunity to see that she was not only readily accepted as who she was but also actively liked.

Cath's house would be ready for occupation in about three months. I needed to put my belief into action and begin a search for our daughter's roommates. The first step was to ask likely candidates from my circle of friends and, if they weren't interested themselves, ask them to think of people they knew who might be. Benjy immediately produced two charming young couples but, although they were sympathetic to the idea, it was generally agreed that neither of them was ready to take on such a commitment. Also, one of the couples was on a grim-sounding diet which seemed to consist almost entirely of brown rice. Benjy and I didn't think Cath would appreciate such limited fare.

So I typed a dozen announcements:

My name is Catherine Schaefer. I'm 25 years old and attend Red River Community College 5 days a week. I have disabilities, so I appreciate assistance in remaining an integral part of my community.

I'm a member of Prairie Housing Co-op, which recently bought a large house overlooking Vimy Ridge Park. It's being transformed into 3 apartments. One will be occupied by a couple with a 3-year-old daughter, and another by a single woman. I shall be mov-

Ben and Cath on the newly-made ramp to Cath's "front" door.

ing into the first floor apartment in mid-July and am looking for a friendly, outgoing couple to share my quarters in return for assistance—including lifting.

I can offer free rent, a monthly stipend and time off. If you are interested, please call (then I put my name and number).

I pasted a recent photo of Cath atop each announcement and then put the finished products in places where I thought likely respondents would see them.

That was how we found Darlene, who ended up living with Catherine for two years and who remains intricately involved in her life and ours to this day. Darlene phoned, having seen the ad in the Mennonite Central Committee office. She'd just returned from a year of volunteer work in Jamaica with that organization, teaching children who were deaf or hearing impaired. Now she was going back to university to complete an Education degree that she'd started before going to Jamaica. I was hesitant even to meet Darlene, because I reckoned that living with Cath was a two-person business. However, she insisted on coming round and my first sight of her was a tall, ginger-mopped, vivacious young woman chatting with Benjy on the front porch. A few minutes later Cath came home and Benjy and I watched a shy but definite friendship being struck. She's the one, Mum, Benjy said later, she's just right for Cath. Get her!

Darlene wrote recently:

I remember meeting the Schaefer clan. This was not an ordinary household. I should have known from my phone conversation with Nicola and by her comment about how this job wouldn't work for me if I didn't have a husband or 'bloke.' Liking the idea of getting a job and a home all in one go, I persuaded her to let me meet her and Catherine. When I got to the house Nicola wasn't there; it seemed she had forgotten about our appointment and had gone grocery shopping. So instead I was greeted by a tall blond guy who was dressed in a towel. He offered me a glass of orange juice and we sat in the front porch discussing our respective lives. Nicola arrived shortly after and proceeded to make tea and offer me a cup. Not knowing that it was 'English' tea, i.e. disgustingly strong, I declined milk and sugar. Wanting to be polite and make a good impression I suffered through it and then Catherine finally arrived. I discovered quickly that Cath doesn't communicate through speech but we got along just fine. By the end of my three-hour visit Cath, Nicola and I decided that we liked each other and I left seriously thinking about the possibility of living with Cath.

Darlene told me later that she had pretty well made up her mind after that first meeting but, very sensibly, didn't make a commitment until she'd told her family and friends, and gotten their support. After that, it was a matter of figuring out how the arrangement could work. Luckily, a friend of hers, Leanne—bouncy, blonde and immensely entertaining—appeared on the scene, said she'd like to join Darlene in this venture, and could she have the little room and bathroom in the basement of the house? The girls had shared an apartment before, so it seemed like a good solution. Darlene would be Cath's primary support person and Leanne, who was studying for a theology degree, would pay nominal rent and help out in return.

Once everything was agreed upon, and Darlene had discussed the financial end of things with Cindy at l'Avenir, Darlene spent many hours with Cath and myself, watching me attend to Cath's physical care, and then having a go at it herself. She and I also talked—and laughed—a lot. I was pleased to discover that she was a strong and perceptive woman who wasn't scared to give me her point of view if it differed from mine. As was to be expected, it took Catherine longer to be comfortable with Darlene and vice versa, but as I increasingly left them alone together their relationship developed.

At the house, renovations were winding up, but because it was now classed as a multi-family dwelling there were endless complications which no one had anticipated. Some of the regulations that cropped up seemed reasonable—like being able to exit the house in the case of fire. Others were completely daft. For example, an empty storage room in the basement had to have a sprung steel door instead of its original wooden one. Eventually we were able to say good-bye to the posse of government and City inspectors, and to Jake and his carpenter colleagues, though the latter group continued to be helpful and friendly towards the household in the years to come.

Darlene, Leanne and I roped in some twenty friends and day after day, to the accompaniment of loud reggae music on Darlene's ghetto blaster, we scraped and scrubbed and painted like mad. Lauchie and Evelyn, our l'Arche friends, and Colleen, who were to move into the upstairs apartments, were similarly occupied, and we'd get together and have huge picnics on whatever clean floor space we could find. One day I walked into the kitchen with a fresh supply of beer and nibbles and found Zana, our family's friend of longstanding, on her knees chipping away at the old linoleum and another couple of friends sloshing paint on the walls. Dominic was painting the hallway and Darlene and Leanne were in the sitting room shouting to each other over the music as they wobbled around on step ladders, painting around the windows.

My God, I thought, it's really happening, Cath is actually going to move in here!

Darlene and Leanne had very little furniture other than their beds, personal objects like pictures and some kitchen equipment, so we went garage sale-ing in a big way. One major piece of furniture I planned to buy new was an adjustable armchair for Cath to sit in when she got uncomfortable in her wheelchair. I told Darlene I'd go hunting for one.

"You mean without Catherine?" she said indignantly.

"Well—"

"We're coming too. She should help choose it." So off we all set in the van (which Darlene already drove and which would be permanently at the girls' disposal once they moved in) while I ruminated once more on the pleasing realization that Darlene was a born advocate, even if it meant standing up to me.

Catherine moved into her new house on July 18th, 1986. Darlene wheeled her through the kitchen and into her bedroom. Cath didn't seem particularly interested; she'd been there often before, so the novelty had

Park picnic, 1986. Left to right: Lauchie, Evelyn, Colleen, Darlene, Cath, Leanne, Sherrill, David Wetherow, Marie.

worn off. Then she saw her bed and chest of drawers, which we'd already moved in, and something clicked. She did the most drawn-out double take I've ever seen. She gave Darlene and myself a bemused look and held up her left hand and stared at it for a long time, as if to check that it, at least, was still where it should be. Finally she smiled, just slightly. I found it difficult to leave and fussed around until Darlene pointed at the door.

"Home," she said. "You know we'll be fine."

"You've got my number?"

"Yes!" We hugged and I managed to leave without too many backward glances.

For months my friends had been informing me that I'd feel lost without Cath. Maybe that's why I didn't; I was almost over-prepared. My daughter was, after all, only minutes away and for the time being, at least, I was still very much part of her life. And I was suddenly able to sleep enough on a regular basis, and was free to go out whenever I wanted—for the first time in a quarter of a century. This was, frankly, bliss. Sometimes I stayed out late purely for the pleasure of knowing I didn't have to get up at 7:30 in the morning. Cath's leaving did have one curious effect, however. Coda, our golden retriever, and I continued to go for long rambles round the neighbourhood, and it shook me to realize that without Cath I'd lost part of my identity. I was just a woman out for a walk with her dog.

The absence I really felt—cruelly—was that of the boys. They flew to England "for a month, Mum" at about the same time that Cath moved out. Dominic ended up staying two years. Benjy, who has now become Ben, is still there.

I didn't feel lost without Catherine for the first few days but I certainly had trouble becoming accustomed to her absence. As did Ted. One evening he put down his light reading of the week, Isaiah Berlin's *The Crooked Timber of Humanity*, and went into her room.

"I thought I heard her grinding her teeth," he said sheepishly when he returned.

I nodded. "I keep hearing her mm-mm-mming."

"She can always come back if it doesn't work."

"She can not. This must and will work."

"Hm."

When I talk with other parents in various parts of the world, I always stress how lucky I was to have had a husband who earned enough for us to live on. Growing up with our children at home without having to get an outside job was a luxury. Then I add that the other form of support Ted gave me was that of an incentive: he invariably responded to my latest idea or plan about Cath with "It'll never work." The nods and smiles I receive in response to this observation tell me that Ted isn't the only such mate in the world.

He had been resolute, refusing steadfastly to go past, let alone enter Cath's house before she moved in. Finally, it was Darlene who lured him over there, well after everyone had settled in. No one could reach high enough to put up curtain rails. "I'll get Ted," she announced (they had gotten on splendidly right from the start—much mutual respect). Twenty minutes later, somewhat to my chagrin, there he was, armed with a drill and a case of beer. And thenceforth, particularly while I was in England that August, he would be a frequent and welcome visitor.

Staying in Sussex with the boys and my English family and friends helped me begin to lose that innate sense of responsibility I still felt about Cath, even though I knew she had officially left home, and was secure, with wonderful roommates. I was now four thousand, five hundred miles away, and couldn't run down to her house to help if she had a choke, couldn't take down little plastic pots of her favourite food, couldn't sneak into her room at night to make sure Darlene and Leanne had remembered to hitch her blankets into a tent over her feet to prevent them being squashed down.

Nevertheless, I thought about Cath frequently every day. While we were on the lawn having lunch—often great steaming heaps, all buttery, of scarlet runner beans from Mum's garden—I would visualize the girls, six hours behind us, rubbing their eyes and starting their day. Later, I would discover that, when I awoke at 8.00ish in the morning and fondly pictured Cath fast asleep and having lovely dreams she was often, instead, floating gloriously in the Jacuzzi with three or four friends while music played, incense burned and wine was imbibed—all at 2 a.m.

I returned to Winnipeg in September and was just settling down for a cup of tea with Ted to report on the boys, when Darlene and Cath came to welcome me home. Cath looked round eagerly as she and Darlene came in, plainly happy to be back in our house. She greeted us with unreserved pleasure. I noticed, though, that it was not Ted or myself whom her eyes followed, but Darlene, and when Ted pushed her up the van ramp she craned her head around frantically to keep Darlene in sight.

A day or two later I went to visit Cath at her house and, standing in front of her and resting my arms on her tray, I beamed at her. I expected a delighted beam in return, but my daughter, crossing her eyes with the effort, ground her teeth and gave me the most ferocious look in her repertoire, while simultaneously sweeping me off her tray with her left arm. Then she stared pointedly at the door, refusing to let me catch her eye.

I was taken aback, but realized she was communicating one of two important messages: either she was saying this is *my* place, so don't you dare move in, or she was saying *this* is my place now so don't you dare take me back! Cath took no chances that her meaning was not clear, and she waited until my fifth visit before she felt relaxed enough to greet me with her usual welcoming smile.

•

Darlene spent two years living with Cath. During that time, an American journalist, Bob Perske, widely known both for his lifetime of work on behalf of people with disabilities and his books on the subject (beautifully illustrated by his wife Martha Perske), came to Winnipeg to collect stories for his book *Circles of Friends: People with Disabilities and Their Friends Enrich the Lives of One Another*. Bob reckoned Cath's lifestyle would be a fitting example of the subject. Rather than

Nicola, Leanne, Darlene, Catherine, Marie and Evelyn. KEN GIGLIOTTI PHOTO

describe what Cath's household felt like from my point of view at the time, I'd like to quote parts of Bob's article, beginning with some comments from people living in the house:

'They pay us well at the hospital,' said Lauchie, 'but I have this other satisfaction, coming home and doing something for Catherine every now and then—doing something that's freely given.'

'We love it here,' said Evelyn. 'We are people who are interested in good, basic living—we're not merely interested in making money and getting ahead.' Little Marie showed her feelings by wanting to sit next to Catherine when I took a picture of the group

Colleen said she liked playing with money during the day, but 'I'm so much happier now that I'm connected to the people in this house, too.'

Leanne spoke of being away from her family for the first time, and how good it felt to be part of this family.

Bob asked Darlene to comment on being Catherine's friend and this was her response:

'I was reluctant to talk,' she said when asked about her speech before the Canadian Association for Community Living. 'When I got up there I told them I thought it was silly to even talk about it. It was just so natural, being somebody's friend. But I talked about Catherine and me going out with people and being with people—about how she annoys me at times—like when she grinds her teeth—and how I get on her nerves and we straighten things out. She really is my friend. She knows more about me than anybody else. (laughs) Gee! If Catherine ever speaks, the stories she could tell! She knows everything that goes on, she just has her own way of communicating, and I don't see that as her disability—it's mine. I have to learn her language. . . . For the last few months I've been going through a lot of different things in my life. And Cath rubs my face or takes my hand and squeezes it . . . she gives, too.'

Darlene then talked about entertainment, and on support from other members of the house.

'We go everywhere; lots of friends drop by to go out with her, too. We go dancing where people aren't worried about the wheelchair. Leanne went with her to a school play. We saw the film **Crocodile Dundee** which she loved—and **Witches of East-wick**—which I loved and she hated. We even go out to four-course dinners.'

'Don't forget about the male strippers,' Leanne added. She and Darlene looked at Nicola and laughed.

Nicola laughed, too. 'I'd never have gone with her,' she said, 'but three of her friends did a couple of years ago, and Cath thought it was wonderful. Giggled all the way through, and nonstop for several days afterward.'

'It's really neat,' Darlene said. 'We never lock our doors. If I have to leave for awhile, I can open my door and let the rest know, and I know everything will be okay. Also, because there's always somebody in the house, no crook would ever try to get away with something.'

During the day I spent at their house, every renter made me welcome. I watched Darlene's concern for Leanne, who was coming down with a cold. I saw her work confidently with Catherine, who suddenly choked on a cracker. She joined with others to borrow some of Lauchie's tools to get a flat tire off Catherine's wheelchair and hustled to various shops until she found one that would fit. Then she fixed a meal for Catherine, Leanne, Colleen, and me.

At dinner, Catherine, who swiped a glance at me every now and then but still refused to make eye contact, let me know her jury was still out on whether to accept me.

At the end of the evening everyone in the house gathered and talked about their life together (for my benefit). They saw great humour in a government licensing man who came with his clipboard to see if Catherine was being cared for properly. Seemingly unable to sense the richness of the personal interactions in the house, he wrote them up for a lack of draperies in the kitchen.

As people began to sum up their experience, Joanne (a friend) touched on something they all seemed to feel: 'Catherine laughs at me a lot. She makes me feel warm. Laughter is her litmus test for accepting one as a friend.'

I can't, of course, resist adding to what Bob wrote. For instance, whenever I dropped by the house during those two years, there was always at least one, often more like four or five, of Darlene's and Leanne's friends around, and Cath was always part of whatever was going on.

Recently I had lunch with two women I've known for years. We each have a daughter with a disability. My friends' girls are teenagers now, and planning is afoot for each to move away from home. I recalled the profound effect Darlene has had on Cath's life, and advised my friends that, as they searched for caregivers to live with their daughters, it would be essential to find people who not only have a good set of personal values but who are well-connected to the community and have a wide circle of friends. Catherine did not, if I'm honest, have any friends of her own (as distinct from people who were also, and usually primarily, my friends) when she left home. Now, through Darlene and other housemates, she truly does have her own circle of friends.

There are many stories that could be told to demonstrate the distinctive and cheerful—albeit sometimes pandemonious—nature of the household.

For instance, when Kedar, the owner of the nearby corner store, had saved enough money to buy a house in the neighbourhood, his wife came from India to join him. They needed somewhere to live for a month before their house became vacant. Darlene, Leanne and Cath invited them to camp out in the basement, with shared use of the kitchen, and it became a mutually satisfying experience (delectable curries, for one thing).

I loved the idea that Catherine, originally predicted by doctors never to be anything but a burden, was now giving refuge to some people in trouble.

A cameo: Marie, Lauchie and Evelyn's daughter upstairs, was overheard introducing two of her nursery school friends to Catherine. "This is my friend Catherine," she said, adding, after a pause, "and she lives with two handicapped women." Apparently she knew the word "handicapped" came into the picture somewhere but wasn't quite sure to whom it applied.

Another cameo, demonstrating that Darlene and Leanne were living with Cath as both helpers and friends:

ME: *Hey Leanne, that's Cath's sweater you're wearing.*
LEANNE: *Sure—I really like it!*
ME: *Oh, I see.*
LEANNE: *And Cath's wearing Darlene's harem pants—they look great on her, don't they? And Darlene's borrowed those crystal earrings Cath got for her birthday. We all wear each other's clothes . . .*

One more cameo: During a prolonged period while Darlene had a bad shoulder, Lauchie and Evelyn lifted Cath several times a day on a regular basis. When I attempted to thank Evelyn for this cheerfully given, long-term assistance, she responded, "You really don't have to thank us, Nicola. Cath's the reason we're living here." Then she added a comment which made me tingle. "Cath," she said, "is the heart of our household."

Joanne and her friend Brad spent many a day with Cath as respite caregivers. L'Avenir's arrangement with Darlene paid room and board, a small (embarrassingly small) stipend, and about thirty hours of time off a week (this was funded through government "respite" funds). Darlene chose to take her time off in the form of a forty-eight-hour weekend every two weeks, plus one evening a week. She was encouraged by Cindy, l'Avenir's General Manager, to find people from among her friends to take over with Cath, and this she had no trouble doing.

Joanne and Brad, like Darlene, were students, and moving in with Cath for periodic respites suited them well. Darlene would then either spend the weekend with her family, or crash with Ted and myself, a real pleasure for us. Several other couples and many individuals have spent time with Cath, and while each person has brought different and inter-esting qualities to Cath's life, they have all had one thing in common: a fondness for Cath and an appreciation of what they could learn from her. "I'd never met someone who was unable to walk or talk," one said, giving voice to what many have indicated over the years. "Cath taught me to value my abilities. She made me think."

Leanne left the house after a year to work in Peru, and I asked a mutual friend of Cath's, Darlene's and mine if he would consider moving in. His name was David, but to distinguish him from the David who had already had such an impact of Cath's life I'll call him Dave. Quiet and thoughtful, Dave was in his mid-twenties and headed for a career in business administration. Prior to our meeting him, he had taken a job sorting out the finances of a forty-bed group home. He was so horrified by the conditions in which those people were living that he started a community agency (similar in ways to l'Avenir) to help them find better housing and daytime activities. Initially, when I asked him if he would be interested in living with Cath, his main concern was whether, with the demands of running the agency, he would have the time and energy he'd like to give Cath as a roommate.

Cath and Marie.

The house agreement, via Prairie Housing Co-op, was that all household members meet and approve any new resident.

Everyone liked Dave. He made the decision to move in, and ended up staying for two and a half years. He made it clear from the start that he was Catherine's friend, which precluded his doing anything she disliked, such as coercing her to drink when she was ill. Cath appeared to appreciate this and I recall many a time seeing her reach out to touch Dave with love and gratitude illuminating her face.

Dave also proved a thoughtful advocate for Cath. When the van developed so many holes in its floor that Cath was in danger of sinking through it, we started discussing a new one. Dave suggested designing the adaptations so that Cath sat in the front next to the driver, rather than being stuck behind the driver with a nonstop view of his or her hair and shoulders. This was a novel idea. I don't think it would have occurred to me. Making the adjustments to the van was tricky, but we did it, and for several years now Cath has shared a front seat view—and coffee—with whoever is driving.

Dave is now a family man and a lawyer (in which capacity he has, among other cases, represented several people with disabilities who are in conflict with the law), so the amount of time he spends with Cath these days has inevitably diminished significantly—part of the ebb and flow of any friendship. Nevertheless, I am so convinced of his fundamental fidelity to her that he is one of the trustees of the fund set up in her name in my will.

In the Jacuzzi (Dave, top left; Cath, floating on her back).

Dave shared these thoughts about his time with Cath:

One of the first times I met Catherine was when I went to her house for a small gather-ing—probably intended to evaluate my worthiness as a potential roommate to Cath. After I had answered and asked questions a number of us, including Catherine, got into the whirlpool. Sitting in the Jacuzzi with Catherine's head on my chest I knew that we would get along well. I remember feeling very peaceful and happy. Catherine's smiles and chuckles and her gentle kicking lifted my spirits.

Catherine has the gift of the subtle. No one else I know can brighten my mood with a smile or a chuckle like Catherine can. When she smiles at me or touches my hand I feel loved—no small gift.

Not only does Catherine give gently, she accepts tenderness and gentleness. She allowed me to be gentle—to speak softly, sit quietly, stroke her hand or let her stroke mine—without any discomfort. I don't feel self-conscious when I'm with Catherine.

I lived with Catherine during a period of inner struggle, and she made me calm. I felt that I could share with her what I was feeling without a lot of words. Being together in contented silence is one of the important mutual gifts of friendship.

As I write, I realize that Catherine provided an anchor for me. She gave me a home that I loved, she is a completely non-judgmental friend, she made me feel loved, and helped me define myself. I am extremely grateful to her for her friendship.

D arlene had made a two-year commitment to live with Cath, after which she was due to practice teaching for a year and knew she would be too preoccupied to be Cath's primary caregiver. As the end of her reign approached I started, reluctantly, to put out feelers for a replacement. Fittingly, it was Catherine herself who found her new housemates.

By this time, l'Avenir had grown considerably, and under its original manager, Cindy, the co-op had moved away from ACL Winnipeg to become a separate entity. Prairie Housing, too, had branched out and now included a twenty-seven-unit downtown apartment block, the acquisition and setting-up of which had been engineered by David Wetherow. Like l'Avenir, Prairie Housing had separated from ACL, and I suspect David may have felt somewhat miffed and concerned as his two gangling "teenagers" struck out on their own. Like any good father, however, he has always been on hand to give support and assistance.

Cindy left l'Avenir when her husband was transferred to the Northwest Territories. Her place as General Manager was taken by enthusiastic and upbeat Sandee, who had been a member of the camping trip to the Rockies years before and had also been connected with the Red River Community College project. Sandee had hired a warm and empathic young woman, Laurie, to act as l'Avenir's individual support worker. This position involved spending time with l'Avenir's members and ensuring that their needs and wishes were being heard and, if possible, met.

It was in this capacity that Laurie had gotten to know Cath. She and her husband Glen decided that, if everyone approved, they'd like to move in with Cath. Cath seemed to think it a good idea, especially when Glen serenaded her with his guitar. Realizing that Laurie would find it difficult to remain l'Avenir's support worker full-time while also fulfilling her responsibilities to Cath, she and Glen (who had experience as a respite worker and as a teacher's aide) decided to job-share, both as Cath's roommates and at l'Avenir. They and their two cats moved into the house.

Soon after, Lauchie and Evelyn concluded they needed to return to the l'Arche community (where they remain—and we're all still friends). An amiable married couple, Eileen and Gerald, whom I'd met through talking to a University of Manitoba nurses' class, moved in upstairs. Both

Cath and I were glad that Dave and Colleen stayed put and provided not only assistance but continuity.

Inevitably, the tenor of the house changed, particularly in Catherine's apartment. Cath probably missed the buzz Darlene and her friends provided, but she seemed content with the quieter atmosphere provided by Laurie and Glen, both of whom were creative people. The basement became a double studio, half for Laurie and her pottery, and half for Glen with his music, although much creativity took place in the kitchen and sitting room. Cath loved it when Glen played his guitar and sang, and when the cats got tied up in the piles of wool that Laurie was weaving into a wall hanging.

All went well for a few months. Then a number of factors combined to create tension. Catherine's health, or lack thereof, was the chief problem, but it was compounded by unexpected and traumatic personal difficulties between Glen and Laurie—which, they have been consistently anxious to assure me, had nothing to do with Catherine. Glen left the house after a year but Laurie remained another few months until the spring of 1990. Although I was aware of what was happening, my knowledge was peripheral, so I asked Glen recently to contribute to Cath's chronicle.

The year that I spent living with Cath was a difficult one personally, but not without its pleasures. I miss the feeling of community and mutual concern that the circle of people around Cath shared. We also had some great, fun times together. I do wonder sometimes if I ever saw Cath at her best. She had such a hard winter physically that year. During those bouts of illness, just getting enough fluids into her became a battle, with her stubbornness more than a match for us. That year Catherine was certainly witness to enough emotional upheaval to last a lifetime. Late at night after we had gone to bed, Laurie and I would often hear Cath happily giving the bunch of us a big raspberry. With a whirlwind blowing around her, I thought she was more than entitled.

Laurie described her time with Cath in a letter:

It was not an easy time for either of us, was it, Cath? You were sick so much of the time . . . and the struggle we had trying to figure out what was wrong with you. Most of the answers came later, after I'd left.

I remember days of knowing you were feeling lousy or hurting, and I'd be desperately searching for every available clue to solve the riddle of what was ailing you. I hated the fact you were in pain and I didn't know how to relieve it. Do you remember the times when

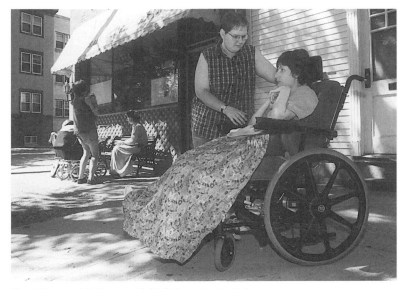

Friend Darcy with Cath outside Tall Grass Prairie Bakery. KEN GIGLIOTTI PHOTO

all else failed and I d settle you on your bed, light up the candles, put Vivaldi on the tape deck and give you a full body massage? Both you and I knew that wasn t getting to the root of the problem but you were gracious in your appreciation and took from it what comfort you could. Do you remember all the horrible treatments and remedies we put you through, Cath? If you re like me you ve probably blocked as much of it from your mind as you could. Let s see now . . . for chest infections there was the treatment consisting of alternating hot and cold packs on your back and cold wet cotton socks covered with warm woolly ones . . . for urinary tract infections there was that extremely effective but thoroughly obnoxious-tasting concoction referred to as your pee-pipe tea . . . and if you started twisting around in your wheelchair and grabbing at us (a sure sign your back was out of whack) it would be time for your favourite treatment of all Tracey the Chiropractor! As bizarre as some of it sounds, it really did help.

Intertwined with all the struggles were some very good times as well; for example, those quiet cozy evenings with your dad, being plied with liqueur and chocolates while discussing philosophy. We also benefited from the experience of living in a communal house with the various exchanges and gatherings that that entailed.

My time with you as your roommate was one of the most challenging of my life. It also facilitated some of my greatest growth.

So thank you, Cath, for sharing yourself and your home with me. Most of all, thanks for hanging in there through all the good times and the bad.

How Catherine's mind works, what her thought processes are, remain a mystery to me. I am, however, certain that she has a lifetime's worth of questions to ask and comments to make. I'm equally certain that the worst aspect of her disability, for her, is when she's in pain, and can't explain where the pain is, its degree and what relieves it. For her friends and caregivers, all of whom want desperately to help her when she's hurting, it's gut-wrenchingly frustrating not to know these details.

Sometimes we're lucky, and it's pretty obvious what's wrong. If, for instance, Cath has a fever and cough, and doesn't want to swallow, it's a safe bet she has an upper respiratory infection, which can include a sore throat. More often, though, there's no discernible reason for the pain, even after—watching her expression carefully—we've manipulated various limbs or joints, and pressed different areas of her abdomen.

Sometimes Cath will really confuse us. For instance, I've more than once slammed her foot against a door frame while wheeling around a corner—something that, if done to me, would cause an outburst of yelling and swearing. Catherine, however, reacts with every sign of riotous enjoyment.

She has had horrible health problems in the last few years. Even when she was in her mid-twenties she would indicate, by biting her hand and by her expression, that she was sometimes in significant pain. Analgesics didn't seem to help and none of us liked the symptomatic approach. She was also getting food stuck in her esophagus more frequently, which often led to pneumonia because she aspirated mucus that collected above the blockage. We discovered her esophagus was being scarred by acid rolling back up it and we fed her huge amounts of antacid glop. As Laurie's letter indicated, Cath also started getting urinary tract or, as we referred to them, pee-pipe infections. Urinary tract problems are common in people who spend much of their time in a wheelchair.

We soon learned to recognize the symptoms and gave her antibiotics at once. The trouble was that she seemed at times to be on the damned stuff for weeks on end before feeling any relief. Then, when the infection flared up once more, we'd have to start the whole process again.

My method of dealing with a jammed esophagus was panic, then panic control and, finally, the induction of vomiting (on Cath's part). While this procedure worked often, it was traumatizing for all concerned. When it failed to work, we made yet another trip to the hospital.

One night Laurie called me to say that Cath had had a choke, but that whatever had been stuck had apparently made its way down into her stomach.

"Well done," I said. "Okay, how? You sound pleased with yourself."

"Candles, soft music and stroking," she replied, and I could hear the beam in her voice.

"The calm approach. Not a bad idea." Sure enough, Laurie's method both worked more often than not and was far less intrusive.

Laurie also introduced Cath and me to an extraordinary naturopath, Dr. Goodheart. He helped Cath by suggesting the hot/cold treatment for chest infections described by Laurie in her letter, and also by prescribing and procuring the special tea for her pee-pipe infections (it's a magical mixture of herbs and berries and smells delicious when it's being brewed, although I agree with Laurie it tastes vile unless camouflaged). The tea also does the trick, on a consistent basis. In the years that Cath has been using it, she's only twice had to resort to chemical antibiotics and both times were due to extenuating circumstances.

•

Laurie, Glen and I may have given the impression that Catherine was constantly ill or in pain during this time. This was not so. Cath appeared healthy, happy, and thoroughly enjoying life much of the time; it was just that when she did have problems, she was so *utterly* wretched. And all of us felt that, even when she did recover from a serious infection, she still had an underlying fundamental problem that we had not yet identified.

Cath has the ability to attract unusual people. Sonja came into her life to lend Laurie support after Glen left. To a greater or lesser extent, she has remained linked to Cath ever since. The first time I met Sonja, she was sporting leather anklets with bells attached. She was unusual with bells on, both literally and figuratively.

Sonja's main responsibility was to ensure that Cath had fun on weekends. My friends would often report seeing Cath and "a lovely young woman with long hair, round glasses and a huge smile" at a farmers' market out in the country or participating in Winnipeg's annual March for Peace. Sonja had the use of a house near Riding Mountain National Park, and she and her friends took Cath up there for holidays. It wasn't easy—no running water for one thing—but Sonja made it work and Cath has photos of herself and friends lying on the grass under a tree, or being wheeled down the beach with Sonja's dogs bounding along at her side.

Here's how Sonja felt:

I had grown up scared of people with disabilities and generally avoided them, so I was apprehensive when I went to meet Cath. (A friend had told me Cath was looking for someone to spend time with her.) During that first meeting in her living room I remember the way she observed me without a smile—but curious all the time. When I looked at her she looked away; when I looked away she looked at me. It was like playing hide and seek. I can't remember what broke through my first layer of concerns. Maybe it was Cath's softness that I sensed even that first time I saw her. Maybe it was the confidence I got from her wonderful housemates.

When I started work two weeks later my heart was pounding and my hands shaking. I didn't want to do the wrong thing or hurt Cath by mistake. It took me a while to learn all her disabilities but during that same time I learned about her abilities—her charm, her softness, her humour.

It wasn't always easy to be there for Cath. The emotional demand was often more than one person could carry. After all, you're constantly trying to talk for someone else, understand her feelings, her desires, her needs. She made me realize that when I was with her I, too, was disabled. At first I made decisions for her—like where to spend our evenings and with whom, without even telling her beforehand where we were going. I apologized to her for this and told her I hoped she didn't mind me taking the freedom to make decisions.

There were many people that I met through Cath, and she shared some of my friends with me. As a rather new resident of the city (I had come from Germany two years previously) I was glad to have Cath as a friend through whom I could without much effort make new friends. Whenever I spent time with her I realized that somehow everybody took to her no matter where we went. Often I would walk down the street—more or less stumbling behind that wheelchair—and someone would walk up to us—or better, Cath—and say 'Hi, I'm so-and-so, I saw you coming down the street . . . I'm a good friend of Cath's, I've known her since she was . . . Cath, it's so good to see you. How are you doing?' It always surprised me how many people knew Cath. It was almost like she was a celebrity.

Many people I've met through Cath have become close friends of mine. These are people like Tandy and Gavin, who once lived in Cath's house and who taught me so much about the 'new age' lifestyle during the 'Year of Aquarius.' We spent many hours in the house philosophizing with these groovy people. Then there was Dave, who would not miss breakfast with us—and we laughed because Cath always reached for his coffee, preferring it to her own. And Laurie, who taught us that drinking lots of water will give us the clean-looking face that we envied her for.

Cath has a charm that attracts people the first time they meet her, and she doesn't even have to smile. During a wondrous week in Riding Mountain among colourful birds, busy bees and the company of friends, we were invited to a big feast and afterwards we roasted marshmallows over the bonfire. I was so taken with this new Canadian discovery that I didn't notice right away that Cath had disappeared. I ran around asking everyone where she was and then I saw her coming down the lane with two of my friends. 'We just went for a walk . . .'

I think that working, spending time with Cath helped me reflect on how I perceive people and what kind of value I put on their abilities or disabilities. My time with her has taken away my fear of disabled people in general and has led me to an understanding of the joys, frustrations and fears of an individual friend.

One of my favourite stories about Sonja and Cath, which Sonja told me with great amusement, was the time they went to a party and a guy came smiling up to their table. Sonja didn't feel like dancing and was preparing to decline politely, but before she could say a word, the guy asked Cath to dance.

Sandee retired as General Manager of l'Avenir at the beginning of 1989, and we held a huge party to bid her farewell. We were reluctant to see her leave but she and her husband were busy preparing for the birth of their first baby. Cheryl, a close friend of one of our members, had been on l'Avenir's board for two years, and she assumed Sandee's position. One of her early responsibilities was to help find a new primary caregiver for Cath. Sonja was not able to live with Cath full-time, so after Laurie left and no one else materialized, we had to advertise in the paper for live-in assistants for the first time since Cath moved into her own home. It made me nervous.

Rika responded to the ad and Cheryl was plainly impressed. "She's a bit young," she told me after the interview, "but I think she'll suit Cath."

When I walked into Cath's sitting room, my daughter was looking down at her left hand and was surrounded by a number of other people, including Rod, her friend of many years standing who now inhabited the bachelor apartment and whose regular assistance to Cath included helping her out of bed each morning before he went to work. Cath loved that. Lloyd, a philosopher/carpenter who shared Cath's apartment for a while, contributing deep thoughts and trails of wood shavings, was also there. As was a striking woman with short black hair, black clothes and a ring in her nose. She looked about twenty, was quiet and wary, and was the only person I didn't know.

Catherine and Rika.

Rika was in fact only just eighteen but, as I was soon to discover, would be one of the most responsible and resourceful people ever to enhance my daughter's life. She took Cath's health problems in her stride and learned quickly that the best way of dealing with me was to high-light the positive and downplay the difficulties—much the same way I dealt with Ted, come to think of it.

Rika was—is—a human rights activist and, like Sonja, an assertive feminist. She had a circle of similarly-minded friends, mainly women, all of whom seemed to wear black, change their hair colour frequently, wear exotic jewelry and clump around either in army boots or black Doc Martens. This group took Cath under its collective wing, giving her lots of attention and always including her in whatever was going on.

My friends were constantly informing me that they'd seen Cath at the Legislature for a Take Back The Night demonstration, or on TV at a neighbourhood rally of some sort. There were sightings all over town, and further afield. In August, 1990, Rika, her friend Christine, and Cath took off in the van for ten days for a women's music camp in Michigan with ten thousand participants. Later, several of my friends reported meeting them there. I myself had a curious experience during Rika's reign. One day when my dog and I were ambling down a local street blocked off to traffic for a street festival, we saw a woman approaching in a wheelchair. She was wearing sunglasses, an elegant velvet hat and a flowing flowery dress. Accompanying her were three other women. The one with orange hair waved when she saw me. It was Rika. I had recognized neither her nor my daughter.

Members of Rika's entourage frequently moved in and out of Cath's house, sometimes because they needed somewhere to stay and sometimes because Rika needed help with Cath. They also often came to visit me singly or en masse with Cath. I found their company stimulating and entertaining, and I realized how, after the boys left, Cath and her friends have consistently helped me keep up with what my mother used to call "the young." I'm grateful.

For the most part when Catherine has needed help at the Health Sciences Centre she and I and the friends who have taken her there have been pleased with the treatment she's received. One day in summer 1990, however, this was definitely not the case. Cath's caregiver called me to say that Cath had part of her supper, a chick pea, stuck in her esophagus and the calm approach hadn't worked so an ambulance had been called. I met them at the hospital and we spent hours suctioning Cath while waiting for medical attention. Normally a surgeon would have checked her, and dispatched her to an operating room within an hour or so, but this time there was no surgeon available.

By midnight, we had been struggling with Cath in the emergency room for over four hours, and Cath's friend was exhausted, so I suggested she go home. About an hour later I realized that Cath was in serious trouble. She was too tired to cough up the constantly gathering mucus, so she quit. The next thing I knew, her mouth was going blue around the edges, her eyes were rolling up and she went limp. I screamed to a nurse for help and finally there was action. Cath had an on-stretcher X-ray, after which she was rushed into the resuscitation room where a medley of medics crowded around her. I was told categorically to keep out ("the doctors are busy"). I phoned Darlene for moral support and she appeared within minutes. We huddled together miserably.

Ted is an inveterate but silent worrier and we came to an arrangement years ago where I tell him afterwards, when things are fine again, that Cath has been in trouble. This time, however, I phoned him too, since we'd been given no assurance by the doctors that Cath would survive. I told Ted that Darlene was coming down and that I'd call when I knew more. He was all prepared to rush right over but, suddenly, one of the doctors swung out of the resuscitation room and informed us Cath was breathing properly again. Darlene and I sped to her side. Cath glared at us crossly and then looked away.

I was too shaken to ask questions, but I did discover that the bloody chick pea was still stuck in Cath's esophagus and that there was still nobody around who could remove it. We all know how horrible it is to swallow something too large and have it get stuck even for an instant on its way down. The idea of having an object jammed for hours at a time is appalling. Cath was scheduled first on the operating list in the morning, but that was still two or three hours away. I have blanked the rest of the night out of my mind, but I suspect I continued to suction my daughter—repeatedly, every ten minutes when necessary—until she was prepared for surgery.

Cath and I hadn't met the surgeon, Dr. T.H., before, but he was friendly. When he came to talk to me after the surgery, he explained that Cath's crisis a few hours earlier had been due to the collapse of her left lung which had, in turn, been caused by being clogged up with mucus. Cath's esophagus was a mess as a result not only of the chick pea's tenacity (over twelve hours) but also of scarring from previous blockages.

Two months later, Dr. T.H. checked Catherine's esophagus again. While she was recovering from her anesthetic, he gave Rika and me a report.

"The good news is that there's no additional scarring. But," he paused, "we took some X-rays and Catherine has a hiatus hernia, which we'll have to repair, and a large growth of some sort either in her uterus or on an ovary which will also have to be dealt with. The pain she's been having is a result of excessive acid re-entering her esophagus." He showed us the X-ray and explained that the diaphragm muscle is supposed to keep the lungs and esophagus up and the stomach and guts down. In Cath's case, there was a hole, so part of her stomach was knocking around in her chest and squashing her esophagus. Very nasty.

The news was horrifying, but it did explain Cath's distress and the pain she had been experiencing for so long—which was obviously far worse than mere heartburn. We consulted a gynaecologist, who gave Cath an ultrasound which showed the cyst, or whatever it was, spread right across her lower abdomen. For some time I had thought I could feel something in that area which, especially after checking my own body, seemed strange, but the doctors I'd consulted earlier had always explained it away.

Dr. T.H. and the gynaecologist agreed to work together, each in their area of expertise, and a mutually agreeable date was set for the operation. In the meantime, we conferred with a dietitian at the hospital who gave Cath a diet excluding fat and acid. Thenceforth, too, Cath had to eat two sorts of pill at frequent intervals; one to reduce the amount of acid her stomach normally produced and the other to speed up the digestive process. The eating aspect of Cath's life, always one in which she took particular pleasure, must have seemed remarkably less interesting for a while, but these measures did reduce her pain significantly.

We awaited the operation date impatiently and were more than a little irritated when it was postponed due to a nurses' strike. Dr. T.H. promised Cath would be at the top of the list once the strike ended, and the operation eventually took place on February 25th, 1991.

Although I gave up playing the cello many years ago, I've subsequently enjoyed music-making vicariously by being on the board of the Manitoba Chamber Orchestra. I also act as what might loosely be called production manager, which means anything from ensuring that the stage goes up and down, the musicians on and off it, and the guest artists in and out (of the airport) at the right times. My job also includes hanging around at rehearsals, purportedly to run errands if necessary for Simon Streatfeild, our esteemed music director and conductor, or anyone else, but really because I just love to be there.

The orchestra was rehearsing for a concert while Cath was in surgery, and I was grateful for the distraction. Sitting in the orchestra's concert hall, Westminster United Church, listening to Gorecki's *Three Pieces in the Olden Style* and Robert Turner's *Manitoba Memoir*, was a far better distraction than the hospital cafeteria.

We had been warned that Catherine would take up to eight months to recover fully from her double surgery but I'd thought this was an exaggeration. Not so. While she slowly gained strength, and was certainly cheerful much of the time, the operation and the period leading up to it must have seriously weakened her body, making her less resistant than usual to infections. I can probably best describe the months after the operation by quoting a letter. I wrote it on October 20th, 1991 at the end of a women's poetry-writing weekend which was accommodated in my house. I can't cope with poetry but realized I did have something churning around inside me that had to emerge. Winnipeg poet Di Brandt, who was leading the workshop, encouraged me to write it down. And here it is:

Cath, my darling girl:

It's been a grim two years for you in many ways, hasn't it? Months of acid burning its way up your esophagus, months of intermittent pneumonia and gurgly coughing, months of pee-pipe infections, months of feeling exhausted, months of doctors and technicians handling—sometimes far from gently—your battered body, months of those (to you at least) needless needles, months of having unwanted food and fluids forced into you, months of blocked bowels and the consequent assaults on your system, months of your mother's face looming gloomily over you as, once again, you were in discernible but indecipherable pain. And perhaps—though none of us can do more than guess what goes on in that mysterious mind of yours—perhaps months of wondering when the people around you would figure out what was wrong and the pain and indignities would end.

Well, we finally did sort out some of the problems, and that resulted in your waking up one day with a row of clips and stitches and pain from your sternum to your crotch. They had repaired your hiatus hernia ('huge,' said the thoracic surgeon, 'I could put my fist through') and removed a (benign) cyst from one of your ovaries. 'It was like eight oranges strung together,' said the gynaecologist.

That was in February '91, and we all looked forward to your gradual recovery, thankful to think that your troubles were over. But it seemed that as soon as we started rejoicing with you as you began once again to enjoy eating, to enjoy going for walks, to enjoy being in the pool, to enjoy going to the bar with friends, to enjoy life, things started to go wrong again. I reached a point where the phone ringing caused my stomach to seize up, where I had to take several deep breaths to listen to the messages on my bloody answering machine, where it took all my courage merely to call your house or drop in to see how you were. And as, time and again, I rushed down—after an alarmed and alarming call from one of your splendid and empathic roommates and helpers—and found you feverish, whimpering, gagging, defenseless, totally wretched, I began to have black thoughts about what your life felt like to you. Were you willing to go through all this pain and discomfort, then to be made better, only to face more pain and discomfort soon afterwards?

Until recently you'd had a pretty good life. Maybe you were saying hey, let's leave it at that, my body seems to be falling apart, let me go. I found these thoughts terrifying and unmentionable.

In the past, my love, I've only worried and grieved when you've actually been ill, and the rest of the time have been joyful about your life. But now I find I worry and grieve not only when you're in trouble but all the time. And I extend that worry and grief into the future. I've almost stopped daring to hope that you'll be well more often than ill. I'm becoming a half-empty rather than a half-full person as far as you're concerned. I find it safer; I expect trouble and can be grudgingly happy when it's absent.

Last week, when you'd been staying with me because I could no longer stand the strain of waiting for the inevitable, it seemed to me, emergency phone call, you seemed to be getting well and happy but suddenly developed a raging fever and shrank with dehydration within a couple of hours. Rika and I took you to the hospital and two doctors said you were fighting for your life. As, trembling, I invaded your armpits with cold wet cloths and a nurse invaded your bottom with Tylenol suppositories—all to reduce your fever—I began again to wonder. Do you want us to do this? Is that sunken-eyed look you're giving me one of anger and despair at not being heard? Have you had enough?

I'm sure my hot tears streaming onto your burning body could hardly have helped you but at least some of the horrors I was and had been having for months were being released.

My black thoughts did not evaporate with my tears and will probably return but you did something for me last night, a week after your recovery from that particular trauma and your return to your home, that greatly ameliorated my misery. I visited you, after managing to be out of touch for nearly forty-eight hours, and was ready to find you experiencing some new wretchedness. Your friend Christine greeted me. 'Nicola! Stop looking so worried, Cath's had a great day, she's been so happy! It's been wonderful, she and Rika and I have been laughing together all day!' And there you were, all pink and healthy and you greeted me with a huge smile and that chirrup of excitement and shake of your body that tells me you're feeling really good.

And that made me remember something of the utmost importance about you, a quality that many, including myself, could and should learn from you: as soon as you've recovered from something nasty you seem able to dismiss it, and are ready to enjoy life again. I know you don't forget it. But you don't dwell on it and worry about its happening again—until it happens.

I think you truly take life not only a day at a time but a moment at a time. Brilliant! I intend to do the same. I am a half-full person, even where you're concerned, and you've reminded me of that. Thank you, my precious girl.

From then on, almost exactly eight months since the operation, Cath's health improved greatly.

•

I was seriously upset when Rika, after living with Cath for a year and a half, told me out of the blue she wanted to quit being Cath's roommate.

"But Rika, you've seen her through all the ghastly stuff—her operations and the aftermath—and things really have improved now, I mean Cath's health has, and surely it's easier now and more fun and anyway I thought you liked being with Cath!"

"Calm down, Nicola, I'm not just walking out. I'll be around to help someone else move in. I love Cath, but I need to move on. Anyway," she added as I yanked another Kleenex out of the box, "I want to stay on as her weekend person. It's time she and I just had some fun." That helped, and I was even able, after calling her a cheeky cow, to agree to being used as a reference for the job she was after.

I whined about Rika's imminent departure to several friends, including Di Brandt the next time she gave a women's writing workshop in my house. Once again we looked for two people, preferably a settled couple. Di didn't know such a combination, but she did suggest that Irene, a close relative who had recently moved to Winnipeg, might be interested. Di recommended her highly, so meetings and interviews were duly set up and ultimately Irene, who was willing to take on the challenge, moved in.

At first blush, she appeared quiet and reserved but, like so many young women from a Mennonite background, including Darlene and Di, she proved to have an intense inner life that was busting its way out. In Irene's case, it was through art, and her distinctive and accomplished work enlivened Cath's apartment during the time she was there. Cath typically took her time sizing up her new caregiver, but I pointed out to both of them that a period of comparative tranquillity and orderliness, which I suspected Irene could provide, might be just what Cath needed after the busy fall. Irene remained relatively retiring with me but her letter describing her time with Cath reveals another warm relationship:

The seven and a half months that I spent as Cath's helper and roommate were filled with learning, laughter and occasional tears as two headstrong, independent-thinking women met head to head, both believing their way was best. Originally I often looked upon this time as an opportunity to help Cath gain more independence; often, however, she became the teacher and I learned things about myself, relationships, and life.

Cath, a young woman who sits unspeaking in a wheelchair watching life go by? Never! She often gets more enjoyment from life than people who are able-bodied. Good-natured, loving, laughing, Cath frequently communicates more in her own way than words do. Caring, giving, she enjoys walks on a summer evening, music, theatre and parties. She has a special gift of acceptance and I often found myself singing, playing and talking with Cath as I didn't do with friends I'd known for years.

I knew that Irene would find it tough going living with Cath without a partner. Although a friend of hers did join them for short periods, she basically had little help—except, of course, when Rika took over at weekends. Conditions of occupancy in Prairie Housing had gone awry of late, as had other aspects of the co-op, and there was unusually little caregiving assistance forthcoming from the people who were now in the upstairs apartments in the house.

In fall, 1992, Irene said she had to leave. Luckily, Cheryl at l'Avenir found Lynell and Brian (Mennonites again—they've been a godsend in Catherine's life!), a young couple who had spent three years studying in a seminary in Indiana and were now qualified as Mennonite church ministers. Lynell and Brian were on the lookout for a Manitoba parish where they could be hired as a team, but were happy to live with Cath in the interim, and this gave us breathing space in which to help Cath find more permanent roommates.

Lynell and Brian's tenure was a peaceful few months and Cath was very contented. Brian was a professional cook on the side, and I was invited to several excellent meals at the house. Lynell's creative instincts had been directed towards parenthood, and the need for her and Brian to find a job became increasingly urgent as her midriff expanded. Luckily, a small country parish decided to welcome them in early 1993, just prior to the baby's arrival, so while they made their plans, we at l'Avenir made ours around Cath. Lynell contributed an interesting and succinct note to Cath's story:

Living with Cath improved our marriage! My own life has been enriched by my encounters with people with disabilities. In our time with Cath, Brian also had the opportunity for the growth that inevitably happens when a person opens his or her life to a Catherine. It was good for me to watch, and it gave us, as a couple, a new common experience and language.

•

Thanks to Cath, I've travelled widely (even twice to Australia) since *Does She Know She's There?* was published in 1978. I've always enjoyed these speaking engagements (or gigs) but early on learned to expect surprises. Once, I was asked to speak at the Annual General Meeting of a local branch of ACL in a small Ontario town. I anticipated about fourteen people at the meeting, mainly parents like myself, with the addition of a service provider or two.

The lone disembarking passenger, I clambered out of the plane, looked both ways and crossed the tarmac to the terminal, which was a shed with two doors marked In and Out. I was about to inquire if there were any buses into town when a charming fellow, aglow with smiles, approached me and took my arm. "Hi there," he said, "I won the draw to pick you up!"

"Well thank you," I murmured as he led me from the shed across an expanse of muddy ruts to his car, "But the bus—"

"Bus! You think we'd let you take the bus? Careful now, we don't want you tripping and hurting yourself." Solicitousness personified, he helped me into the car. Suspecting by now that the local ACL AGM was a bigger deal than I thought, I asked how many people were expected.

"How many? Lady, I got four hundred guys with their tongues hanging out waiting to see you this evening." Steering with one hand, he waved the other in the air. "How 'bout that, eh? Hey," he added while my brain turned somersaults, "I'm Fred, by the way. Guess I was too excited to introduce myself."

I took his proffered hand. "And of course I'm Nicola," I responded with a gracious smile.

It was Fred's turn to be puzzled. "Nicola," he said with a frown. "That your private name, then?"

"Private? It's my only name . . . well, that and Schaefer." Fred's smile vanished and he released my hand abruptly.

"You mean," he said, horror slowly mounting on his face, "you mean you're not Brandy the exotic dancer?"

I shook my head regretfully. The car veered onto the verge and stopped.

Horror turned into panic. "But you were the only one that got off the plane . . . you gotta be Brandy . . . and that was the last plane in today and . . . oh my God. Oh my God, I don't believe this."

I asked Fred what his club was paying Brandy for her services. He asked me when my meeting was over. We nearly came to an arrangement, but I hadn't brought my feather fans.

Fourteen people attended my ACL meeting and I had a unique icebreaker.

It is always fascinating to hear other parents' stories, and to spend time with people who have disabilities, who can be powerful advocates for themselves and for others. I seldom come home without useful information or some good ideas. I recall, years ago, bumping into Judith, a friend of Cath's and mine, who uses a wheelchair. Judith looked different somehow—better than when I'd last seen her—but I couldn't identify why. I told her as much but she only grinned and said I had to work it out

Daughter and mother in conversation. JACK PEARPOINT PHOTOS

for myself. I couldn't, so she looked down at her lap tray, which was see-through plexi-glass, and barely noticeable. That was the point. I realized that the last time I'd seen Judith her tray had been in a solid colour.

I ordered a plexi-glass tray for Cath, replacing the vinyl-covered wooden one she'd had for years. The difference was astonishing. Suddenly one saw Cath as a whole person rather than as a top and a pair of legs. I think, too, she appreciated being able to look down and see her legs and feet, especially since she now knew when to warn whoever was pushing her (by tensing up) not to catch her foot going round a corner in the house. My slide show presentation has pictures of Cath with both kinds of tray and, invariably, someone from the audience will come up afterwards to thank me for the idea.

I should mention at this point that while Darlene was living with Cath we had a wheelchair built for her (Cath) that she uses to this day. It is designed to support her in such a way that she no longer needs a plastic body jacket—a great relief to everyone. The chair can also be tilted back within the frame, giving Cath a choice of angles at which to sit.

When I'm talking about Catherine's life, particularly her living situation, I try to stress that the arrangement we've helped her concoct should not be treated as an inflexible recipe. Carrying the cooking analogy further, we knew that the basic ingredients Cath required were: a good place to live; friends who valued her; the opportunity to pursue activities she enjoyed; and fundamental security. These are the basics for anyone's life but, as with all good cooking, sometimes one needs to vary the ingredients and their amounts, according to taste and availability.

In other words, Cath's situation has worked for her. Had she been a different person, her requirements, and the set-up we created, would also have been different. Sometimes when I return to a city where I've spoken before, people will tell me that Cath's story ignited their imagination, leading them to create similar arrangements for friends or family members who have disabilities. This I find immensely satisfying.

Conferences are useful events at which to exchange ideas, be inspired, begin or elaborate on friendships, laugh, cry and, last but not least, catch up on the latest disability terminology. Recently one particularly keen student asked me the politically correct way to describe my daughter. "Catherine," I answered. Later I relented and we discussed the issue.

When Catherine was small, people used to refer to her here in Canada as "mentally retarded" and "crippled." When I took her to England the terms became "mentally handicapped" and "spastic." Later, the Canadian labels evolved into "developmentally delayed" (implying that, like a train, she would eventually catch up and reach her destination), "neurologically impaired" and "not too swift." I rather like the last one, unofficial though it may be, because it applies to most of us in at least some aspects of our lives. For a while "differently-abled" did the rounds but luckily didn't catch on. We are constantly striving to help people with disabilities be recognized as more, rather than less, similar to everyone else, and that term merely reinforced the difference. Today, of course, the trendy word is "challenged," so Cath has both intellectual and physical challenges. The problem with this and other such well-intentioned terms is that they soon grow quotation marks, and become almost jokey.

I first spoke in public about Cath during the late '70s at a big weekend gathering in Quebec generated by the Canadian Association for Community Living (CACL). It involved parents and other activists from across the country. I introduced myself as the mother of a severely multiply handicapped daughter named Catherine. Afterwards another mother, Audrey, gently remonstrated with me. "You have a daughter named Catherine who has severe multiple disabilities," she said. I got the message and ever since, when necessary, have referred to Catherine as a person who has disabilities, rarely even shortening it to say she's disabled. I also met Barb Goode at that meeting. Barb is one of Canada's leading advocates for people who are intellectually challenged (or whatever the current fashionable term is). "I'm a person first," says Barb, "and I don't like being labelled." "Label jars, not people" is the motto of People First, the organization she helped to found. Incidentally, it was also Barb, and other members of People First, who lobbied for years to have the Canadian Association for the Mentally Retarded (CAMR) changed to the Canadian Association for Community Living (CACL).

I am by nature an optimist, and I find it easy when speaking at conferences to get so caught up in the numerous positive aspects of Cath's life, and the many good things that have happened in Winnipeg for people with disabilities, that I sometimes gloss over the difficulties we've experienced en route.

One of the key words written on the tattered sheet of notes I keep on hand when I'm rabbiting on is "dangers." I've mentioned one of my concerns already, that of making Cath's housing arrangement sound like a recipe. Another pitfall I try to avoid is making things sound too simple.

Cath and housemate, Ken.

Prairie Housing Cooperative (PHC) and l'Avenir Cooperative, how they work and stay afloat, are good examples of complex interconnected institutions which people tend to oversimplify.

PHC nearly collapsed a few years ago. There were several reasons. First, with the exception of the downtown apartment block of twenty-nine units, the co-op's clusters of houses are scattered all over Winnipeg, and the co-op members became isolated from each other. Second, the membership became preoccupied with finances, sometimes to the exclusion of community considerations. Third, there have been, at times, disagreement and a lack of interest in the co-op as a co-op—many members weren't interested in playing their part in running its administration, and the few people who did play an active role tended to burn out. Finally, there have been periods of bad management. I believe the most significant reason for the co-op's difficulties was that even though the original concept was clearly defined, safeguards for ensuring members' commitment had not been defined at all. Put crassly, this meant that if someone moved in and proved to be a lousy neighbour, there was no eviction procedure unless the rent was not being paid. These problems Prairie Housing Co-op experienced have now been addressed but they could have been avoided.

Problems we've encountered in l'Avenir have nearly always been due, directly or indirectly, to inadequate funding. Government funding for small community agencies such as l'Avenir is still nowhere near comparable to that which is provided to agencies operating large group homes, and to institutions. This means that while we're working to give Cath and our other members a vastly superior, in-home, individualized service, we're having to do so on a paltry budget. One of the results of this financial inequity is that l'Avenir can afford to pay its staff far less than they would make working in a large group home or in an institution. We're always saddened and frustrated when a good support worker leaves us, albeit reluctantly, to work in, for instance, St. Amant, because "unfortunately they'll pay me nearly twice what you guys can offer. And I have this student loan to pay off."

While it's draining for l'Avenir's administrators constantly to be seeking good support workers (when they would far rather be spending time working directly with members), the people most seriously affected by staff turnover are, of course, the individuals we serve. It must be horribly upsetting when a trusted and, often, loved support person vanishes and a new one has to be trained. It's also enervating and time-consuming for all concerned, and it certainly doesn't help create for our members the sense of stability and continuity we strive for.

Another danger I need to be aware of is implying that Cath's household has been all love and laughter. Most of the time the house has run according to the original plan and the atmosphere has been truly joyful and co-operative. But, as is true of any large family or mixed household, there have been periods of acrimony between members, and occasionally a person has moved in who has initially appeared to be co-opminded but who has ultimately created serious problems. However, these matters are not insuperable, and were I to be embarking on a new living situation for Cath today, I might well choose the same basic plan.

Or I might do something quite different. If anyone out there is considering housing for someone with a disability and is attracted to the idea of Cath's arrangement, a question might come to mind: where does Cath's primary support person, the one living with her, go during days and weekends off? The answer, since none of the people who have lived with her over the years have been able to afford a separate domicile, is that most of the time they stay at home. This is difficult for the full-time person because it's hard (in an apartment) to escape an innate sense of household responsibility. And for the respite person it's not easy to escape the sense of being in the way or, worse, overseen.

Friends Jenni and Joanne helping Cath in the pool. KEN GIGLIOTTI PHOTO

I've learned that it's of the utmost importance to support in every way possible the people who live and work with Catherine and it's clear, in retrospect, that as well as incorporating time off for the person living with her we should have planned a way of providing a place in which to spend it. Although everyone, from Darlene on, has been creative in coping with this drawback to being with Cath, it hasn't been easy.

Some friends and I in Winnipeg, including Zana and several others who have been involved in Cath's life and mine for years, have recently been investigating a practice known as co-housing, which has been popular in Europe for several decades and is now spreading to North America. It's a form of intentional community in which the residents, who represent a cross-section of the population in terms of age, marital status, education and careers, have equity in their own self-contained unit in the development but also share common space both indoors and out. The average co-housing development has twenty-four units and can be created by converting—to the needs and wishes of future inhabitants—apartment blocks or other large buildings, or by custom designing clusters of houses around a central common house (which usually has a large kitchen and dining room for regular communal meals, guest rooms, maybe a carpentry shop, or whatever the community decides is appropriate).

I'm excited by the idea of Catherine owning and living in a self-contained unit but being surrounded by neighbours whose aim is to create a mutually supportive, inclusive community in which everyone's contributions and needs are appreciated. She would have paid assistants with her on a shift basis rather than living with her (there would be a guest bedroom in her unit, of course) so the problem of private space for her primary support person would be eliminated.

But that's in the future. In the meantime, what does Catherine do during weekdays? This question naturally crops up when I'm talking about her life. I think I know what she'd *like* to do from Monday to Friday: she'd like to have two people, a man and a woman, both of whose company she enjoyed, at her service all day. At 9.00 a.m. they would appear at her door and, depending on her state of health and mood, would either stay at home with her or go with her for a jaunt in the van. If she felt unwell, these people would do whatever they could to help her feel comfortable. And if Cath appeared interested in staying home for some reason other than illness, her friends would entertain her in whatever way most appealed to her. They might read to her, play her electronic keyboard with her (she's pretty good at picking out notes with her left hand), look at magazines with her, leap around or dance wildly to loud music, fall off or over the furniture (including her bed, with her in it), swing her around in her wheelchair, get into the Jacuzzi with her, give her massages, and so on. (It would be necessary, incidentally, for Cath's friends to be slightly eccentric and very imaginative). If it was an out-of-house day, the trio might go swimming, to a movie, to the park, on a shopping spree, to visit friends or anything else that took their fancy—all with frequent coffee and food breaks. Alternatively, the day might be a combination of going out and staying home. Flexibility would be the key.

Cath and friend, Sue.

That's the dream. Reality, of course, is different. When Project Inclusion at Red River Community College concluded after three years, after losing most of its funding (although recently it has been been revived in a slightly different form and for a different group of students), Cath joined a daytime program for some fifteen people with complex disabilities. The Director of the program, Sunny (admirably named), and her ebullient

Cath and Cheryl racing around the Reh-Fit Centre track. KEN GIGLIOTTI PHOTO

assistant, Joanne, would like nothing better than to be able to provide individualized activities for every one of the participants. The problem, it need hardly be said, is a lack of adequate funding.

Most social agencies in Manitoba are expected to provide a "day program" for people who have a disability, and who are unable to compete in the job market, on financing of $22.00 per person per day. Hefty lobbying over the years by l'Avenir and the folks running Cath's program have resulted in Cath and her co-participants not faring as badly as some, but they could, of course, do much better. The program is based in a couple of ordinary offices—with bathroom and kitchen facilities—in a small strip mall next to my bank and local drugstore. Sunny's and Joanne's aim is to have everyone out and about, so as little time as possible is spent in the offices.

Cath is picked up from home by one of several local transportation firms designed for people with disabilities. On Mondays, Wednesdays and Fridays she arrives at the program by 9.30. Weather permitting, mornings are usually spent visiting local stores and coffee shops or walking around the neighbourhood. After lunch, whatever the weather, Cath and a couple of other participants plus their assistants are picked up by bus and travel downtown to swim—or, in Cath's case, happily float on her back, kicking—in the pool at the spanking new YMCA.

Cheryl helping Cath with her physio at the Reh-Fit Centre. KEN GIGLIOTTI PHOTO

Recently a friend phoned me to say that one day she was in a downtown skywalk and found herself looking down at the Y pool: "There were three women getting out," she said. "They seemed to be helping one another, working together, and the effect was that of a choreographed ballet sequence in slow motion. It was beautiful, and I watched, fascinated, until they were on dry land. And then I suddenly realized that one of the women was Catherine—being helped by the other two."

On Tuesdays and Thursdays, for several years, Cath would be picked up and taken directly to a keep-fit place known, exotically, as Body Sculpture. She would be met there by an assistant from the day program and, along with other men and women in search of a more fit physique, she would spend an hour having different parts of her body moved around on padded tables which functioned electronically. This form of passive exercise was invented for people who have had polio, but able-bodied people also use it to work out by pushing against whatever the table is doing; for example, if the top half of the table is sitting the person up and down, he or she will try to move in the opposite direction. I discovered this form of exercise years ago, courtesy of Kevin, a core member of l'Arche, and I took Cath to see if she'd like it. Two businessmen in suits and shiny shoes with bows on them lay on the tables adjacent. Their legs scissored back and forth and they fought the machine with agonized expressions—while having a discussion about the stock market. Catherine, who loves limbs flying round, nearly fell off the table giggling and blowing raspberries.

When the Body Sculpture business closed down, Cath's helpers from her home and her day program organized an alternative exercise program—physio and fun at the Reh-Fit Centre, which proved fairly successful. As with other aspects of Cath's life, we're constantly looking for new ideas to try.

Another daytime pursuit that Cath enjoyed for a while was volunteering, with assistance, at a day nursery a couple of days a week. Cath loves babies and children, and we have a slide of her looking down maternally at a little boy who is showing her a drawing he's done. Ultimately, however, she became disenchanted with the nursery and spent much of the time there sleeping. She stopped going, and we realized later that this was the time when her health problems began and that she was probably sleeping because she was exhausted from the pain, rather than boredom with the children.

•

After Cath moved into her house I started going to England every summer. Harry, my dear stepfather, died in June 1987. I had visited him in the nursing home hours before his death, and my mother and a friend and I were in the pub when my brother Edgar, who had visited his father just after me, phoned the pub with the news. I bought Mum a large gin and tonic and then told her about Harry. She sat absolutely still for a moment and then said firmly, "Good. He'd suffered enough. Good." The nurses and the patients in the home always enjoyed it when Harry turned up in old films on TV. One of the nurses later told me about the last moments of his life: " He was an actor to the end, was Harry. He had the heroin, dear, so he wasn't suffering. I asked him if he'd like a sip of his whisky and he nodded. I helped him with it and afterwards he smiled and said, 'Thank you, that was lovely' and then he was gone."

Harry had been ill for years and Mum had, in her own caring but sometimes brusque way, looked after him. After his death, she missed him sorely and was terrified of becoming incapacitated herself. To ward off her fears, she continued to swim in the pool over at Greatham, to don her men's gumboots and keep the garden more or less under control and,

Cordelia. DOMINIC SCHAEFER PHOTO

picking up where she'd left off years before, to attend painting classes and create oil paintings with a fierce intensity.

I visited Mum the summer after Harry died. One day, an elegantly attired woman came picking her way carefully down the steep, uneven path to the cottage in high-heeled shoes. She was carrying a foil-covered tray. "Ah," said my mother, "here comes Meals on Heels." Mum had always disliked cooking and this was her one concession to old age.

My mother died instantaneously from a cerebral hemorrhage in May 1990, and it was an awful shock. Mum was eighty-two and was as mentally and physically vital as ever, although she had been saying for at least a year that she wanted to die. We had brushed this off, but maybe she knew something we didn't. At any rate, we were glad that she had died the way she wanted to—suddenly, with no fuss.

Dominic was living in Winnipeg when she died, and he and I flew over to join Ben (who'd been living in Oxford for two years) and the rest of Mum's descendants at the cottage. This was the first time ever that my family had been gathered together—my sister Veronica, her son Richard, her daughter Eleanor, and their partners and children, my brother Edgar, myself and the boys. The only person missing, unfortunately, was Cath, but taking her to England would have been well-nigh impossible.

We organized a simple but satisfying memorial service in the nearby country church of Mum's childhood. One of our cousins arranged wild flowers in wine carafes on the altar, a touch we knew Cordelia would have enjoyed, and Dominic and Ben dragged our ancient audio system to the church. After the service everyone trooped out to some of Mum's favourite Louis Armstrong numbers. At the cottage later about eighty friends and relatives of all ages, some with white hair and others with dreadlocks, came from near and far for a celebration of her life that continued until breakfast the next day. We decked the cottage and garden, which was a glory of flowers and nesting birds, with her paintings, one of which she had finished days before and with which she was particularly pleased. I think everyone had trouble realizing she wasn't, as she would normally have been, sitting on a piece of old sacking by her bonfire with a homemade cigarette in her hand and a gin and tonic by her side on the grass.

Nothing gives me more pleasure than travelling to England each year to spend time with Ben and the rest of our British family. We're still hanging on to the cottage and for the last few years Ben has made it his home, along with a small gang of cousins and friends. Ben is also caretaker of the cottage, and as it is some six hundred years old, this is a considerable responsibility. When a new roof became a necessity in 1997, he removed over eight thousand tiles, replaced rotten or deathwatch beetle-infested beams and then reinstalled the tiles. He also knocked two small rooms downstairs into one and put up a magnificent support beam between the two. It was fashioned from an ash tree he'd felled for the purpose three years previously. After attending a nearby agricultural college and a number of carpentry courses, he seems to have found his calling as a man of the land, and a builder/restorer. It pleases me that he has made friends with some of the members of the l'Arche community in nearby Bognor Regis and welcomes them to the cottage for time off and a change of scene.

He seems contentedly dug in, but visited Canada in the summer and fall of 1995. After sending over his motorbike (utilitarian, fast but not fancy) in four massive parcels, he appeared on the doorstep, put the thing together and spent several weeks with us, doing tree work in the neighbourhood (he brought his saws, harness and ropes), spending time with Cath, and whitewater rafting in the wilds of Ontario with child-

Our family, 1999. Left to right: Ben, Ted, Cath (determinedly not smiling), Dominic and Nicola in Cath's sitting room. THOMAS HARDIE PHOTO

hood friends. Then he piled his gear onto, and hanging down the sides of, his motorbike and brrrmed off to explore the Rockies and thence to see Dominic in Vancouver.

Dominic found his calling, photography, way back in 1986 when he first went to England. He'd been acting suspiciously for some time before leaving Winnipeg, spending hours—sometimes days—arranging a feather on top of a broom against the back wall of the house and photographing it from all angles and in all lights. When he returned from Europe after two years he sequestered Ben's room and transformed it into a darkroom. Some stunning prints of Sussex emerged from that period and are still among his best. In 1990 he spent a year at a photography school in Victoria and then moved to Vancouver, where he had his first gallery show in 1993. I attended the opening and basked in reflected glory as his friends and admirers asked if I was really Dominic's mother. I was far less modest in my response than was my son as he received congratulations.

Since then he's been the photographer for a business magazine. Because, like his father, he's a perfectionist where work is concerned, this occupies much of his time but he's managed to make quite a name for himself simply as an excellent photographer/artist on the side. Like his brother, he always wants to know how Cath is and I recently, at his request, named him a trustee of the fund in her name in my will. Being a mere two thousand miles from Winnipeg, he's able to visit us quite often, which is lovely.

For the last few years Ted and I have lived eight blocks, or a good dog walk, apart. We're on very good terms. We share news about our children's lives and our own (after thirty-nine years of hard slogging away at the University, he retired, joyfully, in the spring of 1997), and exchange books and magazines. We also often meet at Catherine's house at get-togethers and other family events. Ted lives in our old house, where his daughter often visits him, and I'm in the lower two floors of a huge old house, similar to Cath's, and have friends living in a separate apartment upstairs. I have official sleeping spots in my part for six visitors, plus floor space and mattresses, so friends from the two main sides of my life, music and the disability field, can *and do* come to stay.

About two hundred and sixty people have bedded down here so far, some for a night, some for up to six months and others on a weekly basis. This last group includes l'Arche assistants. Living in l'Arche is not always a heavenly experience and these young people desperately need a place where they can collapse and regenerate. I consider myself fortunate to be able to provide a bolt-hole. One summer at Folk Festival time I had a nine-piece brass band from New York, hotly followed by the Oyster Band (six blokes) from England, hotly followed by Friends in High Places—brilliant stilt dancers from Manhattan. Somewhere in all of this music and dance, Sister Mary, a nun connected with l'Arche in Syracuse, spent a night or two with us. I love the hustle and bustle and the gains are immeasurable. Ted, a self-confessed hermit, shudders when I tell him about it. He says he prefers the company of books.

Providentially, my new house came equipped with a ramp, so Catherine or friends who use wheelchairs are able to visit easily. I keep her old hospital bed in "Cath's" room (it's also my office) in my house and she has a nifty new one at her place. I bought it second-hand from a hospital for $200. It sits her up or raises her knees at the touch of a button and is a great success, particularly with visiting children. People of all heights attend to Cath's needs when she's on her bed, and over the years several have developed sore backs because the bed is either too high or too low. A particularly useful aspect of the new bed is that the whole thing can be raised or lowered electronically.

One of the happy events Ted and I attended together was Darlene's wedding in the summer of 1991. Catherine was present too, of course, looking rather thin and wan because she was still recovering from her big operation, but happy nonetheless. Darlene had been teaching up north and we had missed her. She and her husband Greg lived in town for several years after their wedding and visited back and forth with Cath, as well as with Ted and myself. I feel a satisfying sense of continuity about the fact that shortly after her marriage, I persuaded Darlene to join l'Avenir's Board. She even spent three years as our super-conscientious president. She and Greg and their son Sam live in Ottawa now, but visit Winnipeg whenever possible.

In July 1993 Ted and I dropped by Cath's house to help her celebrate her thirty-second birthday.

"The garden looks good," noted Ted, nervously jovial, "look at all those tomato plants."

"And I've never seen such a mass of flowers here," I said, "the ramp's almost invisible. Come on!"

There was a crowd of people, and as I sorted through them, I realized that many of the people making music and swilling beer on our daughter's front deck or talking inside the house had been in her life almost as long as Darlene, and in some cases longer. Keith and Kathleen, Catherine's roommates since the beginning of that year, were active and gracious co-hosts with Cath.

Cath and I first met this singular couple in my sitting room in 1992, when Cath was staying with me for Christmas. We and Rika, who insisted, rightly, on being present as Cath's friend and advocate, were conducting informal interviews with a number of people who thought they might like to move in with Cath as her caregivers when Lynell and Brian left in February. Cath, as so often when I wished she would be in an alert and beguiling mood, sat looking completely blah throughout each interview. I realized for the umpteenth time that a person immobilized and speechless in a wheelchair often has no choice in where they're plonked and whom they meet. Maybe Cath didn't want to be there that day. Months later, however, when I asked Kathleen about her initial impression of Catherine, she described Cath as a magnet. "I was drawn to her immediately—it was an almost physical tug. I just knew I wanted to be around her, get to know her, be part of her life."

Kathleen was twenty-two—a lovely, sensitive, practical young woman. She has an outstanding gift for creating beauty wherever she goes. One of the things that warmed me to her immediately was her response to my question regarding Cath's personal care. Would it bother her, I wondered? Well yes, it would, she replied, because Catherine would surely feel it as an invasion of her privacy to have a strange woman washing her. But, Kathleen added, she would be as respectful as she knew how. Keith was forty-two, with a wealth of experience in many occupations, including driving a taxi, managing a bakery, and working with people who have disabilities. Keith told me it was only in the latter two jobs that he felt truly fulfilled. His upright bearing, his somewhat stern look and blunt words belie a sensitivity equal to Kathleen's. Keith and Kathleen had been together (not always, they freely admitted, without difficult periods) for five years and intended to remain so. Both Rika and I, with a few reservations —they really were unusual—liked them. And Cath granted Keith a small chuckle when he carefully helped her with her tea. Keith and I had several friends in common and he encouraged me to request character references. I received the same response from each request. In summary, Keith was hardworking, 100% honest and reliable, and once he'd decided to be one's friend there was nothing he wouldn't do for that person. And Kathleen? A beautiful personality—and bright. And as a couple? They were devoted to each other and complemented one another well; a great team. Would they be good for Cath? Absolutely.

Rika, Cath and I had been invited to participate in an ACL family conference in Edmonton at the beginning of February. This break gave Lynell and Brian time to move out and Keith and Kathleen to move in. It was years since I'd travelled by plane with Cath. It is always a tricky business, involving a transfer from wheelchair to plane seat, with little manoeuvring space. I automatically went into organizing mode and began making one conflicting suggestion after another as more passengers started to queue up behind us. Rika stopped me in mid-muddle and organized the move with quiet efficiency.

The conference was at the Fantasyland hotel, attached to the West Edmonton Mall. We were allotted a huge room with a Jacuzzi, rather than one of the "theme" rooms Rika had pushed for. Catherine, relieved to have arrived somewhere, lay on her bed and looked around the room with wide eyes. Rika, the kid in her suddenly emerging—I kept forgetting how young she was—went around bouncing on the king-sized beds, investigating the basket of "free" toiletries in the bathroom, lying in the

Three beautiful women: Kathleen, Catherine and friend Monica. KEITH CROWSTON PHOTO

empty Jacuzzi while looking at herself in the ceiling mirror ("Cath, you'll love this!") and squeaking with delight at each new discovery ("Hey Nicola, get a load of this mini-bar!"). Later, we moved Cath into her wheelchair and the two of them charged off to explore the West Edmonton Mall, returning hours later armed with such essentials as four massive bottles of Diet Coke for Rika, tea-making equipment for Cath and myself, and bag upon bag of life-threatening snacks, chips and candy, for all of us. There was also a bright red Speedo swimsuit for Cath. I winced at the colour. "She chose it," said Rika, "it's not the colour I liked but it was the one she kept pointing at." And actually, Cath looked pretty good in her new suit, I thought later as we all floated in the Jacuzzi.

When we returned to Winnipeg, Cath's apartment was transformed. Unlike most of their predecessors, Keith and Kathleen had significant amounts of furniture and other possessions which they had integrated tastefully with Catherine's. One of the most striking new aspects of the place was the sudden abundance of greenery, which hung from the ceilings, spilled over the edges of shelves and was draped over doorways. Cath also had fresh herbs growing in a tray on her window sill—"I thought she might enjoy the aroma," said Kathleen—and a large fern curled down from the shelf over her bed. Hanging on a string from the same shelf was a phantasmagorical winged creature made for Cath by Kathleen from bright material and studded with beads and bits of mirror—"It must get pretty boring just looking up at a plain old shelf." Kathleen had spent time in the Middle East as a child, and the apartment now reflected this with adroitly placed exotica—a hand-woven rug on the wall here, an inlaid table there and other smaller items—brass pots, candlesticks, dishes—everywhere.

Kathleen is a whiz with a sewing machine. She made extra cushions for Cath's sofa, and was now working on much-needed new curtains for the sitting room. An orderly woman, she'd noticed the mess around my telephone table and had made me a present; using leftover cushion cover material, she had fashioned a sort of mini-wall hanging with separate pouches for pens, notepad and glasses. Keith, who is almost as keen a reader as Ted, added several new bookcases and shelves around the place and, because he's also a musician, a variety of music-making equipment.

Keith's carpentry materials were stacked neatly in the basement along with his overflow of books. There had been cats in the apartment ever since Glen and Laurie's time. Keith and Kathleen carried on the tradition by bringing their two—one who peered out nervously from behind an arrangement of Keith's antique tins on a shelf in the kitchen, and the other already curled up on Cath's bed. Added to all this visual beauty and coziness, Keith was baking bread, so a marvellous smell filled the kitchen.

The following year was a really good one for Catherine, apart from some illness. She was demonstrably happy with Kathleen and Keith, who loved her and provided a fine combination of stability and entertainment. The apartment always looked, smelled and felt beautifully welcoming and there were frequent parties—Jacuzzi and otherwise—which invariably included music provided by Keith and his friends. At least two of his and Kathleen's friends told me how much they appreciated being able to visit without being hauled up flights of stairs in their wheelchairs. For Cath, one great advantage of parties at home is that if she gets fed up she can retreat to her room.

People dropped in often. One regular visitor was Rika, who had moved upstairs to the bachelor apartment. When Rika quit as Cath's weekend helper, she knew I'd be upset, so she wrote a beautiful letter about her relationship with Cath and her reason for leaving:

Catherine is a teacher, but this ability of hers is separate from who she is as a person. The lessons she's taught me are from being around her and having to adjust and broaden my perceptions about communication, language and friendship.

I never felt very close to Cath until after the first year of our being together, when the worst of her illness was over. That was when I got to see the part of her that Nicola, Sonja and many others had told me about, the part of Cath that is happy, full of life and spirit, the part of Cath that was able to give to me in many touching and wonderful ways. While she was ill, I saw the great deal of pain she went through and I was often the only person she could show it to. She let me know very clearly that she was hurting and I often mistook this as personal dislike for me. I realize now that she was communicating with me the only way she knew how and that I wasn't picking up very well on what she had to say.

With Cath my dependence on words has lessened. I needed to understand how unnecessary words are before I could let go of trying to build our friendship on what I said with them. I had to realize we weren't going to have a close relationship unless we were on equal ground, and we gradually achieved this through living together and sharing numerous life experiences. Many people see Cath as being limited in what she can say because she doesn't use words, but I feel quite the opposite. I can't use words to say half of what I'd like to because I'm using this medium to communicate about a friend whom I don't think of in these terms.

Between Cath and me, language has become an experience of touch, sight and sound. Our shared enthusiasm for sound and music has been one of the building blocks of our friendship. Some of our most intimate moments have been while at a concert, participating in a drumming circle or while on the back porch at dusk listening to the birds. Often, our hands will join in the darkness and between them a dance will take form, creating a tangible link between us and the music around us.

We're at a point now where we don't deal with the details of each other's daily lives and our time together is spent enjoying each other's company. I stopped working with Cath because I didn't want to be paid to be a friend and it's important to me that I spend time with her because I want to, because our time together is what we've chosen to give each other.

In Catherine I have a friend who touches me in a place that others rarely do, a place that's usually vulnerable and hidden. When I think of her and my relationship with her I think of how I feel around her, about touching hands and about the things she says with her eyes that no one could ever say to me with words. I think about the love between us and how precious it is to me, and about how I don't think it would be there except for Cath's abilities, as a teacher and as a friend.

Catherine had a bad spell in the fall of 1993. Keith and Kathleen, with tireless dedication, saw her through a couple of chest infections but, just as in her pre-operation days, Cath was also experiencing bouts of severe pain for no obvious reason. She had been so healthy of late, I'd forgotten she was supposed periodically to have her esophagus checked, and stretched when necessary. Keith and I took her to see Dr. T.H. An X-ray showed that her left lung had collapsed. As Cath happened that day to be in excellent spirits and looking completely well, we were baffled.

During the subsequent investigation of her esophagus (which was fine) Dr. T.H. suctioned out the top part of her lung (the only area one can get at, apparently) and pumped it full of air. However, when Keith took her to the hospital a few days later because she was in extreme pain, another X-ray revealed that the lung was once again flat. We sat there wondering what to do when all of a sudden Cath cheered up, started accepting a few sips of water and was plainly ready to go home, flat lung or not. It was puzzling.

Dr. T.H. suggested I consult a respiratory specialist, who said that, due to Cath's scoliosis, which bends her body to the left, the left lung was under constant compression and would probably never fully reinflate. The specialist did not think, however, Cath's condition would cause her to be in pain. I asked what we could do. "Aggressive physiotherapy," was the response, so that was what Keith and I promptly organized.

Jean, a splendid woman from a local Home Therapy team, began visiting Cath on a daily basis and, through positioning and thumping and squeezing, she helped Catherine to breathe more deeply. Keith quickly learned the techniques, and he and Kathleen incorporated physio into Cath's daily life. Cath seems fine, even with only one lung working well, and my suspicion is that the other had quietly packed up long before it was noticed. Jean continues to work with Cath on a regular basis and has become a valued friend.

•

I was filled with immense satisfaction in the summer of 1996 as I composed the following invitation:

On July 18th, 1986, days before her 25th birthday, Catherine moved from her parents' house into her own home on the ground floor of 822 Preston. It was an exciting, somewhat anxious time, the culmination of about two years of planning and hard work on

Cath and some of the many friends who helped her celebrate her 35th birthday.

the part of many people. Everyone had been eager to help Cath create a home for herself where she would have both the necessary paid, live-in support and the freely given friendship and help of others living in the two upstairs apartments. Could such a novel arrangement work?

In the succeeding years there have been wonderful times at 822 Preston, and many equally wonderful people have been—and in some cases still are—an important part of Catherine's life, and she of theirs. It hasn't always been perfect—what household is?— but we can now say that it not only could work, it has worked, and we hope and believe it will continue to do so.

Catherine invites you to help her celebrate her 35th birthday and the 10th anniversary of her move to her own place. She would also like you to meet her housemates, including Sherrill, her primary support person, who incidentally was already part of her life 10 years ago.

It was a grand party. About fifty of Catherine's friends and former roommates ambled up the sloped path to her front door during the evening, many bearing gifts and foil-covered plates of good stuff to eat. Those who were unable to be there sent regrets and good wishes. There was much music and laughter and storytelling, particularly of the "Hey, do you remember —" variety as events around Cath's life in her house were recalled. Ted was there, of course, and provided a cooler loaded with beer and wine. Darlene made the birthday cake. A good friend, John, kindly lent us his professional services and video'd the whole event. Cath was beautiful, if bemused, throughout but, as is her custom after a hectic happy time, had a long reflective giggle in bed when everyone had gone.

Catherine detests being photographed, incidentally. Immediately upon spotting a camera she will turn away and become resolutely unsmiling. Many of us have hovered for hours trying to catch her out but she's nearly always too quick for us. She seems to regard it as a game, because the moment we give up she will grin and chortle happily—but will instantly look away and turn her mouth down if we try again.

Keith and Kathleen spent nearly two and a half terrific years with Cath before moving to their own apartment nearby. Tracy, a young woman from Newfoundland, took over the role of Cath's primary caregiver. Tracy had a penchant for helping anyone or anything in trouble and during her tenure with Cath at Preston Avenue—a time during which Cath was both well and cheerful—I never knew whom or what I would encounter when I visited: temporarily motherless children, temporarily childless mothers (during child custody imbroglios) and permanently, until they found Tracy, homeless animals.

Tracy unfortunately developed serious health problems and had to leave Catherine sooner than any of us had anticipated. And Cath's succeeding roommate, Sherrill, eloquently described what happened next:

In July 1986 I attended an extraordinary celebration—a house blessing for Catherine Schaefer. Like many young women of 25, Catherine was setting up her own household but, because she was unable either to walk or speak, her family, with the creative assistance of David Wetherow, had designed a unique situation for her. Cath's new home was a lovely white older home, three stories high, with a curving wheelchair ramp leading to a small deck at the back, a columned two-story porch, several leaded glass windows and one of those roof ventilators that give a place the appearance of a Middle-Eastern mosque. There was a warm gathering of friends and Catherine's new housemates, and Catherine herself, of course, as Father Eric Jensen processed through the house sprinkling it amply with holy water, and then we walked across the road to the park and enjoyed a celebratory meal.

I shed a few happy tears that day, reflecting the happiness with which I was surrounded. Although it made little sense at the time, as I was then married to David Wetherow, had three children and a full-time job with the Department of Education, part of me wished I was moving into this place as well. Sitting on the fringe of all the activity as I was, however, I merely wondered at the courage of all the participants, including Darlene, Cath's first roommate.

I had first met Catherine at a New Year's Eve party at the Schaefer family home some time before. She had been enjoying all kinds of wonderful food when something became jammed in her esophagus. I helped Nicola remove the spine-supporting corset Catherine was wearing but I remember my awkwardness and fear that I would unintentionally do more harm than good. Something about Cath made me want to come close but I didn't know how to approach her. I watched the warm ease with which Catherine's and Nicola's friend Zana helped Cath but I remained in the dark. There was no communication device and Catherine neither looked me in the eye nor relished my touch.

In 1991 David and I separated and three years later I moved into the upstairs apartment of Nicola's house with my two sons and a friend. Catherine came to visit quite often but although she joined us for various family celebrations with my children and Nicola, she and I made no strong connection until, with Nicola's permission, I practiced my newly acquired skill of Reiki with her. We sat quietly together watching television as I placed my hands in various positions on Cath's body. At first she only tolerated me, occasionally pushing my hands away, but as we sat in silence over a period of several hours, a warm energy began to form between us. I needed this time alone with her to establish a channel of communication. At Nicola's invitation, I began to visit Catherine in her own home. During these times I spoke little, continuing the Reiki experience and massaging the pressure points in her feet—a practice known as reflexology. Although I was often cold and tired as I went to her house I never failed to emerge from our sessions feeling happy and refreshed. When I first began massaging her feet, we both approached the experience with some caution. Due to her cerebral palsy, the muscles and tendons in her feet are often in spasm, so her feet are very tender. She often jumped or glared at me if I hit a sore spot, but with practice I learned to lighten my touch and she learned to relax and trust. I slowly added new forms of touch and found that she loves having her back muscles, legs, arms and hands massaged. I massaged her spine timidly at first because it's quite curved and I was afraid of hurting her, but she soon began to experience a lot of release and would deepen her breathing as I worked. The last frontier was working on her head and neck. These two, together with her left arm and hand, are the areas of her body over which Cath has the greatest control and she wasn't sure she wanted to 'give' them to me. She would sometimes allow me to touch these areas briefly and then with a glare push me away. We continued in this fashion for about a year.

In the spring of 1996, Catherine's roommate, Tracy, announced that due to persistent personal health problems she had decided to return to her parents' home in Newfoundland. When Nicola told me she was initiating a search for Tracy's replacement, I felt a resurfacing of the desire to move in with Cath that had caught me by surprise ten years earlier. I loved living upstairs in Nicola's house, sharing so much of our lives, but the apartment was too large for one person (my sons were leaving), so I

Sherrill and Catherine trying on hats.

was reluctantly thinking about moving anyway. I was hesitant to suggest myself to Nicola as Cath's roommate; we are good friends and I didn't want to put her on the spot.

Her encouraging response lighted the way through the following months. For one reason and another, including my father's sudden death down in Virginia, my move into Catherine's house was very stressful and sometimes I felt I would collapse in exhaustion. One evening, as yet another thing went wrong, I fell on my knees beside her bed, crying. When I raised my head shamefully, Cath was looking at me with concern and as I moved near her, she reached out and stroked my head. It was in that moment that I knew how truly present she is to others. The opening between us widened in the ensuing days and I began to share with her what I was doing and feeling and to elicit her opinion on what she would prefer to do, eat or wear. I also began to read to her, something she seemed genuinely to enjoy. I wasn't sure how much she was actually understanding but noticed that her reaction changed appropriately with the material content. At one point, while I was reading a poignant story that was particularly pertinent to our circumstances at the time, she began to laugh with a knowing look. I, too, began to laugh, and realized that we were indeed truly present to one another. I knew then my own definitive answer to the question Nicola had first posed with the title of her book.

The bonding process continues. It forms the basis of all the activities we pursue, making our lives together a joyful exploration of fresh possibility. This translates into simple things like making travel arrangements that leave her feeling animated rather than exasperated, or shopping together for a wardrobe that reflects her own colouring and personal taste, or being part of a women's drumming circle. We are working together to cre-

Sherrill and Cath grocery shopping. KEN GIGLIOTTI PHOTO

ate a communal universe in which each of us also has our own space. Catherine withdraws into herself when she needs to and so do I. I'm delighted when she chooses to emerge. And if I am not mistaken, she, too, rejoices in my returning.

When I'm alone with Catherine I feel truly free to play. She often initiates the mood by blowing raspberries, interspersed with hoots. Her beautiful eyes are large and animated at these times. I respond with sounds of my own, dancing and clowning around. She keeps me wound up with an increasing crescendo of noise and excited body springs. High on enthusiasm, she is rarely the one to terminate such sessions. We continue our fun with making sounds as we travel in the van. Sometimes, when she's tired of gadding about, I swear, though Nicola and Ted have yet to hear her do it, she begins to intone the syllable 'home,' obviously happy to be heading there.

In the Jacuzzi, I began to put together our Reiki and sound sessions by placing my hands on the topside and underside of each of her chakras (energy centres) while chanting a sound traditionally associated with each. Since she loves to submerge her ears in the water, the sound vibration is travelling through both the water and my touch. I often make up my own songs at these times, sometimes with words and sometimes just a flow of babble. Her eyes shine and she joins me in experimenting with the sounds she can make.

One of Catherine's freedoms is that of being her own person. When she's tired she sleeps; when she's hungry she eats. Her face and body are true reflections of her state, unmasked by social expectations. In this she is my teacher and I am her slow student. I still eat when I'm full, smile when I'm in pain and generally ignore the signals my body *sends me. I know that one of the quickest ways to heal myself when I'm unwell is to fast but I often fail to act on the knowledge. Catherine, however, tends to refuse any food when she's ill and she's usually the first in the household to finish with the current flu or cold virus.*

Sages have written through the centuries about the art of living and loving simply. Catherine is the first person I have met who actually does those things. The gift of her presence is to allow those of us who are privileged to know her to experience just how simply loving and living is done. Were she to use words, she could say with complete candor, 'I live simply as I am.'

Summer 1997

•

There are several issues I'd like to see addressed in Cath's life. When she was at school years ago she had been introduced to choice-making by means of electronic equipment. A while before she left home a friend had made her a gizmo that would allow her to turn her bedroom light on and off by remote control. It required her to flip a switch and, frankly, she either couldn't co-ordinate her hand to do this or else she wasn't interested. I now think I should have persevered with the idea. Also, she's never owned a powered wheelchair. My excuse—a lame one, I admit—for not having pursued this is that there always seem to be so many absolute necessities to attend to. And finally, we would all love it if we could find a way of helping Catherine communicate more easily. We've tried symbols and letter boards and various methods involving computers and other electronic machines, but none of these so far has helped her much, if at all.

In the meantime, she has become far more determined and successful about making her wishes known. Much of this is due, I know, to the extraordinary sensitivity of the people around her since she left home but I'm not alone in thinking that Cath herself has found a way to transmit many more of her choices and feelings than she did when she was younger. I reckon she has helped make a pretty good and at least partly self-determined life for herself.

As might be deduced from Sherrill's description of her life with Catherine, the two women developed an exceptionally strong bond over the two and a quarter years they spent together and it was a sad day when Sherrill found she was unable to continue living with Cath. Not only was she exhausted from the strain of carrying two jobs—for financial reasons she didn't feel able to quit her job with the government—but also she wanted to live with her new partner, and there simply wasn't room to do this in the apartment (they tried for a few months).

I alluded earlier to the drawback to Cath's living arrangement—lack of privacy —and Sherrill helped me finally face the fact that we should look at a different way of providing support for Catherine: on a shift basis rather than having her primary support worker living in. Sherrill and I spent some time with l'Avenir's superb administrative team since 1995, Dianne and Stephanie, and the result is a new system which is working well—and we believe will continue to do so. From Monday to Friday, Catherine's new primary support worker, a vibrant young woman named Karen, comes to the house when Cath returns from her day program and stays until 11.00 p.m. Karen is responsible for overseeing all aspects of Cath's life—contact with her family and friends, household management, medical appointments, training weekend respite workers, having fun, and so on—and we think and hope that, because she returns home to her husband and two young children each night, she will not easily burn out.

At a large family reunion in Ted's back yard last summer, 1998, I noticed Catherine sitting with a young cousin whom she hadn't seen for a while. She and Sara were holding hands, both with slight smiles on their faces but not actually looking at one another. They sat like that for several minutes, just being together. It was beautiful. I didn't say anything, but later Sara came to me: "I've discovered this wonderful thing about Cath, Nicola. You don't have to entertain her or talk or try to get a reaction. I think she appreciates it more if you just let her know that she has your complete attention, that you're there for her, and that you know she's there for you. There was a whole lot going on between us that no-one could see . . . I'd love to spend more time with her."

Sara'a wish was fulfilled sooner than she expected. When Sherrill moved out in January, 1999, Sara moved in—as Cath's roommate and as a part-time support staff with l'Avenir. Her responsibility, gladly taken, is to be at home five nights a week and to help Cath prepare for her day each morning. It's a brilliant arrangement and Catherine, Karen and Sara all love it. Sherrill, who often drops by, is equally happy that her critical observations have produced such a positive result.

•

As I search for a way to close this chronicle, I find myself pondering some of the many gifts with which Catherine has presented myself and numerous other people.

In a world where we tend to be too busy and too hurried, she helps us to slow down; it's hard to do things quickly around Catherine! Tied to this is her quiet ability to help us appreciate our own capabilities, and also to recognize, and even deal with, our own frailties. She encourages us to be resourceful and creative. She's a good (if captive) listener. She is an understanding and forgiving friend. She has a lovely sense of humour, and the timing with which she falls apart laughing—often at moments of disaster—is frequently just what is needed as a tension-breaker. She's a great introducer; I know of many good friendships between people who have met through her. As I write that I realize that many of my closest and most lasting friendships have been initiated by my daughter.

Cath is a truly marvellous teacher and educator; rottenly paid, but in her own way every bit as effective as a university professor. (I must try this theory on her father one day—he might even agree.) She's also an employer; we need to recognize that our sons and daughters with disbilities have the capacity to provide fulfilling employment for others.

Not a bad list of credentials, I reckon, for someone who was intially written off as a sort of medical dud. Catherine, despite all her difficulties, is a woman of influence and is truly what we all strive to be—a productive member of society. I'm blessed and proud to be her mother.

Summer 1999

Annie's Coming Out, by Rosemary Crossley and Anne McDonald, Penguin, 1984. Anne and Rosemary tell the story of how they met when Anne was living in an Australian institution, and what they went through so that she could move out and live with Rosemary. It's a great story.

Barbara and Fred: Grownups Now, Living Fully with Developmental Disabilities, by Lotte Moise, 1998. To obtain this book call (707) 964-9520. It's a beautifully and entertainingly written account of Lotte's daughter Barbara and Barbara's long-standing and fulfilling relationship with Fred.

Cerebral Palsy: a Practical Guide, by Marion Stanton, Little, Brown and Co., London, England, 1992. This British book is both informative and personal—the author has a young son with cerebral palsy.

Circles of Friends, by Bob Perske, Abingdon Press, 201 8th Ave. S., Tenn. 37203, 1988. Lovely stories, beautifully illustrated, about people with disabilities and their friends enriching the lives of one another. All Bob Perske's books are good.

Co-housing: a contemporary approach to housing ourselves, by Katheryn McCamant and Charles Durrett, Ten Speed Press, Berkeley, Calif. 1989. ISBN 0898155398.

Couples with Intellectual Disabilities talk about Living and Loving, by Karin Melberg Schwier, Woodbine House, 5615 Fishers Lane, Rockville, Maryland 20852. The author has done a wonderful job of discreetly assisting a variety of couples who have a disability to describe their lives together.

Laying Community Foundations for Your Child with a Disability, by Linda J. Stengle, Woodbine House, 6510 Bells Mill Road, Bethesda, MD 20817, 1996. An excellent book about establishing relationships that will support your child after you're gone. Full of vivid examples.

Life as we know it: a father, a family, and an exceptional child, by Michael Bérube, Vintage Books, NY, 1998. While telling the story of his family, the author raises some difficult issues that face families today, such as the impact of negative labels, genetic testing and abortion.

Members of Each Other, by John O Brien and Connie Lyle, Inclusion Press, 25 Thome Crescent, M6H 2S5, Toronto, 1996. An important book about building community in company with people who have disabilities.

Skallagrigg, by William Horwood, Penguin, 1988. A riveting and unusual novel that unites Arthur, a child abandoned to a grim institution in England decades ago, with Esther, a brilliant young woman with cerebral palsy, and with Daniel, an American computer-games genius. I love giving this book as a present. You may have to order it from England   it will be worth the effort.

The Whole Community Catalogue, compiled and edited by David Wetherow, Inclusion Press, 25 Thome Crescent, Toronto, M6H 2S5, 1992. A source book for enriching our communities, neighbourhoods, schools, workplaces and families via the participation and inclusion of people who have disabilities. An excellent collection of articles, ideas and reviews.

Who Cares? Rediscovering Community, by David Schwartz, Westview Press (a division of HarperCollins), 1997. Another important book.

NICOLA SCHAEFER grew up in Oxford, England. She has lived in Winnipeg since her marriage to Ted, a Canadian scientist, in 1960. They have a daughter and two sons.

Cath, her 38-year-old daughter, has significant inconveniences with which to contend, including quadriplegia and lack of speech. She has encouraged Nicola to become an advocate for her and others with similar problems. Cath has taught Nicola to be a passionate believer in real homes, real friends and real lives for people who have disabilities.

Nicola has, for many years, been involved in the production of chamber music in Manitoba.